Cost Estimation
for Software
Development

INTERNATIONAL COMPUTER SCIENCE SERIES

Consulting editors   **A D McGettrick** University of Strathclyde
                        J van Leeuwen University of Utrecht

OTHER TITLES IN THE SERIES:

Programming in Ada (2nd Edn.) *J G P Barnes*

Computer Science Applied to Business Systems *M J R Shave and K N Bhaskar*

Software Engineering (2nd Edn.) *I Sommerville*

A Structured Approach to FORTRAN 77 Programming *T M R Ellis*

An Introduction to Numerical Methods with Pascal *L V Atkinson and P J Harley*

The UNIX System *S R Bourne*

Handbook of Algorithms and Data Structures *G H Gonnet*

Office Automation: Concepts, Technologies and Issues *R A Hirschheim*

Microcomputers in Engineering and Science *J F Craine and G R Martin*

UNIX for Super-Users *E Foxley*

Software Specification Techniques *N Gehani and A D McGettrick* (eds.)

The UNIX System V Environment *S R Bourne*

Data Communications for Programmers *M Purser*

Prolog Programming for Artificial Intelligence *I Bratko*

Modula-2: Discipline & Design *A H J Sale*

PROLOG *F Giannesini, H Kanoui, R Pasero and M van Caneghem*

Introduction to Expert Systems *P Jackson*

Local Area Network Design *A Hopper, S Temple and R C Williamson*

Programming Language Translation: A Practical Approach *P D Terry*

Data Abstraction in Programming Languages *J M Bishop*

System Simulation: Programming Styles and Languages *W Kreutzer*

The Craft of Software Engineering *A Macro and J Buxton*

An Introduction to Programming with Modula-2 *P D Terry*

POP-11 Programming for Artificial Intelligence *A M Burton and N R Shadbolt*

UNIX System Programming *K Haviland and B Salama*

UNIX™ is a trademark of AT & T Bell Laboratories

Cost Estimation for Software Development

Bernard Londeix

STC Telecommunications, UK

ADDISON-WESLEY
PUBLISHING
COMPANY

Wokingham, England · Reading, Massachusetts · Menlo Park, California
New York · Don Mills, Ontario · Amsterdam · Bonn · Sydney
Singapore · Tokyo · Madrid · Bogota · Santiago · San Juan

Cover graphic by kind permission of Digital Pictures, London.
Typeset by Colset Private Limited, Singapore
Illustrations by Chartwell Illustrators.
Printed in Great Britain by T J Press (Padstow) Ltd., Cornwall.

First printed 1987

British Library Cataloguing in Publication Data
Londeix, Bernard
 Cost estimation for software development.
 1. Computer software —— Development ——
 Estimates
 I. Title
 005.1'068'1   QA76.76.D47

 ISBN 0-201-17451-0

Library of Congress Cataloguing in Publication Data
Londeix, Bernard.
 Cost estimation for software development.

 Bibliography: p.
 Includes index.
 1. Computer software —— Development —— Estimates.
 I. Title.
 QA76.76.D47L66   1987   005'.068   87-1026
 ISBN 0-201-17451-0

Foreword

The basic strategy in estimating the cost of developing large-scale software systems rests on two key issues: (1) making the cost decision under uncertainty and (2) controlling by techniques which effectively manage the cost decision. While many useful ideas are presented in this book, we will examine these two issues in the context of the author's approach.

In general, software cost models are based on the premise that the analyst can produce a deterministic solution that can be perturbed to examine its sensitivity not only to environmental conditions but also to measurable attributes of the product itself. Monte Carlo simulation has proved to be very useful for evaluating the chance element in decision making under uncertainty. We use the solution produced under assumptions of certainty and subject that solution to a series of numerical experiments based on a random sampling procedure and linear programming methods.

The reader should be mindful of the fact that the single point solution (that is, person months and calendar months for a given situation) represents the average solution. In other words, it is equally likely to overrun as underrun that 50% probability solution. To estimate any other probability level we can use a Monte Carlo simulation, alter the variables, and repeat the solution as many times as we want until we feel that we have a solution that is about as good as we are likely to get.

To solve problems with Monte Carlo, we need four things: (1) a measure of effectiveness, (2) the relevant variables, (3) the cumulative probability distribution of each variable (that is, the chance of each of the various values of the variable occurring), and (4) a set of random numbers. Tables of such numbers have been prepared by and for computers and are published in the form of multiple-digit columns, each digit of which, because they have been selected at random, has an equal chance of appearing at any place in the entire table.[1]

The first step in using Monte Carlo is to assign random numbers to the possible values of each variable, so that the probability of the numbers in the table occurring is equal to the probability of the value of the variable occurring in actual practice. For example, if there is a 25% chance of a certain event occurring, we assign 25% of the random numbers to that event.[2] Now we are ready to simulate an actual operation. The author shows an effective technique for evaluating the standard deviation of the module size. Extending this technique by Monte Carlo will enable the user to determine statistically a best-bid solution, which is the product of the probabilities of time and person months.

The basic control process involves three steps: (1) establishing standards, (2) measuring performance against these standards, and (3) correcting deviations from standards and plans.

Because plans are the yardsticks against which controls must be formulated, it would seem appropriate to first establish plans. However, since plans vary in detail and complexity, and since managers cannot usually watch everything, special standards are established. Standards are by definition simply criteria of performance. They are the selected points in an entire planning program where measures of performance are made that give managers signals of how things are going without watching every step in the execution of plans. The author gives us a complete software development cycle, with explicit real-world examples, to support our understanding of acceptable criteria of performance.

Standards may be of many kinds. Among the best are verifiable goals or objectives, stated in quantitative terms, regularly set in well-operated systems of management by objectives.[3]

Once a point estimate of person months and calendar months is calculated, Monte Carlo studies performed to give the desired operating point (for example, 90% probability of not overrunning the budget), and the milestones established for the software development process, it is then essential to distribute the resources over time. The basic building block of management by objectives is the *objective* itself: an *objective* is a statement of measurable results to be achieved, by when, and at a cost not to be exceeded.

For example, in the software development cycle it is important to know exactly what is covered (and not covered) in the estimate of resources. Ordinarily, a work breakdown structure is given to show resource allocation and accountability at every level of the development organization from analysis and design, code and unit test, through test and integration, including documentation. Another way to view the problem is a distribution of resources (person months) over calendar time by means of a given distribu-tion, such as the closed form Rayleigh distribution.[4,5] A ramp function, a pedestal function, or a piece-wise linear parallelogram could be used depend-ing on the style of management of the enterprise. The rationale and equations for the preferred distribution are covered nicely by the author.

Measurement of performance against standards should ideally be on a forward-looking basis so deviations may be detected in advance of their occurrence and avoided by appropriate actions.[6] The alert, forward-looking manager can sometimes predict probable departures from standards. In the absence of such ability, deviations should be disclosed as early as possible.

The author, Bernard Londeix, provides the reader with a number of check points in the software development process, such as Preliminary Design Review or Critical Design Review, together with the time allocation and resource allocation formulae, appropriate to well-run, large-scale soft-ware projects. A complete guide for software development,[7] quality standards,[8] and management practices[9,10] that are required by the United States Department of Defense should prove useful for any software project manager who wishes to apply more rigor with less ambiguity to standards for software development. The author's work is consistent with these referenced guidelines.

As managers at all levels develop verifiable objectives, stated in quantitative terms where practicable, these become standards against which all position performance in the organization hierarchy can be measured. Also, as new techniques are created to measure, with a reasonable degree of objectivity, the quality of management itself, useful standards of per-formance will emerge. This book promises to assist the manager or analyst in making real progress in this area.

Corrections of deviations in performance is the point at which control is seen as part of the whole system of management. Managers may correct departures from plan by reformulating the plan or modifying their goals in terms of cost and schedule impact. Or they may correct observed departures from plan by reassignment or clarification of duties. Also, they may correct by additional staffing, by better selection and training of subordinates, or through better leading or more effective leadership techniques. These are the standard tools of management by objectives and results as previously cited.

The author provides examples of immediate usefulness to the reader, from fundamentals of resource allocation, through a comprehensive exercise in reusability, to the Technology Factor and productivity index which is influenced by appropriate use of tools and modern programming practices.

One of the outstanding features of this book is the definition of the size of a software product in terms of delivered source lines of code together with a mutually exclusive, collectively exhaustive Venn diagram and table that illustrates the cost impact of software reuse. A checked-out, error-free line of code that is reused in another software product has a unique effect on the pro-ject cost and schedule, which is treated by the author in a very clear manner.

That treatment alone is worth the price of the book.

Perhaps it is the vigor and enthusiasm of the author, in his work at STC Telecommunications over the last five years, that underlies the experience reflected in the book, and most commends it to the software engineering professional. Obtaining valid data, applying it in a cohesive cost model, comparing actual outcomes with those predicted, instilling the concept at every level in the organization, and creating a comfortable mood for change from old ways of ambiguous software cost estimating to modern ways of cost modelling and quantitative management are illustrated by hard-won experience. This book reflects solid work by a respected practitioner in software engineering, Bernard Londeix, and is highly recommended for the library of the serious software engineer and manager.

Ray Wolverton
Chief Scientist
Defense Information Systems Division
Space and Communications Group
Hughes Aircraft Company
Los Angeles, California
January 1987

[1] Williams, J. D. *The Compleat Strategyst: Being a Primer on the Theory of Games of Strategy*, McGraw–Hill, New York, 1954.

[2] Rubinstein, Reuven *Simulation and the Monte Carlo Method*, John Wiley & Sons, New York, 1981.

[3] Koontz, H., O'Donnell, C. and Weihrich, H. *Essentials of Management*, Fourth Edition, McGraw–Hill, New York, 1986.

[4] Putnam, L. H. and Wolverton, R. W. *Tutorial, Quantitative Management: Software Cost Estimating*, COMPSAC 77, IEEE Catalog No. EHO 129-7, Chicago, November 8–11, 1977.

[5] Putnam, L. H. *Tutorial, Software Cost Estimating and Life-Cycle Control: Getting the Software Numbers*, IEEE Computer Society, COMPSAC 80, IEEE Catalog No. EHO 165-1, New York, NY, October 27–31, 1980.

[6] Wolverton, R. W. *SDE: The ITT Software Development Environment*, The National Institute for Software Quality and Productivity Conference, Methodologies and Tools for Real-Time Systems, Washington, DC, March 10–11, 1986.

[7] Draft Standard, *Defense System Software Development*, DOD-STD-2167A, 15 August 1986.

[8] Draft Standard, *Defense System Quality Standard*, DOD-STD-2168, 1 August 1986.

[9] Air Force Systems Command, *Software Management Indicators*, Management Insight, AFSCP 800-43, 31 January 1986.

[10] Draft, Air Force Systems Command, *Software Quality Indicators*, Management Quality Insight, AFSCP 800-XX, c. June 1986.

Preface

This book has been written to communicate an understanding of the estimating practice involved in developing large-scale software projects to software managers and consultants, project managers, marketing and technical executives as well as to students interested in software development. It is based on the experience gained by the author in estimating the cost and time of software developments at STC Telecommunications. This software was used mainly in large telephone exchanges, which require a great deal of real-time programming.

The term 'project' is used here to indicate the development of all (or part) of a new product to be included in a product line, as soon as it is recognized as a viable business proposition. The 'project manager' is regarded as the person who has complete (or almost complete) authority over the development of such a new product.

'Software development', on the other hand, represents all the phases of the product's life cycle, starting from the point at which a 'requirements' definition is submitted to a development team and ending at the point when the software product is recognized as being valid on the target processor. The development phase is the most expensive of all the phases, and professionals have experienced spiralling development costs and even the most skilful project manager might be tempted to sacrifice quality to meet a schedule already several times revised. Software development is still a labour-intensive activity, often involving hundreds of man.years in large telecommunications projects, and some of the most critical management decisions have to be taken in terms of manpower. For this reason, the term 'cost' is used in this book to signify the amount of manpower effort necessary for developing software, and is usually expressed in man.years. The consideration of the cost of related acquisitions, such as machinery, work space and energy, is not within the scope of this book, unless considered as part of the overhead for software development.

Several examples are given in the text to illustrate the application of the estimating method. Some of these are representative of software projects that are either currently in development or have been under consideration. However, to protect the commercial confidentiality of the organizations involved with these projects, all names of projects, functions and modules have been changed. Furthermore, performance data that might be deduced from these examples are those commonly found in real-time software projects. Hence, these data are not typical, nor do they relate to any specific business organization.

Synopsis

The book's structure is didactic. It starts by surveying the role of estimation in the software development process and then takes the reader through the actual estimating practice, outlining various methods that can be used. As different types of reader will find specific subjects in which they are interested, the following is intended to highlight those areas that may be of special interest. However, it should be noted that the role of the 'Consulting Estimator' has been introduced into the estimating method, as this character has an important part in the practice of estimating.

- Chapter 1 introduces the technique of software estimating, outlining the role of the Consulting Estimator, the elements of the Product Life Cycle and the concept of estimating time and software size.
- Chapter 2 reviews models currently used in industry in estimating software and introduces the concept of micro and macro models.
- Chapter 3 presents an overview of COCOMO, an example of a micro model, giving an insight into the software development environment.
- Chapter 4 introduces Norden's theory of project modelling and the extension made by Putnam for the Software Life Cycle. The conjunction of their efforts resulted in what was probably the first dynamic macro model of software projects that directly exploits the main management parameters, such as time and manpower cost.
- Chapter 5 extends the ideas of Chapter 4, introducing the concept of project scale and describing how the modelling can be carried out for small- to large-scale projects.

- Chapter 6 develops a method for software development estimating.
- Chapter 7 looks ahead to advances and improvements in cost estimating methodology.

For the Project or Software Manager

Chapter 1 is targeted at project and/or software managers. This chapter provides a rational basis for setting up a relationship with their Consulting Estimator, and guidelines for controlling and assessing the estimating process. It also provides guidance on how to establish a measurement baseline, and which data to deliver (and when) during the development life cycle.

The Product Life Cycle described in Chapter 1 should be considered a high-level management tool. It has to be refined for large-scale software projects and simplified for small-scale ones. However, it is important to realize that it covers many software development practices. The choice of these practices is the project/software manager's responsibility. However, the estimating method should not influence this choice, unless it is a question of promoting efficient software methodologies.

Project/software managers will also benefit from reading Chapter 6, which outlines the estimating process as conducted by their Consulting Estimator. It will be to the project manager's advantage to assimilate the concept of 'planning zone', which represents clearly the phenomenology of the cost–time trade-off.

For the Consulting Estimator

The recommended practice is for the estimating work to be done by a software specialist – called here the Consulting Estimator – who is not directly involved in the development of the software product. The Consulting Estimator is assumed to be familiar with the estimating context. If this is not the case, Chapter 1 gives some overall guidance.

The Consulting Estimator is invited to make a thorough study of the model presented in Chapter 5 to gain maximum benefit from the estimating method. The main results are outlined, requiring only an elementary level of mathematics. Some tools for this purpose are provided in the appendices, of which the SM10 program could be particularly helpful.

Chapter 6 fully explains the estimating method, and the Consulting Estimator should master this. Understanding is aided by several practical examples.

For the Software Engineer Student

Students in software engineering will benefit from reading the chapters in their natural order. By working through all the calculations, they will gain a better understanding of the techniques involved, in addition to the results provided by the estimating tools. The technique of software estimating is still being improved, and more developments need to be carried through. This book introduces a practical step in this evolution.

Students should remember that the model used in a method is fundamental to its success or failure. A way of comparing the two classic models, COCOMO and the Norden/Putnam model, is proposed in Appendix 4. The method used in this comparison, and the results obtained, are detailed in such a way that the student can draw his own conclusions on their respective effectiveness.

The exercises given in this book are intended to illustrate some of the questions that arise during estimating work. Their solutions require an elementary level of mathematics and application of the formulae provided in the text. For some exercises, the student might find it convenient to use the SM10 program given in Appendix 1 or a spreadsheet. Selected solutions are provided at the back of the book in addition to a Glossary of important definitions.

Acknowledgments

I would like to thank Mr L. H. Putnam, to whom I am indebted for his consistent support since I first told him of my plans to write this book. I would also like to thank my colleagues who enthusiastically reviewed a draft manuscript and provided constructive comments, especially Mr S. F. Smith, Mr D. G. Phillips (STC), Mr C. Mills (ICL), Mr D. Snow (Plessey) and Dr B. Kitchenham (ICL). Mr R. Wolverton, who I had the good fortune to meet, has been a most supportive presence behind the book, and it is indeed my pleasure to acknowledge his help and many creative suggestions.

At the crucial time of putting the book into its final shape, Mr D. G. N. Hunter read the manuscript and contributed many valuable and constructive criticisms. I cannot thank him enough for his thorough assessment of the manuscript. I would also like to thank Addison–Wesley's team of reviewers for their detailed and most helpful comments, as well as STC Telecommunications for their cooperation.

Finally, I am very grateful to Ms S. Perrin, Ms C. Yankey, Ms J. Richards and Ms N. Chamberlain, for their excellent typing assistance, and to Mr A. Toogood for his editorial care and advice. To them and everyone who helped with this project, may I express my heartfelt thanks.

Bernard Londeix
STC Telecommunications
June 1987

---

* For reasons of simplicity, the pronoun 'he' is used to relate to both male and female throughout the book.

Contents

Chapter 1
The Estimate and its Context

1.1 Introduction

In the software profession it is well known that large-scale software projects, once started, get steadily and surreptitiously out of hand. It is not unusual for a project originally estimated to cost ten man.years to double its cost by delivery time. The project manager is not always in an enviable situation: managing on a quicksand has become a way of life. As far as the customer is concerned, he becomes progressively accustomed to being ready for anything, as far as the budget is concerned. It is therefore important to devise techniques that help the project manager keep the project under control.

One of the conditions that has to be satisfied for this to happen is that the development plan is based on a realistic estimate. This is the point at which most software professionals might be worried; perhaps they have rarely seen a realistic estimate. Nevertheless, adoption of the method outlined in this book will facilitate the production of such estimates.

The software-estimating process requires a basic understanding of the fact that software development is not a 'mechanistic' process – like that which occurs in building-construction. There, tasks are concrete, visible, measurable by simple means and of finite quantity. By contrast, software development is a 'probabilistic' process, consisting of a large number of tasks of undetermined complexity. Software tasks are not always rationally

1

measurable: at best, they can be assessed by experts in the software field. Current techniques to test software products are not always completely reliable, and this leads to uncertainty in determining whether a software product is really achieved to full customer satisfaction. Until better methods of software development are made available, cost and time predictability will remain no better than a probabilistic estimating method. Nevertheless, recent experience in the telecommunications industry tends to suggest that it is possible to render software development less anarchic by the use of an estimating method throughout the development cycle.

1.2 What is an estimate?

'Estimate' is a very loaded word in an engineering environment. According to the *Concise Oxford English Dictionary*, an estimate is an approximate judgement, a contractor's statement of the sum for which he will undertake specified work. And when in a management meeting, the senior manager asks the project manager 'How much will the such and such development cost?' a reply of 'My best guess is...' sends the project manager quickly back to his business plan.

Let us clarify the concept of an estimate by contrasting it with a 'guess' and an 'educated guess'.

1.2.1 Guess

Engineers are always embarrassed when the moment comes to make an estimate. The practice of estimating covers three kinds of processes: guess, educated guess, estimate. Furthermore, because of their education, engineers do not like to guess. They feel, quite rightly, that guessing is not compatible with a serious engineering way of thinking. The higher the level of professionalism, the stronger the need is felt for passing from a guessing process to a real estimating process.

To guess is to form an opinion, to give an answer based on supposition, not on careful thought, calculation or definite knowledge. In this sense, an estimate given by a newcomer into a discipline is more a measure of his own enthusiasm than an estimate.

1.2.2 Educated guess

An educated guess is a guess based on expertise – that expertise may be within a particular field or as a result of available knowledge. This expertise or knowledge is normally built up by means of personal experience; however, the educated guess still contains emotional components.

1.2.3 Estimate

An estimate, although a judgement, is still an opinion about something. As such, the process of estimating makes use not only of expertise and knowledge but also of a set of rules that are universally recognized.

The difference between an educated guess and an estimate is that an estimate pretends to be true within certain limits. To arrive at this result, the estimating activity must be based on an **estimating method**.

Estimating and costing always go together, as costing is the purpose of estimating. We cannot cost without estimating. Estimating a software development involves estimating both the size and the cost. By cost we mean the effort spent in person.years to develop the software. For ease of expression and understanding we will use the usual abbreviation, MY, for man.year or person.year.

An estimating method is successful when:

(1) The early estimate is within ± 30% of the actual final cost: this is the accuracy currently obtainable at an early stage of the development.

(2) The method allows refinement of the estimate during the Software Life Cycle. A higher accuracy can be achieved by monitoring and re-estimating the development each time more information is available.

(3) The method is easy to use for an estimator. This enables a quick re-estimate whenever it is necessary; for example, during a progress meeting, the evaluation of alternatives in strategic choices.

(4) The rules are understood by everybody concerned. Management feels more secure when the estimating procedures are easily understandable.

(5) The method is supported by tools and documented. The availability of tools increases the effectiveness of the method, mainly because results can be obtained more quickly and in a standard fashion.

(6) The estimating process can be trusted by software development teams and their management. This helps in gaining the participation of everybody concerned with the estimate.

The method presented in the following chapters is intended to demonstrate these principles.

1.3 Elements of Product Life Cycle

Either intuitively or by experience, we all have a notion of what a project is; nevertheless, a project is only a part of a wider business process whose aim is to provide the market with products that will generate profit. A correct estimate will inevitably contribute to the business goal by avoiding costly project replanning. This can be accomplished by viewing the software project in the context of its product line.

An organization has generally more than one product as a going concern. When the market's interest for a given product weakens, an organization generally makes plans for developing a new product, just before phasing out the old one. Several promising ideas are considered and rejected until one becomes the object of a **Product Plan**. This product then has to be developed, made available to the market and, at the end of its market life, has to be terminated. The decision to develop a product is made partly on the basis of the results of an initial estimate. A flawed estimate is responsible for either starting a software project that is out of proportion with the development capability or, on the other hand, for rejecting a perfectly valid venture, both of which options can result in missed business. At any given time, an organization may have several products at different stages of their life cycle: some may be in the planning stage, others in development, while others may be being manufactured for delivery in the market. To control this complex product simultaneity, management uses the concept of the **Product Life Cycle** more and more.

It is important to realize that the 'notion' of a product differs from one organization to another. For example, the product of a software house is a software package, composed of a program delivered on a magnetic tape and its associated documentation (for example, a user guide, at least). On the other hand, the product of a telecommunications business might be a Packet Switching System, which is composed of hardware parts, some bought in and others locally developed, on which runs some software, locally developed or subcontracted to a software house.

It is perhaps the right moment to mention that as far as an estimator is concerned, his product is a correct and complete estimating service, which takes into account a customer's business environment (for example, stand-alone or embedded software, technological and business constraints).

Let us now return to the Product Life Cycle and describe it in its general form. Note that we could simplify this form whenever simple products are involved or, alternatively, make it more detailed when we consider complex products (for example, large-scale software developments).

The Product Life Cycle describes the life of a product by means of eight sequential **phases**. Moreover, each phase must end with a **milestone**. A milestone is a demonstrable event; that is, something has been produced and delivered, in a fashion that can be verified independently of the producer, at a definite time. For example, 'code of module $B1$: 90% complete' is not a milestone, it is merely a (subjective) statement of progress. Completion of the last 10% might take as long and require as much effort to complete as the first 90%. On the other hand, 'code of module $B1$: 100% complete' might be a milestone if this code is delivered for testing on an appropriate medium accompanied by the compilation listing showing no compilation error and proving that module $B1$ is really made up of the algorithms defined in the design document.

The phases of the Product Life Cycle are outlined in the following sub-sections. These phases trace the product from its conception to its termination all the way through its development and marketing. When appropriate the role of software estimating is emphasized (see Figure 1.1).

1.3.1 Product planning

A. Conceptual planning (phase 1)

The first phase of the Product Life Cycle, conceptual planning, is initiated by a statement of need. This need can be expressed by a customer under the form of a 'Requirements Definition' (or 'Statement of Requirements') or can be the result of business objectives. Applied research and market research efforts are then required to evaluate the concept and assess its business potential. A rough analysis of the concept can also be carried out to enable a sizing up of the cost of software development. If the concept is promising, a **Product Proposal** is documented and submitted to a management review. When approved, the Product Proposal becomes a basis for further definition [16].

B. Product definition (phase 2)

The Product Proposal now enters a phase of product definition, which should result in a concrete definition of the product. A detailed analysis of customer requirements is carried out by a product team, a **Product Functional Specification** is prepared and a **Product Plan** is set up. This Product Plan must include an estimate of the time and cost of the software to be developed. The estimate produced in this phase must be more accurate than it was in phase 1, since the Product Plan should convince management that the product can be developed, marketed and serviced within acceptable cost and time constraints.

Note During the first two phases the software estimate has, inevitably, a large degree of uncertainty, since the interest is more in the magnitude (or size range) of the software to be developed, rather than in an accurate and definitive size value.

Frequently, for business reasons, the Product Proposal is rejected and phase 1 has to be repeated. Similarly, the Product Plan might be rejected by management or require improvement. In such cases, the estimate, obviously, has to be re-evaluated.

1.3.2 Product development

A. System design (phase 3)

The project is staffed in accordance with the **development plan** part of the Product Plan. The project then proceeds in two steps. Firstly, the **system**

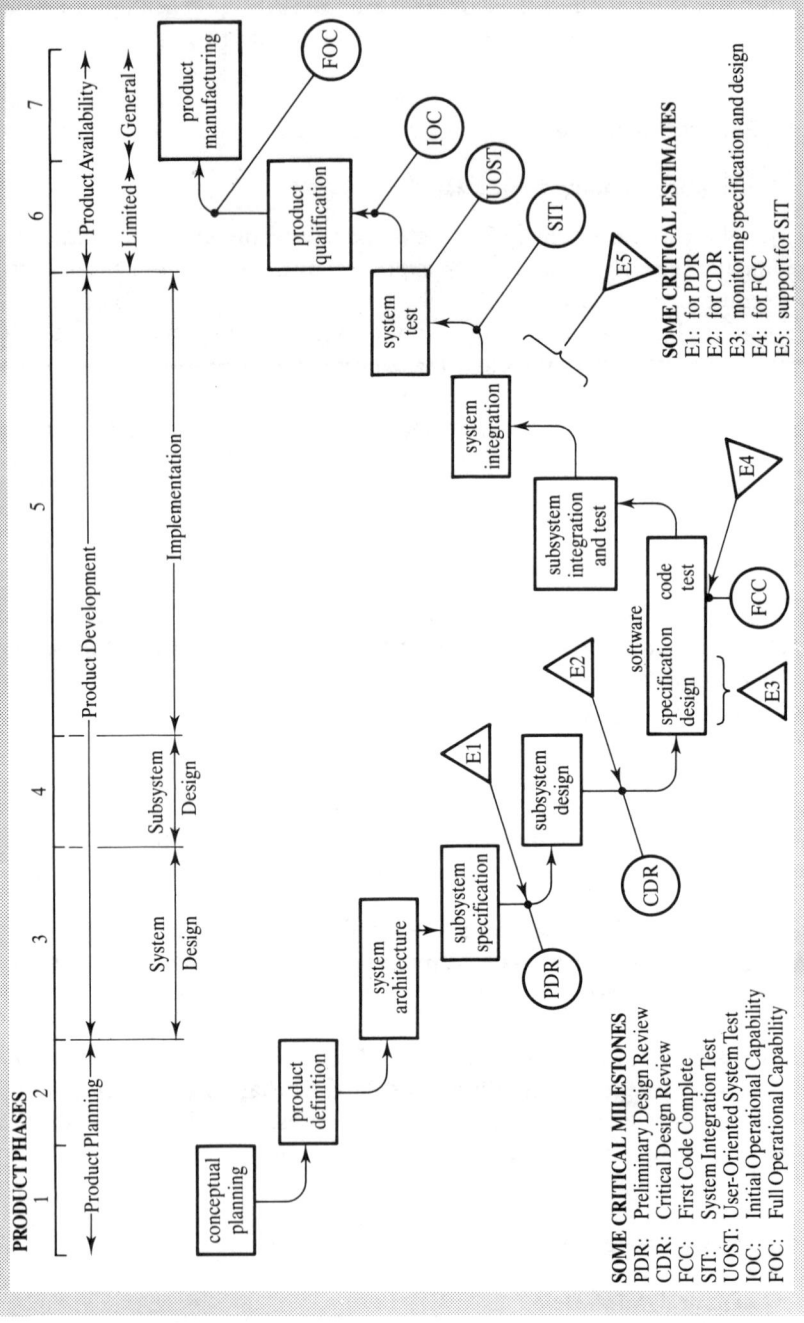

Figure 1.1   A Product Life Cycle.

architecture is established: this determines the hardware and software trade-offs. Then, each subsystem is specified to satisfy the Product Functional Specification. As a result, the **subsystem specifications** are produced which allow the Product Plan, or more specifically the development plan, to be refined. The software cost and time estimate plays an important role here as it can influence the hardware and software trade-offs. During this phase, the estimate becomes accurate enough to permit the scheduling of the end of product development. After having been through a successful **Preliminary Design Review**, the next phase can be started.

B.   Subsystem design (phase 4)

In this phase, each subsystem is designed; that is, the successive specifications and designs of each subfunction and module are obtained by any appropriate method of hierarchical decomposition or reification. The result is a description of how the product is to be implemented. At the end of this phase the product is very well defined and is submitted to a **Critical Design Review**. After refinement of the cost and time estimate, a decision is made whether to proceed to the implementation phase, based mainly on the value of the estimate.

C.   Implementation (phase 5)

During the implementation phase, the software modules are coded and tested; the tested modules are integrated into subfunctions, which are then tested; subsystems are integrated and tested in their target processors; and then the system is integrated and tested.

A critical stage for the software estimate is when the product is fully coded. The product at the **First Code Complete** stage provides enough information to refine or re-adjust the previous estimate, while the accuracy of the revised estimate is sufficient to predict the end of the **User-Orientated System Test**, which completes the implementation phase.

Note   During the implementation phase it is very important to use estimating as part of the monitoring of the software development. The implementation phase is the phase by which the way the estimating method was applied to this particular project can be assessed. Of course, it is important to assess how well the estimating method is suitable for the project, but it is also very important to be able to predict how the project will behave at successive stages.

1.3.3   Product availability

A.   Product qualification (phase 6)

Once the implementation phase has been completed – that is, the Initial Operational Capability stage is entered – the product is installed in selected customers' sites. (The availability of the product is restricted to these sites.) Qualification testing is then performed on the product. The aim of the qualification process is to prove that the product functions in accordance with its requirements at a customer's site. Constant monitoring of the qualification process helps to refine the estimate of **Full Operational Capability** time.

B. Product maintenance and manufacturing (phase 7)

When the product has been qualified, it is freely available for installation without any restriction. During this phase the product is manufactured and installed throughout its market. In addition, new versions may be developed incorporating features or capabilities not provided in the generic product. When this is the case the product has to be recycled through all the development phases. The product maintenance and manufacturing phase lasts for the whole of the product's operational life time.

Note   During the product availability phase some modifications or variants will, inevitably, be required. What has been learned about the project by previous estimates will be essential for correctly estimating the development of the product variants.

1.3.4   Product termination (phase 8)

Product termination, the last phase of the Product Life Cycle, removes the product from general marketing and service. The conditions of product withdrawal are negotiated with the customer. After a re-assessment of the needs, the customer is either oriented towards a new product or assumes full responsibility for the old product.

1.3.5   Role of estimating

Naturally, the estimates carried out during the first three phases are very important as they determine the framework for project planning. As any replanning is a costly exercise, managers of large-scale projects should give the greatest attention to their project plans, thus guaranteeing a workable first estimate. However, the estimating done at the beginning of a software development is not intended to be the once-for-all estimate. Estimating is a continuous process, throughout the Product Life Cycle, that makes use of the data collected during the monitoring of the development phases. By comparing the actual data with the estimated data at each step the accuracy of the next step estimate can be improved. A large-scale project can often take a few years to complete, and during that time the development capability might change or an improved awareness of the initial conditions might be obtained.

Thus, there is a great deal of scope for improving the estimate. At each step there is a need to be able to better predict future steps. This is particularly true at the macro level when developing large-scale projects, rather than small-scale ones. A close correspondence between continuous estimating and project behaviour monitoring seems to be a contributing factor for successful large-scale software developments.

1.4 The Consulting Estimator

The estimating process presented here uses a set of rules based on a model to offer guidance to the estimator. However, despite being provided with such a set of rules, the reasoning capability of the estimator can still be influenced by some emotional aspects. This is particularly true when the estimator is too involved in the software development; thus, he is more likely to produce a flawed estimate. For this reason, management should delegate the task of estimating to an external specialist, to be called hereafter the **Consulting Estimator**. Such a practice, aimed at minimizing the non-rational aspects, serves to give an objective view of the project, as far as is possible.

1.4.1 Who should avoid estimating?

It is an assumption, often validated by practice, that anyone directly concerned with the result (cost, time) of a project should not do the estimating. The deviation from actual performance of the software development reflects the state of mind of this 'preoccupied' estimator.

Those people who are best not selected for the role of estimator for various reasons are as follows:

(1) *Project managers* Good project managers are interested in meeting a contract in terms of cost and time, and sometimes they might aim to complete the project in a shorter development time and for a lower cost. Therefore, their estimates are likely to be over-optimistic and may lead to subsequent replanning during the development, which will result in spiralling costs and a longer development time.

Project managers tend to carry out estimating and contract negotiation simultaneously. Thus, it is possible for project managers to confuse the project issues, and so try to estimate from poorly defined requirements and to negotiate requirements using flawed estimates.

(2) *Software managers* Software managers are often submitted to political pressures from their project managers. Consequently, they will probably be biased towards an objective time–cost estimate.

(3) *Software analysts and engineers* The natural expectations and

enthusiasm of software analysts and engineers will probably lead them to bias their estimates on the optimistic side.

These professionals are also submitted to hierarchical pressures, such as doing the job as quickly as possible and at minimum cost.

1.4.2   Who can estimate?

The Consulting Estimator can be any professional estimator who has no direct or indirect interest in the results of the software development, except that of professional excellence. He might be a consultant working for a specialist consulting firm or an internal consultant employed by the organization developing the software. His main objective is the quality of his estimate, which does not necessarily meet the management's expectations in terms of time and cost.

A Consulting Estimator should fulfill the following attributes:

(1)   An educational background and professional experience to help him to understand project management problems.

(2)   A business or organizational position that enables him to exercise independence of judgement.

(3)   He should have a documented method that can be explained, questioned, discussed and audited by other experts.

(4)   Whenever he is using a tool, he should be able to do so in a way that the tool meets its declared purpose and supports the method; also the tool should be documented and controllable.

(5)   Be able to describe his estimating experience: when the method was successfully used; the problems he had to face.

(6)   Be able to document his estimate, including the results and any necessary background information that makes the estimate repeatable and verifiable.

1.4.3   How to use a Consulting Estimator

Project managers might feel somewhat undervalued by the preceding discussion. However, it should be pointed out that as a manager it is more important to know how to use a Consulting Estimator rather than to do the estimating work itself. The following are some guidelines on how to use a Consulting Estimator:

(1)   Invite the Consulting Estimator to key product definition meetings. The discussion carried out during these meetings will give him the necessary information to better understand the product to be developed.

(2)   Openly describe the objectives and strategies. By doing so, the Consulting Estimator will be able to understand what practical results are required and what the preferred methods of working are. He will then be able to obtain a better idea of the possible risks and make a better assessment of the predictors.

(3)   Provide the Consulting Estimator with the measurement baseline of past projects. A measurement baseline gives a sound basis for determining the predictors and it also provides the level of confidence to be given to these values (for example, Environment Factor and Manpower Build-up, see Chapter 4).

(4)   Offer the Consulting Estimator the service of the software engineers during the size-estimating phase. The practice of software estimating starts by doing a size estimate. Estimating sizes is best done as a group activity, as each participant can give his reasons for being optimistic or pessimistic in the sizing process. (See Section 1.7 for a discussion of the role of brainstorming as applied to size estimating.)

(5)   Discuss the estimate report with the Consulting Estimator. This will ensure that the strategies have been clearly understood and taken into account in the estimate. It will also serve to confirm an understanding of the estimate, and provide a means of bargaining and making the Consulting Estimator justify his estimate.

The next step is to assess the performance of the estimating process.

1.4.4   How to assess the estimating process

Software development is a discipline that has not yet attained (in the industrial sense) the state of a technique. It still involves a large degree of personal judgement – from both the project manager and the team members – as well as many tasks that are not directly measurable. Therefore, an estimating method should be based on a probabilistic principle, rather than trying to be mechanistic.

It is rarely possible to establish definitively at the start of a development project what its performance is going to be. The Consulting Estimator can only provide a range of performances, and this range is wide during an initial estimate (stage $E1$, see Section 1.6). As more information is collected on the process during the development, the more accurate the estimate becomes. This is why the estimating process is carried out throughout the development.

The last stage, $E5$, is the stage of development amenable to an assessment of the estimating process. At this stage the development has been completed. Thus, the development can be measured and it becomes easy to compare how well the successive estimates predicted the measured actual. This comparison can be expressed by the coefficient ϵ and determined by means of the formula given in Equation (1.1).

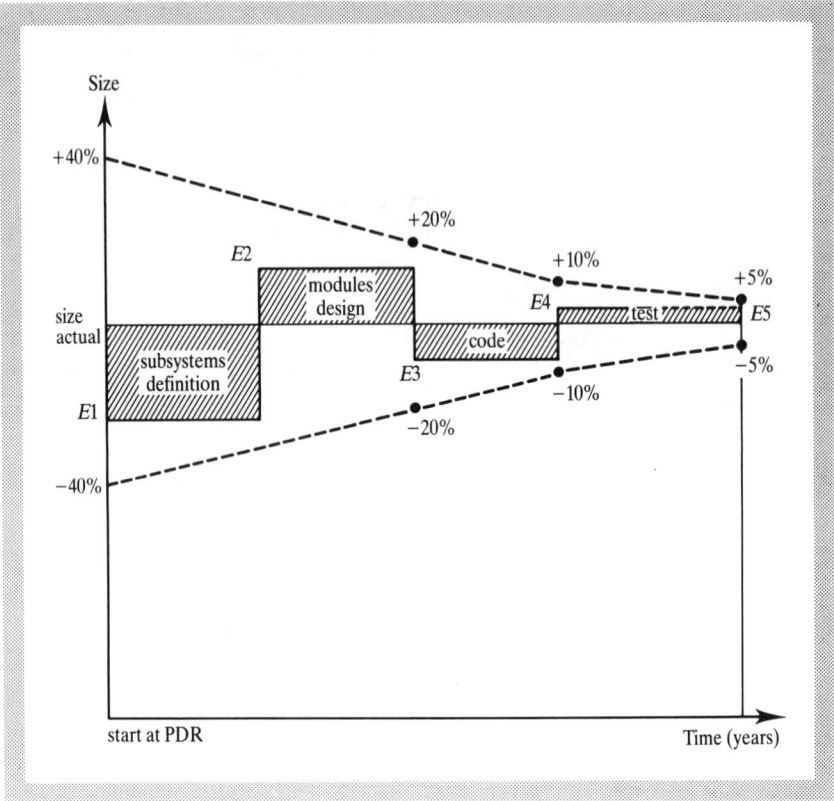

Figure 1.2   Typical size variation during successive re-estimates.

$$\epsilon = \frac{1}{n} \sqrt{\sum_{i=1}^{n} \left(\frac{V_i - V}{V}\right)^2} \qquad \text{(1.1)}$$

where V is the value of the measured variable, V_i is the estimated value at stage E_i and n is the number of estimating stages. If we compare estimates carried out on two projects, the estimate having the lowest ϵ would be the one that had been conducted more effectively. The dotted lines of Figure 1.2 represent the worst case – if no change has occurred in the requirements. In this case, we would expect a maximum value of $\epsilon = 0.14$.

Equation (1.1) can also be used to assess delivery time and software size estimates. In this way, the Consulting Estimator can compare his performance on several projects. A high value of ϵ would indicate that something had gone wrong during the estimating process of a specific project. Thus, by backtracking his actions on this project he would be able to identify the problem and so improve on it for future project estimates.

EXAMPLE

The following example compares the successive estimates of manpower cost (expressed in man.years, MY) with the actual manpower cost.

A 27 MY project ($V = 27$) was estimated:

35 MY at stage $E1$ (before specification)
23 MY at stage $E2$ (after specification)
30 MY at stage $E3$ (end of design)
24 MY at stage $E4$ (end of code)

By applying Equation (1.1), we obtain:

$$\epsilon = \frac{1}{4} \sqrt{(0.30)^2 + (0.15)^2 + (0.11)^2 + (0.11)^2}$$
$$= 0.09$$

1.5 Measurement baseline

As has been already stated, estimating should be carried out not only for the preparation of the Product Plan (see Section 1.3.1) but throughout the project, and more especially at each milestone, when the estimate is supported by the measurement baseline. Therefore, the Consulting Estimator will be interested in the major events of the past and present projects, and the data related to these projects. The material presented here is not intended to provide a method of measurement; rather, it aims to outline what the Consulting Estimator needs to find in a measurement baseline. Those readers who are interested in more advanced software measurement techniques should consult references [9] and [14] on software metrics.

1.5.1 Project journal

The project journal is written by the project manager. This is the journal of the project and not the journal of the project manager; therefore, it must be written from the project's point of view.

The project journal is used to record all events affecting the software development project:

- personnel involved;
- methods and tools used;
- customer's relationship;
- decisions taken and observed results, etc.

1.5.2 Team leader log book

This is prepared by any person who has responsibility for a part of the project. The purpose of the log book is to record all events affecting the work carried out by the team.

1.5.3 Project data

Project data encompasses any numerical information related to the product at the various stages of its development.

Once the Preliminary Design Review is accepted by the customer, each subsystem is designed. The set of subsystem design documents is then presented to the Critical Design Review. After approval of these documents the software development can start. In general, a top-down structuring process is adopted, which results in a hierarchy of software parts. The construction of each of these parts involves the following activities: specification, design, coding, unit testing, and integration and system testing. All of these activities must be carried out on each part of the software being developed and each activity can be the object of measurement.

A. Specification

The purpose of the specification is to describe in a technical fashion what is going to be designed. The following items might be recorded:

- number of functions;
- methods used;
- supporting tools;
- when a formal method is used, the number of states, invariants, operations and functions [20];
- number and types of defects detected during the reviews;
- manpower (number of analysts, number of man.hours, elapsed time).

B. Design

The aim of the design activity is to describe how the software part is to be implemented. The following items need to be recorded:

- number of modules;
- method of design and supporting tools;
- when a formal method is used, the number of states, invariants, operations and functions [20];

- number and types of defects detected during design reviews, cost of repairs in man.hours;
- manpower (number of designers, number of man.hours spent on each module, elapsed time).

C. Implementation (coding)

This task involves coding (writing the source code) what is described in the design document. The task is completed only when there is a clean compilation of the source code – that is, there is no remaining compilation error.

At this stage, the size in number of Non-Commentary Source Statements can be measured (see Section 1.7.3) and compared with the estimated size.

Measurement of the following items is also important:

- number and types of defects detected in each module during the code inspection;
- manpower and time spent on each module;
- cost of defect repairs in man.hours.

D. Unit testing

This task consists of testing each module separately, repairing the modules and updating the documents. Thus, the following items can be measured:

- size;
- number and types of defects;
- cost of repair for each defect;
- manpower and time.

E. Integration and system testing

This task involves putting all the modules together in working order. The following data can be collected:

- the number of defects and cost of repair for each pass of the test routine;
- manpower and elapsed time for each pass and repair.

1.6   Estimating time

During the establishment of the Product Plan, which occurs during phases 1 and 2 of the Product Life Cycle, the software needs to be estimated. But as the information available is not accurate enough at this stage, the sizing can only be expressed in terms of a pessimistic (S_p) and an optimistic (S_o) size. The expected size of each identified software part can then be expressed as $(S_o + S_p)/2$. (Alternatively, a more detailed method for evaluating the size can be used and this is outlined in Chapter 6.)

During product development (phases 3, 4 and 5 of the Product Life Cycle), the product becomes progressively better defined, mainly because more and more activities are being measured (see Section 1.5), and this permits more accurate size estimating.

There are five periods during which estimating or re-estimating must be done. They correspond to the five main activities of the **Software Life Cycle** (see Figure 1.3). An estimate (or re-estimate) will be necessary at the end of each of these activities, which are outlined in the following subsections.

1.6.1 System design

The system design phase produces a complete architecture of the product and a specification of each subsystem. In addition, hardware and software trade-offs are performed, and the product's design is submitted to the Preliminary Design Review. During this review the stage $E1$ software estimate should provide enough information for the management to decide whether the intended

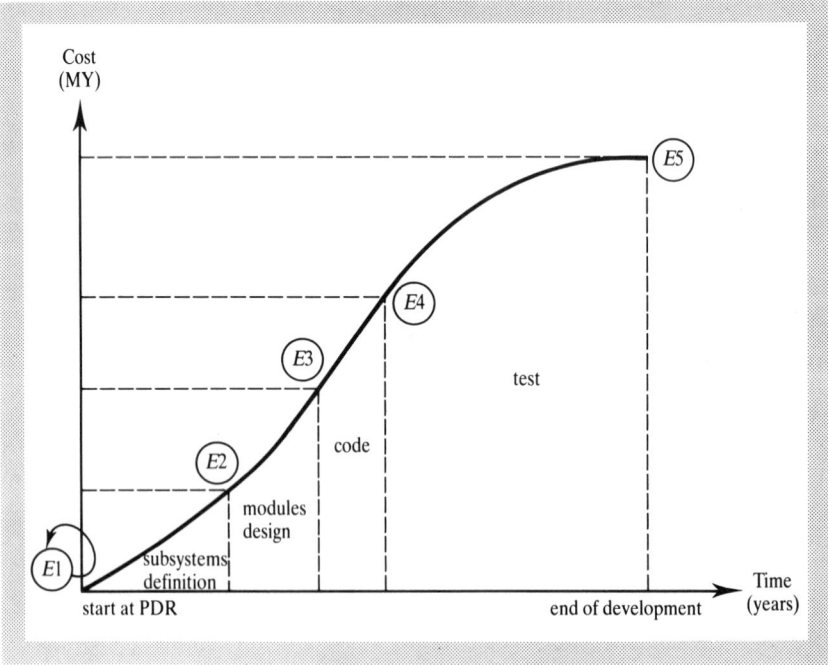

Figure 1.3 Main estimating stages.

project is in the interests of the organization. If so, the estimate leads to a confirmation of the Project Plan and the next phase is authorized.

1.6.2 Subsystem design

The second phase of product development involves refinement of the system design: the subsystem specifications are analyzed and re-interpreted using techniques of the software profession. Consequently, a better understanding of the problem is inevitable. At this time, approximately 17% of the project resources will have been utilized. Thus, a decision to continue or not has to be made during a Critical Design Review, taking into account what has to be developed in software terms. This decision needs to be backed up by a stage $E2$ software estimate, which is a refined version of the stage $E1$ software estimate.

1.6.3 Modules design

In the process of software development, design can be hierarchically structured, according to the methodology chosen by the project manager and the problem to be solved, into generic design, high/low/detailed level design, etc. The most important aspect of the design period for estimating purposes is that it determines:

- how the software is to be developed;
- what problems have been overlooked.

  At the end of this period:

- approximately 33% of the project resources will have been expended;
- a decision has to be made during a design review, although a decision to stop is unlikely;
- the decision made will affect the resources to be applied to the remaining part of the development (stage $E3$ of the estimating process).

Therefore, a stage $E3$ software estimate is produced. This estimate demonstrates that the measurement of previous phases has been taken into account to explain the progress made so far. In addition, the values of predictors are adjusted to the project's actual values and used for predicting the next phases.

1.6.4 Code production

Once the authorization to continue has been granted as a result of the Critical Design Review, the coding starts. As this activity requires extra manpower –

that is, programming technicians – the development manpower level will pass through a peak and then subside.

At the end of this activity:

- the first concrete view of the software product will be available for measurement and testing;
- the elapsed time and manpower cost, as captured during previous activities, and the actual software size can be added to the measurement baseline, and so the estimated size can now be adjusted;
- around 50% of the project resources will have been expended, leaving 50% for various levels of testing;
- a testing strategy has to be proposed, supported by a stage $E4$ software estimate.

This new estimate is now very accurate, as the size is known at the First Code Complete stage, and it plays an important role in the hierarchical planning of the testing activity, which follows.

1.6.5 Test

This last activity of software development can be tactically divided into module testing, unit testing and (sub)system testing, covering all the work from the First Code Complete stage to the Initial Operational Capability stage. It is a series of stepwise integration and testing. At the end of this activity, a valid generic product is available for manufacturing (Customer Application Engineering, Certification, etc.).

A final measurement leads to stage $E5$ of the estimating process. The overall software size is now stable: most of the measurement activity consists in tracking the removal of defects and refining the estimate so that the Initial Operational Capability date can be set. Stage $E5$ is, in practice, an assessment of the estimating process: the actual manpower expenditure and elapsed time are compared with their successive estimates (see Section 1.4.4).

1.7 Software size

The first problem to occur when estimating a software project is that of evaluating the volume of software to be produced. By its nature, this evaluation is generally done from either a customer's statement of requirements or a description of product objectives, which describes the program in terms of what it must do, and not by means of its internal constituents. The result of this evaluation should be a number that is clearly the volume of the software that will satisfy, once developed, the statement of requirements.

It is very important to be as accurate as possible when estimating the volume of the software since the figure obtained is used at later stages to estimate, not only the cost and time of the project, but also to determine such things as:

- the memory occupancy in the target processor (that is, the computer on which the delivered software should run);
- the choice of the host processor (that is, the computing facility used for developing the software); and
- the choice of all the methods used for developing the software, controlling the configuration of the software during the development, the delivery to the customer and the maintenance of possibly numerous variants.

1.7.1 Source and object programs

Before proceeding further, it is important to understand what is meant here by 'program'. During the Software Life Cycle, there is a phase, known as implementation, during which the programmer transforms the design document (produced during the previous phase) into a program. Thus, we can say that a program is simply a sequence of statements written by the programmer in such a way that each statement, once appropriately translated, directs the computer to do a specific task – for example, write, read a memory, add-up, subtract figures, evaluate logical expressions, take decisions, etc.

In a first step, the programmer writes the directives issued by the design document by means of a programming language of his choice. This language might be a high-level language such as Cobol, Pascal, Ada, etc., or a low-level language such as any assembler language appropriate to the target or host processor. When this work is completed, the programmer has, on punched cards or in a computer file, a program made up of statements expressed in one of the programming languages mentioned. Although this program is presumed to give instructions to the computer so that it behaves as prescribed in the design document, this program, composed of language statements, is generally not yet understandable by the computer. This program is called a **source program**. The computer file in which the source program is stored is called a **source file**. Analogously, the statements that compose the source program are called **source statements** – that is, they are not usable by the computer.

In a second step, the programmer transforms the source program into a program the computer can understand and can, therefore, be run on the computer. This transformation is carried out by means of special software tools called **compilers** for high-level languages – for example, a Pascal compiler is used for transforming source programs written in Pascal – or **assemblers** for programs written in assembler languages.

The result of this transformation is a program called an **object program**.

The object program is made up of a sequence of bytes (or eight-bit words) that can be used directly by the computer. In general, a large program is written in parts and before being run on a computer all object program parts need to be linked together by means of another software tool, called a **linker**. Obviously, the completion of the object program, also called the **object code**, is the signal for the testing to start, the purpose of which is to detect and remove eventual defects. When a defect is discovered in the program – this generally occurs while running the object program – the source program, also called the **source code**, is modified and recompiled, and the object program is rerun to verify that the defect has been effectively removed. Once fully tested, the programmer can be certain that the program behaves as required and so it can be delivered to the customer.

Thus, the same program has two different forms: the source program, composed of source statements, and the object program, composed of bytes, which effectively runs on the computer.

1.7.2   Programs description

Let us now look at the constituents of both kinds of program just introduced – namely, the source code and the object code – and elucidate their relation to the programming effort, which, for estimating purposes, is the cause of project cost and development time.

A.   Source code

We have already seen that the source code is a succession of statements written in a programming language. There is an interesting point here as far as the nature of the statements is concerned in view of evaluating the software volume; that is, the text of most source programs contains blank lines, commentary statements, declaration statements and executable statements. Let us review the role of each of these, as the distinction between these various entities will be useful later.

Blank lines   A blank line is a line without any text written on it. Blank lines are important because by using them the programmer can create a clear layout in the text of his program. This increases the readability of the source program; thus, less effort is required to localize a fault or to modify a program. It is also worth noting that it does not demand any programming effort to create a blank line (obviously).

Commentary statements   A commentary statement (or comment) is one or several lines of text written in a natural language, such as English, by the programmer for the purpose of providing explanations about the remaining part of the program. A judicious choice of comments helps the programmer to quickly understand what a source program does, even if it is a program he has not written himself.

Some languages such as Pascal require fewer comments because they allow a choice of almost self-commenting executable statements. In contrast, other languages such as Basic or Fortran require more commentary statements. In general, although good comments require effort from the programmer, they need less effort than that required by executable statements.

Declaration statements   In simple terms, the role of the declaration statements can be said to introduce and define the variables to be used in the executable statements, the data and constants, as well as their types – integer, characters, records, etc.

For a program to be efficient, the programmer sometimes needs to write very complex declaration statements, and this cannot be done without effort, both in terms of time and manpower cost.

Executable statements   Executable statements are those statements that are directly responsible for the production of the object code, after compilation.

Depending on the level of performance of the language used, the source program might be structured by means of constructs called subroutines, procedures, subprograms, packages, tasks, etc.

All the set of statements and their structuring declarations constitute the algorithms defined by the designer in the design document. Executable source statements can be very complex and require most of the programming effort.

B.   Object code

Once the source code exists and is correct it does not take too much programming effort and time to produce the object code. Only source code errors detectable at compilation time require some **debugging** effort and time from the programmer during the compilation process. An effective inspection of the source code, carried out by the programming team, can detect most of these defects and can therefore drastically reduce the amount of debugging effort.

A point worth mentioning at this stage is that at delivery time the total volume of object code produced should be loadable on the target computer. Furthermore, in some systems the amount of memory is strictly limited by the customer's requirements. Therefore, the programmer sometimes has to write the source code in such an efficient manner that the object code is within its size limit.

In practice, the ratio between the volume of object code to source code, sometimes called the **expansion factor**, ranges between 6 and 10, depending on the language and the compiler. Thus, this ratio can be used to determine the source code size limit. Sometimes, the source code development is constrained by its size limit, a situation that can lead to a higher manpower cost and design code time. Thus, this aspect must be taken into account during the software development estimating work.

C.   The scaffolding

The scaffolding (or thrown-away code) is that program (or series of programs) written to facilitate the verification or testing of the software product. At delivery time the scaffolding is not generally supplied to the customer, as it is not part of the product. It is either thrown away or kept for maintenance purposes. Note that, during size estimation, this type of code is not mentioned since the effort of producing it is implicit in the total development effort.

1.7.3   The sizing of software

A.   Lines of code

The measurement of the software volume by number of lines of code (that is, source code) was probably one of the first methods used by software developers. Once written by the programmer on coding sheets, the program was given to a key punch operator who punched each line of code on punch cards. When packs of punched cards were stored in a deck, the volume of software was easily evaluated in terms of the number of decks or number of punched cards. Both of these numbers can be related to a number of **lines of code** (or **LOC**). Note that this definition of size includes all the text of the program – that is, blank lines, commentary, declaration and executable statements.

This size definition has been and is still very much in use because, however tedious, it is relatively easy to count punched cards. Another reason for the popularity of this definition is that the source listing obtained after compilation provides a systematic count of all the source lines of code, usually on the left-hand side of the document. The measurement is carried out by reading the number associated with the last line of the listing of each compilation segment. Then, by adding up all the segment sizes, the program size is obtained, expressed in a number of LOC. Some practitioners sometimes prefer a derived unit, the KLOC, meaning one thousand LOC.

B.   Non-Commentary Source Statements

Although measuring the software volume by the LOC method is simple, it does have a disadvantage; namely, the number of LOC gives as much importance to comments (and blank lines) as it does to executable statements. The number of comments depends a great deal on a programmer's style. Some programmers find it superfluous to comment more than three words per page; on the other hand, some programmers abundantly comment each line of executable statement. Furthermore, the amount of comment does not appear to have any link with the effort spent on specification, design and test.

On the other hand, the number of executable statements is more likely to reflect the specification, design, coding and testing effort, and time scale. This is because, not only do the executable statements implement what the program must do, but also because writing them requires most of the programming effort and time. Therefore, throughout this book, it is recommended that sizing a piece of software is done in **Non-Commentary Source Statements** (or **NCSS**).

The measurement of a piece of software in NCSS might seem problematic to some programmers. For example, considering a compound statement, the programmer might wonder about the count of statements. A method often used for languages such as Coral or Pascal is to count the number of semicolons and to subtract the number of comment identifiers. This can easily be achieved by running a small counting routine on the source file. Some recent operating systems have very effective facilities for constructing such a routine.

1.7.4 Estimating software size

The previous section has introduced a means of measuring the volume (or size) of an existing piece of software. But, for the purpose of estimating program size, the inverse problem has to be tackled. The situation of the Consulting Estimator can be described as follows: there is a statement of requirements and, at best, a preliminary design; there is no code (indeed) and he is required to estimate the size the software will have when developed.

Estimating size is already a difficult task in organizations where a software metrics activity exists, but it is made particularly hard when there is no measurement baseline of previous projects.

Let us first examine what can be done when there is a total absence of software metrics activity within the organization, or if software development is a completely new activity within the organization. In the latter case, it is recommended to involve a group of software engineers with the best possible knowledge of both the statement of requirements and the preliminary design, and then to ask them for their estimates about each part of the software to be developed. Intuitively or not, the engineers would refer to their own experience of past projects or data heard of on some other projects. They would then proceed by similarity and difference, adjusting each time for the language, the perceived complexity, the writing skills of their programmers, etc. They would find great advantage in using the brainstorming technique, which creates a shared awareness of their respective experiences and produces, in favourable cases, an avalanche of data. This data can then be used at a later stage by the Consulting Estimator to construct the definitive estimate. Chapter 6 introduces an appropriate technique that the Consulting Estimator can use to deal with this situation.

A.   Brainstorming as applied to size estimating

The brainstorming technique, created by Alex Osborne [30], has become very popular as an aid to stimulating creative thinking. Because of this stimulation, brainstorming can be very useful in the size-estimating process, as software practitioners are more likely to find project similarities and to assess the real or apparent difficulties of the software development in terms of size.

This technique also provides an alternative to the traditional bottom-up approach, where the team leader conveys the sets of sizes generated by his engineers in an isolated fashion to the project manager. Such an approach cannot only lead to both over-optimistic or pessimistic figures, but also to the loss of a significant piece of code induced by another team member's objective.

It is recommended that the size-estimating process be structured in two sessions; namely, the productive session and the evaluative session. In this way, the generation of ideas is not blocked by the natural tendency to criticize each idea as it is proposed.

Productive session   For the session to proceed smoothly, the Consulting Estimator should act as a chairman, defining the objective in terms of the piece of software to be estimated and keeping the group centred on its objective.

It is useful to have a ten-minute warm-up session during which the Consulting Estimator gives a brief presentation of the software under estimate. This helps to create the right ambience and ensure that all the session members have the same objective in mind.

The duration of the session itself is best limited to about 45 minutes, since beyond this the session members start to feel tired.

The people involved in the group should, if possible, be those who are likely to be concerned with the project to be estimated. However, it is an advantage if the members of the group also represent a diversity of interests; for example, some might be invited to participate because of previous experience in similar projects, others because of their knowledge of software methods or simply because they are programming language specialists.

The Consulting Estimator should set out from the start the non-evaluation rule and enforce it when necessary. He should record the various size estimates, whether optimistic, likely or pessimistic, and the reasons why they are so classified. Finally, when the flow of ideas starts to dry up, he should restate the estimates generated by the group.

Evaluative session   The productive session should be followed up a few days later by an evaluative session. During this session, the Consulting Estimator and team leader or software manager should go through all the estimates generated. Then, considering the reasons and the figures, they should apply the usual critical analysis to select the correct set of figures.

B. Metrics assistance to size estimating

Let us now consider how the Consulting Estimator could be assisted in experienced organizations having a software metrics activity.

It is appropriate at this point to mention the work done by Allan J. Albrecht of IBM Corporate Information Systems and Administration, White Plains, New York. Albrecht analyzed the statement of requirements of 24 data processing programs in terms of the following [1]:

- inputs – number of unique user data input types;
- outputs – number of unique user data output types;
- inquiries – number of unique input/output combinations;
- files – number of file types used and shared;
- interfaces – number of logical groups of information that are entered or output.

He then adjusted these numbers according to three levels of complexity – simple, average and complex – to within a range of ± 25%. Subsequently, he carried out a statistical analysis on these numbers in relation to the size of the programs and the effort they required for development. During the course of this work, Albrecht discovered a high degree of correlation between the size of the data processing type of programs his company had developed and a measure called the **Function Points** [1]. This measure is defined as the linear combination of the five adjusted terms such that:

$$F_p = a.\text{inputs} + b.\text{outputs} + c.\text{inquiries} + d.\text{files} + e.\text{interfaces}$$

where a, b, c, d and e are constants as determined by his statistics.

Albrecht also determined a series of simple equations, using the Function Points, that enable the calculation of the estimated size and cost for the two languages used in his organization, Cobol and PL/1. As an example, here is the formula used to estimate the size of a Cobol program when its Function Points count is known:

$$S = 118.7 \, F_p - 6490$$

In practice, once a software requirement is known, a top-level analysis can provide the Function Points count. Then, by using the appropriate formula – the size formula in this case – the size estimate can be obtained.

Albrecht's metrication has some interesting advantages but it is not yet applicable to real-time programs.

- It is directly linked to the statement of requirements. Any change of requirements can be followed up by a quick size re-estimate.
- The statement of requirements and possibly some high-level analysis are needed; thus, the estimating process can be carried out at an early stage.
- The size-estimating process can be carried out directly during the preparation or revision of the requirements. This helps to rapidly build up a common understanding of the development between the customer and the developing organization.

Moreover, a consensus has to be made as to whether these advantages counterbalance the lack of involvement of the software designer at the early stage. Later chapters stress the importance of involving some members of the development team as early as possible.

Albrecht's method is only one case of application of software metrics to size estimating; indeed, it needs to be further validated on more applications and in areas other than data processing. Although there might be some other equally effective ways of defining a metrics for estimation, it can nevertheless be seen from this example how much estimating effort would be saved and how much more accurate the estimate would be by any use of them.

It is expected that when more and more software organizations have created such metrics for their application areas, even if it is based on different terms from Albrecht's, the process of software sizing will become much easier.

1.7.5 Conclusions on software sizing

Like most of the estimating methods currently in use, the estimating procedure described in subsequent chapters starts by estimating the size of the software. The size can be estimated or re-estimated at various stages of the Product Life Cycle. However, the earliest stage at which the size estimate is meaningful is at the system design stage for the preparation of the Preliminary Design Review. The size unit retained here is the NCSS standing for Non-Commentary Source Statements.

An estimating method based on software size expressed in NCSS presents numerous advantages:

- the size is measurable with reasonable ease by using simple counting tools;
- it is deliverable in the form of object code;
- compared to the number of lines of source code, the NCSS size is more closely related to the object code size;
- it is comparable across organizations on the basis of problem similarity without depending on the commenting capability of the individual programmers;

- it does not depend on the design methodology;
- it can be evaluated in a probabilistic fashion by a group of knowledge-able engineers (this particular technique is introduced in Chapter 6).

But there are also some disadvantages:

- high-level languages do not require as many NCSS as low-level languages or assembler languages, so care should be taken when relating to the language while comparing software products;
- the size is not measurable early enough in the Software Life Cycle.

These disadvantages will be taken care of during the presentation of the method (see Chapter 6). At present, the absence of a valid alternative to size seems to be the main justification for using this method.

EXERCISES

1.1 Select a small to medium-size software project in your organization. Go through its PERT chart, identifying software tasks in terms of work related to specification, design, code and test for at least two hierar-chical levels (one level and its dependent). (*Note*: The rationale for this exercise is that project managers sometimes structure their development plan in a fashion that is not always clearly software methodology oriented. It is useful for the estimator to be aware of this underlying motivation.)

(a) Analyze the problems you encounter.

(b) Discuss your findings with the project manager, and list and analyze his reasons.

1.2 Extract 20 consecutive pages/screens out of a source program listing/file. This extract should be a representative sample of the full program; at least, you should be reasonably convinced that it is so.

(a) Count the total number of:
- lines of source code;
- commentary lines;
- blank lines;
- declaration lines;
- executable statements.

(b) Give the size of source code corresponding to this extract in LOC and NCSS.

(c)　Write a program that counts the number of executable statements; for example, in Pascal programs, it is sometimes the practice to count the number of semicolons not associated with commentary statements. Run your program on this extract and compare the results with those obtained in (b). Evaluate the performance of this measurement method.

1.3　Consider a medium-scale software project you are familiar with. Assume that this project is just starting. What would be your prediction level – guess, educated guess, estimate – for the following elements:

actual completion cost, problems to be encountered during qualification, development time, number of defects to be detected on module *Xxy*, project peak manning, date of the Critical Design Review (CDR), decisions to be made at the CDR, types of defects to be detected during the CDR of module *Rst*, name of the integration manager, host processor for module testing, name of the participants of the code-inspection group for module *Zxy*, specification effort for module *Zxy*, number of customer's representatives at the CDR.

1.4　The software package FOUR56 has been estimated to have a size of 4800 NCSS almost uniformly distributed on five modules. The development productivity for this kind of program is usually 1200 NCSS/MY.

(a)　Draw a Gantt chart showing the development activities in terms of specification, design, code and test on two hierarchical levels (for example, package and module levels).

(b)　Express in man.weeks (mw) the manpower necessary for the development of FOUR56 (take 1 MY = 52 mw).

(c)　Using Equation (6.5) and Equation (6.6), allocate manpower to each task.

(d)　How would you man each task? For example, investigate some heuristics such as not leaving a person alone on the same task for more than two months, or allocate a partner to form a small team which shortens the time scale. Discuss your choice considering the nature of the task.

(e)　Establish the manning profile with respect to the time. Discuss the average manning in terms of the desirability of conducting the five modules in parallel or not.

(f)　Indicate on the FOUR56 chart the main milestones (for example, CDR, FCC, SIT, IOC and FOC of Figure 1.1) and the re-estimating times. Discuss these events in relation to the manning strategy adopted in (e).

1.5   The development of SWITCH87 requires the concurrent development of hardware and software.

   (a)   Specific hardware development tasks are not mentioned in Figure 1.1. How would you add them?

   (b)   Explain how the Software Life Cycle is embedded in the Product Life Cycle.

   (c)   During which phases would you consider the hardware/software trade-off? Investigate the critical positioning of this problem, justifying your choice.

   (d)   Investigate the reasons for which the software of SWITCH87 would be more difficult to develop than if it were a software-only development.

1.6   (a)   Consider the 800 NCSS program, SMALLSTAR, you have written on a Personal Computer, to be run by yourself at home. Which activities of the Product Life Cycle were the most important?

   (b)   You developed SMALLSTAR for another computer expert living a few thousand miles away. Which activities of the Product Life Cycle would you retain?

   (c)   In reality, you have developed SMALLSTAR as a product to be sold on the consumer market. Which activities of the Product Life Cycle would you retain and which would you extend?

   (d)   SMALLSTAR was a success and the market is ready for BIG-STAR, a 8000 NCSS program running on a Personal Computer. Describe the main activities of the Product Life Cycle.

   (e)   The capital goods manufacturing industry, having noticed BIG-STAR, is ready to take on board a more elaborate version, MEGASTAR, a 80 000 NCSS program running on a mini-computer. What new problems will you have to face? What is the impact on the Product Life Cycle?

   (f)   For each case, assess the role of the estimating process in view of the need for a sound time, cost and manning prediction. Using the Product Life Cycle's description, discuss the reasons for which and the extent with which the project grows in time and manpower.

1.7   Prepare a software data collection plan for a small-size project. Define an objective (verification of an estimating model).

   •   Which data is needed with a view to implementing the objective (prepare a list)?

- Where can this data be obtained (documents, source files, listing, people)?
- How can you get the data without burdening the development process (automatic measurement or transfer, recopied by self)?
- When can this data be collected (depending on the nature of the data, which milestone, which task)?
- How is the raw data to be processed (which statistics, manual, automatic)?
- What is to be done with the results (management report, feed back to programming team, actions to be considered)?
- Testing the data collection process, establish a set of testing points.

Chapter 2
Estimating Methods Survey

2.1 Models

When facing an estimating task the estimator always has a model in mind. However, as there is considerable danger in keeping the model at an intuitive level – it can be too easily interacted with by emotional aspects – the model should be formally established. The surest way of doing this is to involve mathematics, as will be shown during the course of this chapter. A survey of models in use in various areas of the industry will help the estimator to understand the respective advantages of bottom-up and top-down estimating methods.

2.1.1 General

The model is concerned with the representation of the process to be estimated. As there are various forms of models, let us first briefly review them, according to the classification of V. R. Basili (University of Maryland) [3]. His classification considers the mathematical form of the equations used, the nature of the data used as the predictor and the assumptions made during the software development process.

A model may be **static** or **dynamic**. In a static model, a unique variable (for example, the size) is taken as a starting element for calculating all the others (for example, cost, time). The form of the equation used is the same

31

for all calculations. In a dynamic model, on the other hand, all variables are inter-dependent; there is no basic variable as in the static model.

When a model makes use of a single basic variable to calculate all the others it is said to be a **single-variable** model. In some models, several variables are needed to describe the software development process, and selected equations combine these variables to give the estimate of time and cost. These models are called **multivariable**.

The variables, single or multiple, that are input to the model to predict the behaviour of a software development are called **predictors**. The choice and handling of the predictors are the central concerns in estimating methodology.

Static, multivariable models make use of adjustments by means of data. An **adjusted baseline** model uses a single-variable baseline equation adjusted in some way by a set of other variables, whereas an **adjusted table-driven** model uses a baseline estimate adjusted by a set of variables whose relationships are defined in tables built from historical data.

The rest of this section is devoted to a description of the main model categories in use in current estimating methods (see Figure 2.1).

2.1.2   Static, single-variable models

Methods using this model use the same basic equation to estimate the desired values – for example, effort, documentation, time. They all depend on the same variable used as a predictor (for example, size). An example of the most common equation is:

$$C = a L^b \tag{2.1}$$

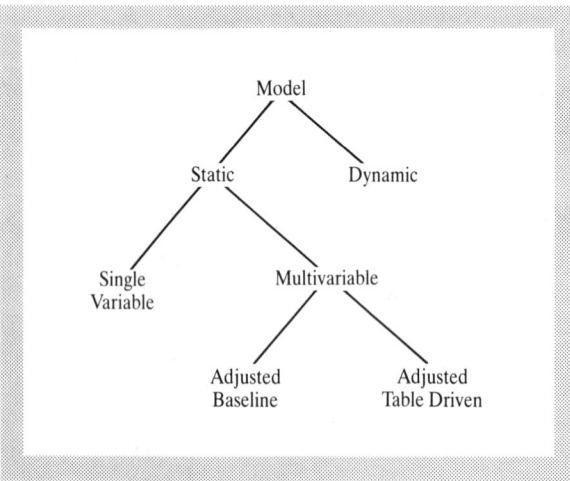

Figure 2.1   Model relationships.

where C is the cost (effort expressed in any unit of manpower, for example, man.months) and L is the size generally given in the number of lines of source code (see Section 1.7.3). The constants, a and b, are derived from the historical data of the organization. Since a and b depend on the local development environment, these models are not transportable to different organizations.

EXAMPLE

The Software Engineering Laboratory of the University of Maryland has established a model, the SEL model, for estimating its own software productions. This model (reported by V. R. Basili in [3]) is a typical example of a static, single-variable model:

$$E = 1.4\ L^{0.93} \tag{2.2}$$
$$DOC = 30.4\ L^{0.90} \tag{2.3}$$
$$D = 4.6\ L^{0.26} \tag{2.4}$$

Effort (E, in man.months), documentation (DOC, in number of pages) and duration (D, in months) are calculated from the number of lines of source code (L, in thousands of lines) used as a predictor.

2.1.3 Static, multivariable models

Although these models are often based on Equation (2.1), they actually depend on several variables representing aspects of the software development environment – for example, methods used, user participation, customer-originated changes, memory constraints, real time.

EXAMPLE

The model developed by Walston and Felix at IBM provides a relationship between delivered lines of source code (L, in thousands of lines or KLOC, see Section 1.7.3) and effort (E, in man.months). This is given by [38]:

$$E = 5.2\ L^{0.91} \tag{2.5}$$

In the same fashion, the duration of the development (D, in months) is given by [38]:

$$D = 4.1\ L^{0.36} \tag{2.6}$$

To these equations is associated a method for estimating the productivity. Data collected on 60 software projects, representing a wide variety of applications and size (ranging from 4000 to 467 000 lines of source code), shows a relation between the productivity (expressed in number of lines of source code per man.month) and a productivity index, I.

The productivity index uses 29 variables, which are found to be highly correlated to productivity as follows [38]:

$$I = \sum_{i=1}^{29} W_i X_i \qquad (2.7)$$

where W_i is a factor weight for the ith variable and $X_i = \{-1, 0, +1\}$. The estimator gives X_i one of the values $-1, 0$ or $+1$ depending on whether the variable decreases, has no effect or increases the productivity, respectively.

The terms of Equation (2.7) are then added up to give the productivity index. A productivity range can then be obtained for the project by using a productivity versus productivity index chart [38]. Finally, this productivity range can be used in conjunction with Equation (2.5) to refine the estimate.

Other models that are built along the same lines include:

- B. W. Boehm's COCOMO Model [4];
- The Doty Associates Model as in [17];
- The GRC (General Research Corporation) Model.

These models will be briefly introduced in Section 2.2.

2.1.4 Dynamic, multivariable models

The most interesting approach in this family of models is one based on a theory of problem solving as applied to software development.

The work of Norden [28] describes a development as a problem-solving effort. The goal of this effort is the progressive exhaustion of the problems, according to a linear-learning curve. Putnam applied this concept to software development and produced a method which will be discussed further in later chapters.

The Putnam/Norden Model uses the following set of assumptions:

(1)   the number of problems to be solved is finite;
(2)   the problem-solving effort makes an impact on the unsolved problem set;

(3)   a decision removes one unsolved problem from the set;

(4)   the staff size is proportional to the number of problems ready for solution.

A theoretical development of these assumptions leads to a representation of the staffing by means of a Rayleigh function, and, in fact, this representation has frequently been verified in industry on large-scale project developments involving high technology.

Putnam, having carried out a statistical analysis on a large quantity of software developments in the US Air Force and later on in QSM (Quantitative Software Management, Incorporated), discovered a relationship between the three main elements of software estimating – that is, size, time and cost – which resulted in the **Software Equation**. (See Figure 5.6 for examples of the Rayleigh manpower function. Notice that the curve starts at the origin.)

Parr [31] describes the process of developing software as solving successively a large number of small problems. As in the Norden description, each elementary problem-solving effort removes one unsolved problem from the total number of problems. But, while Norden assumes an independence between problems, Parr observes that there are some dependencies between them: some problems have to be solved before their dependents can be dealt with, while, fortunately, some other problems do not have any dependency. The development stops when the last problems have no dependents.

Put in a different way, the solving of a problem might make visible a series of other problems which were hidden behind the solved one. An obvious example of this type of phenomenon is the corrections of defects (hidden problems) detected during a code inspection (primary problem). This process of problem discovery occurs throughout the development: at the beginning, the solving of the first problems uncovers a number of other problems. Then, at the end, there are no more dependents and the number of problems is completely exhausted.

One of the merits of Parr's description is that it captures a certain software-management's practice by which the rate of effort applied at any time to the development is approximately proportional to the number of visible problems at application time. This in turn reflects the natural (and tactical) attitude of reacting to immediately perceived threats (or opportunity to carry out tasks in parallel) by opposition to a planned (and strategic) development action.

Parr's analytical study of the manpower distribution shows that:

• it could be modelled by a sech-square function and not by a Rayleigh function, as proposed by Norden;

• the overall shape of both models, Parr and Norden, would be similar in their medium and final parts;

- some level of manpower would be needed at an early stage of the software development, while Norden's model accepts a null manning level at starting time.

2.1.5 Conclusions on models

At this point, it is interesting to briefly re-examine the notion of a model. The line of thought adopted in this book is not to predict exactly the manpower distribution of future projects, but more importantly to capture in the model the intrinsic relationships between cost, time and product.

Furthermore, it should be remembered that a model is only a model; that is, its purpose is to offer guidance to the decision makers and not to act as a substitute for the decision-making process. In other words, the project manager is quite entitled to deviate from the model, not only because it is his own responsibility, but more especially because he can capture intuitively people-related data that cannot be represented by any model, however perfect.

For these reasons, it is important to appreciate the originality of the Parr concept, but, nevertheless, in the rest of the book it is assumed that the Norden/Rayleigh model is powerful enough for our estimating purposes. However, it should be noted at this point that the Parr model is still undergoing tests (at the time of writing) and its methodology is not yet available for use in the software industry.

2.2 Survey of existing models

In 1981, S. N. Mohanty gave a description and a comparison of well-known models in use in the software industry [26]. For completeness, a short description of each of the major models now follows.

2.2.1 Farr and Zagorski Model

Reported in 1965 at an ICC Symposium on Economics of Automatic Data Processing, this model is probably the earliest known. The model involves 13 predictors (for example, delivered statements, document types, size of database) in a static, multivariable model represented by three linear equations, which give the manpower required in man.months to design, code and debug a system. The effort starts when a programmer is given a complete operational specification for a program and it ends when the program is released for integration and system testing [11, 14, 41].

2.2.2 Naval Air Development Centre Model

The Naval Air Development Centre (NADC) used a group of equations similar to those of Farr and Zagorski for avionics systems. However, the predictors were not quite the same, as they were also intended to cover costs for research, development and testing. This model (reported in 1971) tried to capture all sources of cost, such as number of delivered instructions, number of miles travelled and document types [8, 26].

2.2.3 Wolverton Model

In this model, R. W. Wolverton (at TRW Systems Group in 1974) suggests that manpower is directly proportional to the size of the software developed. His model is strongly related to command and control, and real-time systems, and a historical cost-per-instruction data base is used. The difficulty is considered by means of a scale, easy–medium–hard, for old/new software. A matrix of ratios is used to allocate the total cost to seven phases with each phase divided into up to 25 activities. The model is then a combination of formal algorithm and judgement. R. W. Wolverton cautions that this matrix is given for illustration only and users should be prepared to set up their own ratios [40].

2.2.4 Kustanowitz Model

In this model, the software development is structured in phases. For each phase, the cost is estimated using productivity factors based on experience, environment and the programming language used. The size is estimated at the end of the conceptual design and is used to determine the total cost of the project. The work of A. L. Kustanowitz (1977) covers a large variety of application programs such as real-time, numerical analysis and operating systems [21].

2.2.5 ESD Model

The approach of this model, formulated in 1975 at the US Air Force Electronic Systems Division, is similar to Wolverton's. The cost per line of source code is established for the organization and the total manpower cost is proportional to the number of lines of source code to be developed [26].

2.2.6 Tecolote Research Incorporated Model

This model relies largely on the estimated size of the program, and also on the computer system speed and memory size. All code size measurements are in terms of machine instructions. Tecolote Research Incorporated applied this model in 1974 to tactical software systems [12].

2.2.7 Aerospace Model

Aerospace is the name of a static, single-variable, non-linear model reported by T. G. James at the National Aerospace Electronic Conference in 1977. This model uses the size of the delivered software as a predictor. It involves separate calculations of effort for real-time and support software [18].

2.2.8 GRC Model

In 1974, GRC (General Research Corporation) used a static, single-variable, non-linear model based on the size of delivered software. This model also recognized the role played by the host processor. An excess capacity reduced the required effort [26].

2.2.9 SDC Model

SDC (Systems Development Corporation, Santa Monica, California) uses a static, multivariable, linear model involving 11 predictors. The size is not explicitly used but the model produces a cost per thousands of lines of source code [27].

2.2.10 RCA Model (Price-S)

Price-S is a proprietary software cost-estimating model developed and maintained by PRICE Systems Division of RCA, New Jersey. From an estimate of size, type and difficulty of the project, the model computes project cost and schedule. It is based on a historical cost data base which is used for estimation of new projects [13].

2.2.11 Walston and Felix Model

In the late 1970s, C. E. Walston and C. P. Felix carried out an extensive analysis of the data gathered by a Software Measurement Program at IBM Federal Systems Division, from which they developed a productivity model. This static, single-variable, non-linear model uses nine equations. One of these equations computes the cost from a size estimate; the others show the relationship between the various parameters of the software development, such as project duration, total effort, documentation, delivered code, staff size and computer cost [38].

2.2.12 Aron Model

During the NATO Conference on Software Engineering at Rome (Italy) in 1969, J. D. Aron introduced the basis for a software-estimating practice. However simplistic, his contribution has the merit of leading the way towards more realistic views on software estimating. He observed that the manpower demand increases gradually during the first phases of the development, reaches a peak and then decreases to zero. His method relied very much on experience and he asserted that an intended project should be compared with similar projects in a similar environment. A standard productivity (500, 250 or 125 instructions/man.month) is used according to the estimated difficulty of each module (easy, medium, hard). The size estimate plays an important role in the determination of the manpower demand [2].

2.2.13 Putnam Model

In 1977, L. H. Putnam produced a complete analysis of the data collected from the software projects of the US Army Computer Systems Command, which resulted in a software estimation model, since known as the Putnam Model. This is a dynamic, multivariable model based on a Norden/Rayleigh function. There is a non-linear trade-off between the cost, the delivery time and the size. L. H. Putnam offers a complete methodology for which the size estimate is one of the starting points. SLIM (Software Life Cycle Model) is a proprietary software cost-estimating tool offered by Quantitative Software Management, Incorporated, Virginia [32–36]. (The Putnam Model is presented in Chapter 4 and some practical aspects are developed in subsequent chapters.)

2.2.14 Boehm Model

During the 1970s, B. W. Boehm at TRW Incorporated, Redondo Beach, California, analyzed more than 60 software projects from various application areas. This resulted, in 1980, in an estimating method called COCOMO [4]. COCOMO is based on a static, multivariable model, in which the size and the environment play important roles.

2.2.15 Doty/RADC Model

Doty Associates, Incorporated, produced, in 1977, a software cost-estimating study of the software developed for the RADC (Rome Air Development Centre), New York. This resulted in a set of recommendations for estimating software, grouped in a model called the Doty model. Four application areas are covered: command and control, scientific, business and utility. The Doty Model is a static, multivariable, non-linear model. The size is estimated and then used for computing a cost, which is further refined by means of 14 predictors describing the environment [17]. These predictors are yes/no multipliers that cover aspects of the software development environment.

2.2.16   Daly Model

In 1977, E. B. Daly reported some software development experiences related to three large-scale, real-time software projects developed at GTE-Automatic Electric Laboratories, Northlake, Illinois. His findings are what constitutes the Daly Model, which is a static, multivariable, linear model. The size is estimated and then used in a linear formula based on ten predictors to arrive at the cost of designing and testing a software module [10].

2.3   Comparison of the models

Siba N. Mohanty [26] compared 15 of the models used in current estimating methods and the overall result of his comparison is shown in Table 2.1. His comparison is based on a set of 49 attributes which cover all possible aspects of the software development.

For the purposes of demonstration, these attributes can be grouped as follows:

Size	=	8 attributes
Data base	=	1
Complexity	=	10
Type of program	=	3
Documentation	=	3
Environment	=	15
Other Items	=	9

For each model and within each group, Table 2.1 shows the number of attributes used by the model. For each group of attributes, the number of attributes is added and compared with the total number of times these attributes are used.

It can be seen from this table that the three major concerns when estimating a software development are:

1 – Environment	36%	
2 – Size	20%	
3 – Complexity	19%	
	75%	

All the other attributes are only involved for 25% of the estimating process.

Table 2.1 Comparison of estimating methods by the attributes method.

Models	Number and Type of Attributes							
	Size	Data Base	Complexity	Type of Program	Documentation	Environment	Other Items	Total Attributes
	(8)	(1)	(10)	(3)	(3)	(15)	(9)	(49)
Farr–Zagorsky	5	1	1	–	2	3	1	13
SDC	2	–	1	1	1	6	1	12
Aron	–	–	3	–	–	1	–	4
NADC	5	1	1	–	2	3	1	13
Putnam	2	–	3	–	–	2	–	7
Wolverton	1	–	3	1	–	4	6	15
GRC	1	–	1	–	–	2	–	4
Tecolote	1	–	–	–	–	1	1	3
ESD	2	1	1	–	–	2	–	6
COCOMO	2	1	7	3	–	12	4	29
Daly	2	–	6	1	1	5	1	16
Aerospace	1	–	1	1	–	1	–	4
Walston–Felix	1	–	–	–	–	–	1	2
Doty	2	–	–	2	–	5	–	9
Kustanowitz	1	1	–	–	–	3	1	5
Price-S	2	–	1	2	–	4	1	10
Total	30	5	29	11	6	54	17	152
%	20	3	19	7	4	36	11	100

Adapted and reprinted from S. N. Mohanty, 'Software Cost Estimation: Present and Future', *Software-Practice and Experience*, **11**, by permission of John Wiley & Sons, Inc. ©1981.

2.3.1 Environment

These models show a significant concern for evaluating the environment by allocating 36% of the attributes to it. By environment, it is meant all the equipment and methods that help the programmer to develop the software. This could refer to the host computer and its terminals, and also the familiarity of the programmer with the utilities (for example, compilers, languages). We will later see how estimating models offer a method for measuring the environment.

2.3.2 Size

All models use an estimated size in terms of either source code or object code. Although Aron [2] does not explicitly mention a size estimate it is implied in the comparison with similar past projects. The advantage of using the size is that it is measurable and corresponds to a physical delivery. The disadvantage of the size is that it only becomes measurable rather late (generally when 40% of development effort has already been expended).

2.3.3 Complexity

Significant effort has been put into evaluating the complexity of a piece of software. This evaluation has been the subject of a lot of discussion. Halstead proposed a measure of complexity [15], but this cannot be carried out until late in the project as it requires the prior existence of the source code. McCabe [22] suggests a procedure aimed at evaluating complexity at an earlier stage, but this seems to be too dependent on the development method. Thus, it appears that software complexity represents the main difficulty, and so in what follows we will use the word complexity in its intuitively loose meaning.

The development of a complex piece of software is reputed to be difficult. When this is the case it is not possible to rush the development: a slow and steady manpower build-up is unavoidable, and the time scale is necessarily long. A useful estimating method should take this 'difficulty' aspect into account.

2.4   The micro model versus the macro model

The modelling of software development can be approached in two different ways: the top-down way or the bottom-up way. The factor common to both approaches is the size estimate. We will return to this in Chapter 6, but at this stage we can say that it could be performed by a quick and approximate design which determines all the parts of the software to be produced down to the level of the modules. The size of each part is estimated by a combination of experience and intuitive consensus by a group of knowledgeable engineers.

Then, the size of the software product is arrived at by adding up the sizes of all the modules.

2.4.1 The traditional approach for estimating

The differences between the modelling approaches occur at the stages when the overall manpower cost, the development time and the manpower distribution need to be estimated.

Before introducing the micro and macro models, let us examine the traditional approach. Once the size of each small part is ascertained, the experienced software engineers assess the effort and time necessary for its design, coding and testing, and the dependency between each activity. When this is done, the same procedure is applied to determine the effort and time necessary for linking each group of small parts together and testing them. These groups are sometimes called **subsystems**.

Going one level higher, the same procedure is applied to determine the manpower effort and time to build the system, testing and qualifying the software product. Sometimes the initial system design effort and time are omitted, but when this is not the case they are the front end of the estimate so obtained. Then a bar chart or a PERT chart is constructed taking into account the dependencies between tasks. This chart represents the development plan of the software project.

Thus, we can see that the traditional way of estimating uses a bottom-up approach. The natural advantage of this practice is that the group who contributed to the estimating process is likely to be committed to its implementation. On the other hand, the obvious disadvantages are:

- This procedure takes time. Experience shows that between one and four weeks is needed to estimate a project of 9000 statements.

- Whenever strategic choices are discovered to be wrong at the end of the process, all the estimating work has to be carried out again. Thus, still more time is necessary.

- This procedure does not offer any guarantee against optimism. Experience of under-estimating cost and time are very well known.

2.4.2 The micro model

To improve the efficiency of the estimating process, more rational methods of estimating have been developed. The survey reported earlier showed that a great amount of effort has been involved in capturing all possible data on the small software parts and on their structuring, in such a way as to offer a set of equations, numerical information and rules for operating the traditional bottom-up procedure in a more systematic fashion. Models resulting from this approach are called **micro models**, as they aim at constructing the estimate of a system from the knowledge accumulated about the small software parts and their interactions. The leading method using this approach is the Constructive Cost Model (COCOMO) of B. W. Boehm.

The great advantage of the micro model is that it permits the software group to handle an estimate in an almost traditional fashion (although guided by the rules) and to handle estimate components (for example, modules, data base size, processor turnaround) for which the group has a feel. Moreover, the micro model can easily give an impression of security. Nevertheless, the micro model often obliges an estimator to manipulate a lot of data, and this can significantly increase the time necessary to set up an estimate.

2.4.3   The macro model

The top-down method has a quite different approach in principle. Instead of directly using the estimating data base, the model is constructed in such a way so that only the most important variables remain in the equations (for example, project cost, time and size), the estimating data base being hidden and implicit in the relationship between these variables.

Therefore, the need for considering small software parts has completely disappeared. This approach results in a model that offers a macroscopic view of the software project. It is therefore called a **macro model**. It is certainly necessary, once the system estimate is done, to provide an estimate for each small part. This is carried out by a top-down procedure based on the size structure of the software product. The leading macro model is the Putnam Model which has been developed from Norden's theory of the project life cycle.

The effectiveness of the macro model comes from its global view, mathematically representable, so that even though the computations are sometimes complex, they can be easily computerized and estimates carried out quickly. The disadvantage of this model might be that human participation is kept to a minimum. However, because the macro model offers a global view of the software project, it embodies some very effective features, such as the cost–time trade-off capability that exists in the Putnam Model.

2.4.4   Conclusions on modelling approaches

In the following chapters, two important models for software estimating are introduced. Chapter 3 describes the Constructive Cost Model of B. W. Boehm. This is a very popular example of bottom-up estimating. Then, from Chapter 4 onwards, the main features of the top-down Putnam Model are described in depth. The reader will be able to carry out his own estimates and to select whichever model performs in the most appropriate fashion for his purposes.

EXERCISES

2.1 Regression models are often of the type represented by Equation (2.1), which can be restated as:

$$y = a \, x^b \tag{2.1.1}$$

Data collected on past projects gives a set of values for y and x, and we want to formalize this knowledge by a regression model. This problem involves determining a and b for this series of N projects.

(a) Linearize Equation (2.1.1) by taking the natural logarithm of both sides. (Use $Y = \text{Log } y$, $X = \text{Log } x$ and $A = \text{Log } a$.)

(b) The series of N past projects provides a set of N pairs of values: X_i and Y_i. Express the sum Z of the squares of the deviations of the measured data, Y_i, from the model, $A + b \, X_i$.

(c) The objective is to find the values of A and b that minimize the sum Z.

- By differentiating Z relative to A and setting it at zero, find an expression between ΣY_i, ΣX_i, N, A and b. (*Note*: ΣX_i means here the sum of all the N values X_i.)

- By differentiating Z relative to b and setting it at zero, find an expression between $\Sigma X_i Y_i$, A, ΣX_i, ΣX_i^2 and b.

(d) Re-arrange the expressions obtained in (c) and express:

- A as a function of ΣY_i, ΣX_i, b and N.

- b as a function of $\Sigma X_i Y_i$, ΣX_i, ΣY_i, ΣX_i^2 and N.

Then, b is directly determined, a is obtained by $a = \exp(A)$ and the regression model is defined.

2.2 A data collection carried out on four projects has given the following information:

Function	Project 1	Project 2	Project 3	Project 4
Size (KLOC)	38	25	15	30
Manpower (man.months)	235.97	142.77	77.34	177.69

(a) Define the regression model $E = a \, L^b$ by using the results of Exercise 2.1.

(b) The size of a software product to be developed in the same environment has been estimated to be 22 000 LOC. Predict the manpower cost in man.months.

2.3   Compare the Walston–Felix Model [Equation (2.5) and Equation (2.6)] with the SEL Model [Equation (2.2) and Equation (2.4)] on a software development expected to involve 8 MY of effort.

   (a)   Calculate the number of lines of source code that can be produced.

   (b)   Calculate the duration of the development.

   (c)   Calculate the average manning.

   (d)   Calculate the productivity in LOC/MY.

Chapter 3
The Constructive Cost Model

3.1 Introduction

The Constructive Cost Model (COCOMO) [4] gained rapid popularity following the publication of B. W. Boehm's excellent book *Software Engineering Economics* in 1981. COCOMO is a hierarchy of software cost-estimation models which includes basic, intermediate and detailed submodels.

   This chapter introduces Boehm's model and identifies its advantages and limitations. The reasons for introducing COCOMO are two-fold: (1) its popularity and (2) it is an outstanding example of bottom-up estimating. COCOMO is a typical example of a micro model (see Section 2.4.2). For detailed COCOMO, the estimating process starts at the lowest level of the software structure (the module), and then the estimate is progressively constructed by considering higher levels, subsystems and, finally, the system level. For reasons of consistency with subsequent chapters the original notation has been slightly changed, but great care has been taken to preserve Boehm's ideas.

3.2 Basic model

The basic model aims at estimating, in a quick and rough fashion, most of the small- to medium-sized software projects. Three modes of software development are considered in this model: organic, semi-detached and embedded.

47

3.2.1 The organic mode

In the organic mode, a small team of experienced programmers develop software in a very familiar environment. The size of the software development in this mode ranges from small (a few KLOC) to medium (a few tens of KLOC), while in the other two modes the size ranges from small to very large (a few hundreds of KLOC). In this mode, as well as in the other two modes, the cost increases, as the size increases, and the development time becomes longer.

Two equations are used for determining the manpower cost and the development time. The cost is given by:

$$K_m = 2.4\ S_k^{1.05} \tag{3.1}$$

where K_m is the manpower cost expressed in man.months and S_k is the size expressed in thousands of delivered source statements. The development time is given by:

$$t_d = 2.5\ K_m^{0.38} \tag{3.2}$$

where K_m is the manpower cost as derived from Equation (3.1) and t_d is the development time expressed in months. It should be noted at this stage that these two equations, and others yet to come, have been determined by a curve-fitting exercise carried out on data collected from about 63 software projects at TRW Incorporated by Boehm. These software projects include a large variety of languages and application areas.

3.2.2 The embedded mode

In the embedded mode of software development, the project has tight constraints, which might be related to the target processor and its interface with the associated hardware. The problem to be solved is unique and so it is often hard to draw on experience, as it does not necessarily exist.

The time and cost estimates are based on the same equations as for the organic mode, but with different constants. Thus, the cost is given by:

$$K_m = 3.6\ S_k^{1.20} \tag{3.3}$$

and the development time by:

$$t_d = 2.5\ K_m^{0.32} \tag{3.4}$$

The units used for K_m and t_d are the same as those defined for the organic mode.

3.2.3 The semi-detached mode

This is an intermediate mode between the organic mode and the embedded mode. Depending on the problem at hand, the team might include a mixture of experienced and less experienced people with only a recent history of working together.

The time and cost equations are again of the same form as for the two previous modes:

$$K_m = 3.0 \ S_k^{1.12} \tag{3.5}$$
$$t_d = 2.5 \ K_m^{0.35} \tag{3.6}$$

The units used for K_m and t_d are the same as for the organic mode.

3.2.4 Remarks on the basic model

With the basic model, the software estimator has a useful tool for estimating quickly, by two runs on a pocket calculator, the cost and development time of a software project, once the size is estimated. Naturally, the software estimator will have to assess by himself which mode is the most appropriate.

Considering the three modes in the order of increasing project complexity, it can be seen that the constants used for the cost calculation increase from 2.4 to 3.6, which corresponds to a manpower increase. The reason for this is obvious: the more complex a project is, the more effort is required for its development. However, we should be very prudent when drawing conclusions from the use of the basic model, since in the same mode the equations will give the same cost and development time whatever the quality of the software environment (for example, methods used, tool effectiveness, management methods).

EXAMPLE

Consider the case of a software project whose size has been estimated to be 30 000 NCSS. The manpower cost and development time estimates can be calculated by means of the equations previously given. Thus:

Mode	Manpower Cost (man.months)	Development Time (months)
Organic	85	13.5
Semi-detached	135	13.9
Embedded	213	13.9

If this project is a real-time project (embedded), it would require 2.5 times more effort than if it were an easy, straightforward data-processing project (organic). Furthermore, the basic model shows a relatively constant development time, 1 year and 1 month. The conclusion then is that as the project becomes more complex more people must be involved to achieve the development within the same elapsed time. Hence, these equations should be handled with some care.

3.3 Intermediate model

The basic model permitted the estimation of time and cost of software development in three modes (organic, semi-detached and embedded) by using a single predictor – the size. This model allowed for a quick and rough estimate, but it resulted in a lack of accuracy. In contrast to the reality of software development, the same equation giving the development time in an embedded mode gives the same result independent of whether the project is carried out by a team of young graduates working with a small PDP-11 or by a more experienced team using a large IBM-370 with interactive terminals. For this reason, Boehm introduced an additional set of 15 predictors called **cost drivers** in the intermediate model to take account of the software development environment.

Cost drivers are used to adjust the nominal cost of a project to the actual project environment, hence increasing the accuracy of the estimate.

3.3.1 Nominal cost equations

For each development mode, the 15 cost drivers intervene as multipliers on the nominal cost, K_n, to produce the adjusted cost. It is therefore difficult to retain the same cost equations as in the basic model.

The nominal cost equations for the intermediate model are:

Organic mode	$K_n = 3.2\ S_k^{1.05}$	**(3.7)**
Semi-detached mode	$K_n = 3.0\ S_k^{1.12}$	**(3.8)**
Embedded mode	$K_n = 2.8\ S_k^{1.20}$	**(3.9)**

Note here that:

- the exponents are the same as for the basic model, confirming the role played by the size, and the effects of size sensitivity remain unaffected;
- the coefficients of the organic and embedded modes have changed in

order to maintain an equilibrium around the median mode (semi-detached) with respect to the multiplying effect of the cost drivers.

3.3.2 Cost drivers

Cost drivers aim at capturing the impact of the project environment on the development cost. From an extensive statistical analysis of more than 100 factors influencing the development cost, Boehm retained 15 of them for COCOMO.

The cost drivers are grouped into four categories: product attributes, computer attributes, personnel attributes and project attributes. They are listed hereafter by their shorter, alternative names, as defined by Boehm, for ease of reference.

(1) *Product attributes*
  - Required Software Reliability (RELY)
  - Data Base Size (DATA)
  - Product Complexity (CPLX)

(2) *Computer attributes*
  - Execution Time Constraint (TIME)
  - Main Storage Constraint (STOR)
  - Virtual Machine Volatility (VIRT)
  - Computer Turnaround Time (TURN)

(3) *Personnel attributes*
  - Analyst Capability (ACAP)
  - Application Experience (AEXP)
  - Programmer Capability (PCAP)
  - Virtual Machine Experience (VEXP)
  - Programming Language Experience (LEXP)

(4) *Project attributes*
  - Modern Programming Practices (MODP)
  - Use of Software Tools (TOOL)
  - Required Development Schedule (SCED)

Each cost driver is rated for a given project environment. The rating uses a scale very low–low–nominal–high–very High–Extra High which describes to what extent the cost driver applies to the project being estimated. Table 3.1 gives the multiplier values for the 15 cost drivers and each rating, as provided by Boehm [4]. These 15 values are multiplied together and then to

Table 3.1 Multiplier values for manpower cost.

Cost Drivers	Ratings					
	Very Low	Low	Nominal	High	Very High	Extra High
Product Attributes						
RELY	0.75	0.88	1.00	1.15	1.40	–
DATA	–	0.94	1.00	1.08	1.16	–
CPLX	0.70	0.85	1.00	1.15	1.30	1.65
Computer Attributes						
TIME	–	–	1.00	1.11	1.30	1.66
STOR	–	–	1.00	1.06	1.21	1.56
VIRT	–	0.87	1.00	1.15	1.30	–
TURN	–	0.87	1.00	1.07	1.15	–
Personnel Attributes						
ACAP	1.46	1.19	1.00	0.86	0.71	–
AEXP	1.29	1.13	1.00	0.91	0.82	–
PCAP	1.42	1.17	1.00	0.86	0.70	–
VEXP	1.21	1.10	1.00	0.90	–	–
LEXP	1.14	1.07	1.00	0.95	–	–
Project Attributes						
MODP	1.24	1.10	1.00	0.91	0.82	–
TOOL	1.24	1.10	1.00	0.91	0.83	–
SCED	1.23	1.08	1.00	1.04	1.10	–

the nominal cost, K_n, to provide a manpower cost adjusted to the environment. An example of this estimating process is outlined in Section 3.3.5.

3.3.3 The pragmatics of the cost drivers

This section aims at giving an outline of the practical meaning of each cost driver.

A.   RELY: Required Software Reliability

The RELY rating indicates the possible consequences for the user when some defects still exist in the product. A 'very low' rating is used when the defects just need to be removed by the developers without any other consequences. The 'nominal' rating indicates a moderate loss and a 'very high' rating is used when there is a possible loss of human life.

B.   DATA: Data Base Size

The DATA rating indicates the size of the data base to be developed relative to the program size. Four segments are delineated by the ratios 10–100–1000. They determine the ratings from 'low' to 'very high'.

C. CPLX: Product Complexity

CPLX rates the complexity of each module and is then used to determine the composite complexity of the system. Hence, the rating can vary from 'very low' if the module is made of simple mathematical expressions to 'extra high' for modules dealing with multiple resource scheduling.

D. TIME: Execution Time Constraint

It is always more demanding for the programmer to write a program that has an execution time constraint. The TIME constraint rating is expressed in terms of the percentage of available execution time. It is 'nominal' when this percentage is 50% and 'extra high' when the constraint is 95%.

E. STOR: Main Storage Constraint

A certain volume of main storage is expected to be used by the program. Programming effort is increased if the program has to be made to run on less volume of main storage. The STOR rating captures this extra effort from 'nominal' when the reduction of main storage is 50% to 'extra high' for a reduction of 95%.

F. VIRT: Virtual Machine Volatility

During the development of the software the machine (hardware and software) on which the program is developed might undergo some changes, more or less frequently. The VIRT rating assesses the resulting effort multipliers from 'low' to 'very high'.

G. TURN: Computer Turnaround Time

The TURN rating aims at assessing the computer response time as seen by the programmer. The longer the response time, the higher is the manpower cost. The TURN rating can vary from 'low' for an interactive system to 'very high' when the average response time is more than 12 hours.

H. ACAP: Analyst Capability

The capability of the analyst team, in terms of analysis ability, efficiency and ability to co-operate, has a significant impact on the manpower cost. The more capable the analyst team, the less the effort necessary. The ACAP rating might vary from 'very low' to 'very high'.

I. AEXP: Application Experience

The experience of the project team on a similar application has a great influence on the manpower cost. The AEXP rating can vary from 'very low' (less than four months experience) to 'very high' (greater than 12 years experience).

J. PCAP: Programmer Capability

This rating is similar to the ACAP rating, but in this case it relates to the programmers themselves. PCAP can vary from 'very low' to 'very high'. It is worth noting that this rating applies to programmers as a team and not as individuals.

K. VEXP: Virtual Machine Experience

The virtual machine is defined as for the VIRT rating and excludes the programming language experience (see LEXP). The more experienced the programming team with its host processor, the less the manpower needed. The VEXP rating can vary from 'very low' when experience is less than one month to 'high' when this experience exceeds three years.

L. LEXP: Programming Language Experience

A programming team with extensive experience in a given language will program in a much more secure fashion, hence limiting the number of defects produced, and the manpower requirements. The LEXP rating can vary from 'very low' to 'high' for a team with one month to three years experience, respectively.

M. MODP: Modern Programming Practices

The extent to which modern programming practices are used by a team is rated by MODP from 'very low' to 'very high'. These practices include, for example, structured programming and top-down development.

N. TOOL: Use of Software Tools

The use of adequate software tools is a productivity multiplier. The TOOL rating varies from 'very low' when only basic tools are used to 'very high' when special-purpose tools are used.

O. SCED: Schedule Constraint

It is recognized that the nominal development time, as defined in the basic mode, is the schedule requiring the least manpower. Any accelerations (rated 'very low') or dilatations (rated 'very high') will demand more manpower.

3.3.4   Remarks on the intermediate model

The intermediate model provides a very powerful way of capturing the influence of the environment on the project. Most of the project management concerns and the most critical multipliers are represented by the 15 cost drivers.

3.3.5   The Module Controller Project: An application

The Module Controller Project consisted of developing the software used to control the switching of subscribers in a Digital Switching Subscribers System of a Local Telephone Exchange.

The project started with an estimation of the size. Naturally, the group of people who were brainstorming on the sizing did not often agree on the module sizes. The reasons for and against were vigorously debated in the group, giving the impression that the project requirements were not understood in the same fashion by everybody (which was indeed true in some cases). Furthermore, almost everybody had different ideas about a possible implementation. The silences were also long and oppressive when some critical subsystems were under discussion. Nevertheless, an expected size of 30 000 NCSS for the full project was accepted as realistic on the condition that a possible variation from about 25 500 NCSS to approximately 34 500 NCSS was not discarded.

After sorting out the size, the group was set the task of selecting the appropriate program mode, which turned out to be very easy in comparison with the size. The memory constraint, the real-time aspects of the program and the numerous interfaces with the hardware all contributed to the strong consensus to use the embedded mode. Then, the discussion on the cost drivers started.

A.   Cost drivers

The determination of the cost drivers gave rise to a very heated discussion. Consequently, it was not possible to select a unique rating for most of the cost drivers. Thus, it was thought more appropriate to determine a range when there was no obvious choice.

The cost drivers were determined as follows:

- *RELY*   This was rated 'high' as the group wanted the system to have a long time between failures (1.15). The rating 'very high' (1.40) was also considered, for security reasons.
- *DATA*   Information related to the data base was initially uncertain. It was likely to be 'nominal' (1.00), but there were strong suspicions that it could be 'very high' (1.16).

- *CPLX* It was clear from the beginning that the product complexity was going to be 'extra high' (1.65) at least, because of the real-time aspect of the software.
- *TIME* This was rated 'nominal' (1.00) as no time constraint was apparent.
- *STOR* There were not excessive constraints by the main storage so this was rated to be 'nominal' (1.00). However, it turned out that management had decided to fix the main storage from the start, which meant that a 'high' rating (1.06) would be likely.
- *VIRT* It was promised that the host processor would be normally operational, which encouraged a rating of 'low' (0.87). However, it was discovered at testing time that the target processor was also used for hardware debugging, so much so that it should have been rated 'very high' (1.30).
- *TURN* This was rated 'nominal' (1.00) at the start of the project (before the team had been fully built up). However, it later became apparent that the host mainframe had a limited availability because of increased demand and failures. This factor encouraged the group to revise the rating to 'high' (1.07).
- *ACAP* The analysts involved were certainly capable, but the analyst team had only recently been formed, and most of the analysts were new to the company; therefore, ACAP was rated 'nominal' (1.00).
- *AEXP* There was a kernel of experienced analysts, but more software engineers needed to be recruited. Furthermore, the experience of other people in the group was not established. Therefore, the group hesitated between the ratings 'low' (1.13) and 'high' (0.91).
- *PCAP* Most of the programmers were going to be recruited, so the team would not have a good capability of working together. Therefore, it was felt that PCAP could be between 'low' (1.17) and 'nominal' (1.00).
- *VEXP* An ICL-2900 was in the process of being acquired. However, as almost nobody in the team was familiar with this host machine, the rating agreed on was 'very low' (1.21).
- *LEXP* The language to be used (Coral) was new for everybody, necessitating most of the engineers attending a language training course. Consequently, this was rated 'very low' (1.14).
- *MODP* The use of modern programming practices was just starting, but because of schedule pressure the group was not likely to be very good at them. Thus, this was rated 'low' (1.10).
- *TOOL* The group was going to be supplied with adequate tools. However, it was soon discovered that these new tools still had a few internal problems. The first move was to rate this 'nominal' (1.00); but a 'low' rating (1.10) was also likely.

- *SCED*   This was rated 'nominal' (1.00) at first (as the group felt the plan was good), but because of the time spent in training the group discovered that it had to accelerate the development. Therefore, for good reasons, this was rated as 'low' (1.08).

B.   Cost multipliers

Taking all the previous considerations on the cost drivers into account, it was decided to have two sets of cost drivers: pessimistic and optimistic. The higher values of the cost drivers were considered pessimistic because they contributed to a higher manpower cost. On the other hand, the lower values of the cost drivers were regarded as optimistic as they contributed to a lower manpower cost. By multiplying all the pessimistic values together and all the optimistic values together, both cost multipliers were obtained; namely, the pessimistic cost multiplier, P, and the optimistic cost multiplier, O. They were as follows:

P: $1.40 \times 1.16 \times 1.65 \times 1.00 \times 1.06 \times 1.30 \times 1.07 \times 1.00 \times 1.13$
$\times 1.17 \times 1.21 \times 1.14 \times 1.10 \times 1.10 \times 1.08$
$= 9.42$

O: $1.15 \times 1.00 \times 1.65 \times 1.00 \times 1.00 \times 0.87 \times 1.00 \times 1.00 \times 0.91$
$\times 1.00 \times 1.21 \times 1.14 \times 1.10 \times 1.00 \times 1.00$
$= 2.28$

At this point, the group felt alarmed at the ratio (greater than 4) between the optimistic multiplier, $O = 2.28$, and the pessimistic multiplier, $P = 9.42$. It was therefore decided to include the arithmetic average ratings as well, to give a central rating. The average ratings were obtained by calculating the arithmetic average for each rating. Thus, the average ratings were multiplied together to produce an average cost multiplier, M, as follows:

M: $1.27 \times 1.08 \times 1.65 \times 1.00 \times 1.03 \times 1.08 \times 1.03 \times 1.00 \times 1.02$
$\times 1.08 \times 1.21 \times 1.14 \times 1.10 \times 1.05 \times 1.04$
$= 4.73$

The average multiplier was, then, $M = 4.73$.

C.   Manpower cost

When it came to calculating the nominal manpower cost, the uncertainty about the group's initial sizing had to be taken into account. On the initial estimate of 30 000 NCSS, an uncertainty of approximately $\pm 15\%$ was assumed. Considering the manpower cost, a worst case was with 34 500 NCSS and a best case with 25 500 NCSS.

A set of manpower costs in man.months for the three sets of multipliers was obtained by using the embedded mode equations [see Equation (3.9)], as follows:

Size	K_n (man.months)	$O = 2.28$ (man.months)	$M = 4.73$ (man.months)	$P = 9.42$ (man.months)
25 500	136	310	643	1281
30 000	166	378	785	1564
34 500	196	447	927	1846

Thus, the central estimate for the manpower cost was 785 man.months or 65 man.years. However, it was noted that because of the uncertainty on the development conditions the manpower cost could be between 378 man.months (31 MY) and 1564 man.months (130 MY). This meant that the manpower cost could be somewhere between half and double the central cost estimate for the nominal size, and the range even wider if the uncertainty on the size was considered.

D. Development time

The development time was calculated by using the embedded development time equation of the basic mode. Thus, from Equation (3.4), the following was obtained:

Size	K_n (man.months)	$O = 2.28$ (months)	$M = 4.73$ (months)	$P = 9.42$ (months)
25 500	136	15.7	19.8	24.7
30 000	166	16.7	21.1	26.3
34 500	196	17.6	22.2	27.7

The central estimate (21.1 months) therefore corresponded to a development time of 1 year and 9 months. However, because of the uncertainty on the multipliers the development time could vary from 1 year and 4 months to 2 years and 2 months, for the nominal size of 30 000 NCSS. When the uncertainty on the size was added, a wider range defined by 1 year and 4 months at one end and 2 years and 4 months on the pessimistic end was obtained.

E. Conclusions

(1) At the time when this estimate was carried out (early product definition), the group felt that it had good reasons for being uncertain about the cost drivers, and for being doubtful about the size estimate. But despite this, it was decided to plan according to the central estimate of 65 MY and 1.8 years. This gave an average manning of 36 people.

(2) The group did not pay any attention to the manpower build-up of this project. Even a simple triangular hypothesis would have shown that the average manpower build-up would be seven persons per month and that it would be too difficult to build up the team at this rate. Then, the subsequent slippage experienced would have been foreseeable.

(3) The group believed that the uncertainty on the cost drivers was quite legitimate. This emphasizes the importance of monitoring the development by means of thorough data collection. This monitoring would have permitted the group to re-estimate and to gain progressively a better view of the project.

(4) At this stage, one of the most remarkable advantages of Boehm's method can be singled out. The values of the cost drivers provide the project manager with a powerful management tool. It is possible to have a clear view of the role played by each aspect of the software development (that is, product, computer, personnel or project attributes) and also to determine early on which cost driver to act on to improve the situation (for example, personnel attributes are very sensitive).

3.4 Detailed model

A large amount of work has been done by Boehm to capture all significant aspects of a software development. The COCOMO detailed model offers a means for processing all the project characteristics to construct a software estimate. The purpose of this section is to present the underlying principle of the detailed model.

The detailed model introduces two main capabilities:

(1) *Phase-sensitive effort multipliers* Some phases (design, programming, integration/test) are more affected than others by factors defined by the cost drivers. The detailed model provides a set of phase-sensitive effort multipliers for each cost driver. This helps in determining the manpower allocation for each phase of the project.

(2) *Three-level product hierarchy* Three product levels are defined. These are module, subsystem and system levels. The ratings of the cost drivers are done at the appropriate level; that is, the level at which it is most susceptible to variation.

3.4.1 Manpower cost estimate

A. Development phases

A software development is carried out along four successive phases: plans/requirements, product design, programming and integration/test.

Plans/requirements   This is the first phase of the development cycle. The requirement is analyzed, the Product Plan is set up and a full product specification is generated. This corresponds to phases 1 and 2 shown in Figure 1.1. The plan/requirements phase consumes from 6% to 8% of the nominal manpower cost, K_n, and lasts from 10% to 40% of the nominal development time, t_d. These percentages, and those given later, depend not only on the mode (organic, semi-detached or embedded), but also on the size, from small sizes (2000 NCSS) to very large sizes (512 000 NCSS).

Product design   The second phase of the COCOMO development cycle is concerned with the determination of the product architecture and the specifications of the subsystems. This is very similar to phase 3 (system design) of Figure 1.1. Product design requires from 16% to 18% of the nominal manpower cost, K_n, and can last from 19% to 38% of the nominal development time, t_d.

Programming   The third phase of the COCOMO development cycle is divided into two subphases: detailed design and code/unit test. It is comparable to subsystem design and software implementation of the Product Life Cycle (see Figure 1.1). This phase requires from 48% to 68% of the nominal manpower cost, K_n, and lasts from 24% to 64% of the nominal development time, t_d.

Integration/test   This last phase of the COCOMO model that occurs before delivery consists mainly in putting the tested parts together and in testing the final product. This is equivalent to the remainder of phase 5 of the Product Life Cycle (see Figure 1.1). From 16% to 34% of the nominal manpower cost, K_n, is involved and it can last from 18% to 34% of the nominal development time, t_d.

Note   Taken together, product design, programming and integration/test amount to 100% of the nominal manpower cost and nominal development time. Therefore, the plan/requirements phase is a preliminary addition to the nominal manpower cost and development time.

B. Principle of the manpower cost estimate

Size equivalent   As the software might be partly developed from software already existing (that is, re-usable code), a full development is not always required. In such cases, the parts of design ($D\%$), code ($C\%$) and integration ($I\%$) to be modified are estimated. Then an adjustment factor, A, is calculated by means of the following equation:

$$A = 0.4\ D + 0.3\ C + 0.3\ I \qquad\qquad (3.10)$$

The size equivalent, S (equ), is obtained by:

$$S\ (\text{equ}) = \frac{S \times A}{100} \qquad\qquad (3.11)$$

Calculating the manpower cost   The size equivalent is calculated for each module. Naturally, the size equivalent of modules that are not built on reusable code is the estimated size itself.

The manpower cost allocated to the development of each module is then obtained by:

(1) selecting the appropriate values (see Table 3.1) of the cost drivers for each phase (product design, detailed design, code/test and integration/test);

(2) multiplying the cost drivers for each module and phase, to obtain a global set of four multipliers;

(3) multiplying the global cost drivers by the nominal manpower cost for each phase and summing up to obtain the total estimated manpower.

Note   This detailed procedure gives the manpower allocation for each module and each phase, providing useful guidance for manpower planning.

C. Principle of the schedule estimate

The nominal development time is split up between product design duration, programming duration and integration/test duration according to a procedure that calculates time variations due to the variation of manpower cost relative to the nominal distribution of manpower cost. The time variations so obtained are used in a linear fashion to obtain the estimated time durations for each of the three phases when applied to the nominal time distribution.

3.5 Conclusions on COCOMO

The COCOMO model is certainly the most thoroughly documented model currently available. It is also very easy to use. And by doing so, the software engineer can learn a lot about software productivity, particularly from the very clear presentation of the cost drivers [4]. Most aspects of software development are so methodically introduced in the work of Boehm that there is no doubt as to the correctness of the model, in relation to the 63 projects baselined in the COCOMO data base.

However, how does it stand up from an estimating point of view? The COCOMO model implies that what is correct for the 63 projects measured at TRW should be correct for any other software projects. Unfortunately, this line of thought cannot be accepted, mainly because there is not enough validation work done to support this postulate. Obviously, a large-scale measurement campaign could be carried out to completely validate the COCOMO process, but such an extensive measurement exercise across software organizations seems unrealistic at the moment. Therefore, the view proposed in this book is to produce a first estimate at the start of the development and then to monitor the development with reference to the model. In so doing, it would be possible to progressively establish a reasonably accurate estimate of the development duration and project cost. But does an estimating method based on COCOMO make such monitoring practical? Let us try and answer this question.

The size and the cost drivers, because of their clear definitions, can, in fact, be progressively adjusted to realistic values (to some extent). However, the mode choice offers some difficulties, since it is not always possible to be sure which of the three modes is appropriate for a given software development – it might be a mixed mode. The fundamental difficulty resides, all things considered, in the nature of the equations themselves. For simplicity, an exponential function has been selected in the analytical representation. As the reasons for this choice are not clear, it is difficult to know how to handle these equations when adapting them to a specific organization.

In contrast to the COCOMO approach, the next chapter introduces a theory of software development modelling, based on the Norden/Rayleigh model of the Software Life Cycle. This model will be used and developed in subsequent chapters to build up a formal macro model for software development estimating.

EXERCISES

3.1   The objective of project ALPHA is to develop software for a Packet Switching System. As such, ALPHA will have to receive, store and send data packets according to various transmission protocols. Some parts of ALPHA will have to react in real time. There is no memory constraint as long as the volume of storage remains reasonable for the minicomputers used. The development team is moderately experienced – a few junior programmers have been recently taken on the team. The size of the software has been estimated by the team using the knowledge they had at the time of product definition. Thus, the expected size is

27 500 NCSS with a standard deviation of $\sigma = 1550$ NCSS. (The role of the standard deviation is outlined in Section 6.2.)

(a)   Using the basic model, calculate the expected manpower cost and development time, in person.months and months, respectively.

(b)   Determine, for a probability of 99.8%, the likely range for the project manpower cost and the development time.

(c)   How would you set the project objectives in terms of cost and time?

3.2   Assume that the project productivity is the ratio, Pr, of delivered software size, S, to the manpower, K_m, expended on the project until delivery.

(a)   Express Pr as a function of S_k for each of the three modes of the basic model, represented by Equation (3.1), Equation (3.3) and Equation (3.5).

(b)   Describe the variations of the project productivity with the scale of the project.

(c)   Define your approach, based on the basic model, to productivity minded clients.

3.3   A method sometimes used in project manpower planning is to represent the manpower distribution by means of a trapezoid, as follows:

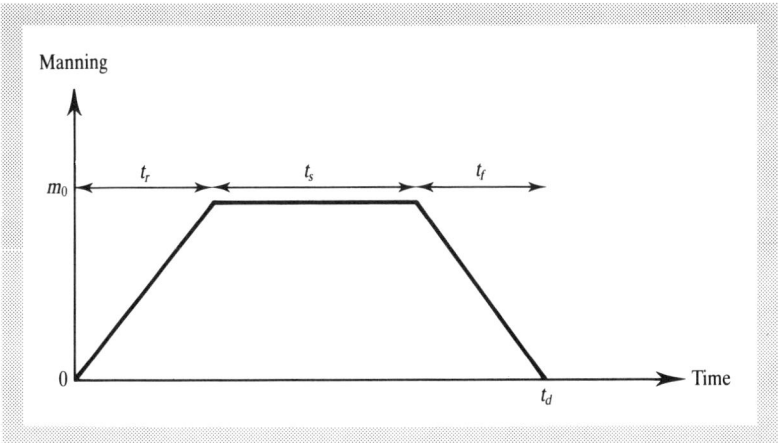

During the rise time, t_r, the team is built up at a constant rate, $r = m_0/t_r$. The manning remains steady at m_0 persons during the steady time, t_s, then falls at a constant rate, r, during the fall time, t_f. Usually, $t_r = t_f$. Referring to the basic model equations:

$$t_d = t_r + t_s + t_f = 2 t_r + t_s$$

and the manpower cost, K_m, measures the area outlined by the trapezoid.

(a)   From the geometrical properties of the trapezoid, find the trinomes, M, Tr and Ts, such that:

$$M (m_0, t_d, r, K_m) = 0$$
$$Tr (t_r, t_d, r, K_m) = 0$$
$$Ts (t_s, t_d, r, K_m) = 0$$

(b)   Let $B = K_m/(t_d/2)^2$ and find the necessary condition on the growth rate, r, for which the steady time, t_s, exists.

(c)   Express m_0 and t_r as functions of r, t_d and K_m.

(d)   Considering the embedded mode of the basic model, from Equation (3.3) and Equation (3.4), express B as a function of S_k.

(e)   For each of the three following software project sizes, calculate the minimum rates of manpower growth, r, in persons per month and the associated peak mannings. In each case, calculate the peak manning for a growth rate of eight persons per month. Identify the team-building problems in management terms.

$$S_1 = 30\ 000\ \text{NCSS}$$
$$S_2 = 50\ 000\ \text{NCSS}$$
$$S_3 = 90\ 000\ \text{NCSS}$$

3.4   Consider the four classes of attributes as shown in Table 3.1; namely, product, computer, personnel and project attributes. By defining for each class a worst case and a best case and producing their ratio, rank the attribute classes in terms of their effect on productivity, from the most influential to the least influential. What recommendations would you give to increase productivity?

Chapter 4
The Basics of Project Modelling

4.1 Introduction

The previous chapter discussed in detail a micro-estimating method. This chapter, by contrast, presents the foundation of a macro-estimating method. The main intention is to familiarize the reader with the work of Peter V. Norden and Lawrence H. Putnam in such a way that the power of the macro-estimating method becomes accessible as introduced in Chapters 5 and 6.

4.2 The Norden/Rayleigh Manpower Distribution Model

It is generally due to Norden that we have a definition amenable to further analysis for what we currently call a 'project'. Very interestingly, this definition is about development projects, and we will assume that what is workable for the IBM Development Laboratory in Poughkeepsie, New York, is also acceptable for the description of our software development projects. The definition of a development project is stated as follows by Norden [29]:

> *A development project is a finite sequence of purposeful, temporally ordered activities, operating on a homogeneous set of problem elements, to meet a specified set of objectives representing an increment of technological advance.*

Reprinted from P. V. Norden, 'On the Anatomy of Development Projects', *IRE Transactions on Engineering Management*, PGEM, **EM-7, 1**, pp. 34–42, by permission. ©1960 IEEE.

Obviously, each new software project is a technological advance, at least as far as the team members are concerned. Because of market competition, a communications system developed in 1985 must have more functional features than one developed in 1984. For example, when a customer requires a conference-call capability added to the two-party call, this is sufficient reason to incite the developer to use better techniques.

Project planning consists of scheduling a great number of activities, each of them having their own purpose; this might be the design of a module, its coding or its testing. All these activities contribute to the overall purpose of developing a software system that works – that is, meets an overall objective.

The Norden project definition further describes the project as a set of problems, and the development work consists of solving all these problems. The development ends when all the problems are transformed into solutions and these solutions, once implemented, are tested. The transformation process requires manpower, time and creativity. The notion of problems is the central point of Norden's theory of development projects and it is used for the determination of the project's demand for manpower. When the manpower available meets the manpower required, it is reasonable to assume that the software development has been optimized in terms of development time and cost.

Norden makes the following assumptions about the problem-solving activity:

- The number of problems is unknown but it is *finite*. A perfect knowledge of both the project objectives and the nature of the development process would allow the number of problems to be determined. However, in practice, this cannot be done, as it is very difficult to have a consistent and practical definition of what a problem is in this context.

- Problems are detected, recognized, analyzed and solved by means of the creative effort of the manpower involved.

- Every problem-solving effort made as a result of planning or design decisions is an event that removes an unsolved problem from a finite list of problems. The occurrence of these problem-solving events is *independent* and *random*. It is assumed to correspond to the Poisson distribution well known in probability theory.

- The number of people who are working usefully in the project team at any given time is approximately proportional to the number of problems ready for solution at that time.

4.2.1   Analytical interpretation

The number of problems to be solved during a development project, however unknown and finite, requires problem-solving effort. Therefore, the total manpower effort, K, expressed in man.years, is an indicator of the number of problems. The cumulative manpower effort (or cost) involved, $C(t)$, expressed in man.years, is null at the start of the project and grows monotonically towards the total effort, K. The rate of variation of the cumulative manpower effort involved, dC/dt, represents the number of persons involved in the development at any time, $m(t)$. The cumulative cost at time t is therefore:

$$C(t) = \int_0^t m(\varsigma)\, d\varsigma \tag{4.1}$$

One of Norden's assumptions was that the number of persons optimally involved in the project team at any given time is proportional to the number of problems to be solved (that is, to the effort remaining to be employed). If this is now included, the following equation is obtained:

$$\frac{dC(t)}{dt} = k\,[K - C(t)] \tag{4.2}$$

where k is a proportionality factor.

Since the effectiveness of a group of engineers increases progressively during the life cycle of a project, the concept of team learning needs to be incorporated. The trend of increasing capability to solve problems is also a factor that contributes to the addition of effort. This effectiveness can be represented by a function $p(t)$. Hence, the rate of application of effort can be assumed to be proportional to $p(t)$.

Norden's assumptions can now be restated by the following first-order differential equation:

$$\frac{dC(t)}{dt} = p(t)\,[K - C(t)] \tag{4.3}$$

By integrating this equation from $t = 0$ (start of the project) to any given time, t, the following is obtained:

$$C(t) = K \left[1 - \exp\left(- \int_0^t p(\tau)\, d\tau \right) \right] \tag{4.4}$$

[*Hint*: Separate the variables and substitute $u(t) = K - C(t)$. Then, $du = -dC(t)$. As $u(0) = K$, then:

$$\mathrm{Log}\left(\frac{K - C}{K} \right) = - \int_0^t p(\tau)\, d\tau$$

and the solution becomes easy.]

At this point, some further assumptions have to be made about the learning function, $p(t)$. Norden, by observing a reasonable number of development projects and trying several types of learning function, arrived at the conclusion that the most representative learning function is linear (that is, proportional to the time). This linearity can be represented by:

$$p(t) = 2\,a\,t \tag{4.5}$$

where a will be left undefined for the present purposes. It is only necessary to assume it is a positive number.

Now, by integrating the exponent of Equation (4.4), the expression $C(t)$ of the cumulative effort at any given time, t, becomes:

$$C(t) = K\,[1 - \exp(-a\,t^2)] \tag{4.6}$$

The manning of the project can now be calculated by differentiating the cumulative cost function relative to the time:

$$m(t) = 2\,K\,a\,t\,\exp(-a\,t^2) \tag{4.7}$$

This function represents a Rayleigh-type curve. It is zero at the beginning of the project ($t = 0$) and then increases towards a peak of manpower, after which it steadily decreases towards zero (see Figure 4.1). This is the manpower model put forward by Norden [28], and is often referred to as the Norden/Rayleigh Model.

It can be seen from Figure 4.1 that the parameter a, which has the dimensions of time^{-2}, plays an important role in the determination of the peak manpower. The larger the value of a, the earlier the peak time occurs and the steeper is the manning profile. By deriving the manpower function relative to the time and finding the zero value of this derivative, the relationship between the peak time, t_d, and a can be found to be:

$$t_d^2 = \frac{1}{2a} \tag{4.8}$$

Furthermore, by substituting the value of a in the manpower function, the value of the peak manning, m_0, can be obtained:

$$m_0\,t_d\,\sqrt{e} = K \tag{4.9}$$

Norden uses this relationship to determine the total manpower required by the project, once the peak manning has been reached. For example, a project whose manning reaches a peak of 50 persons after 1 year and 6 months of development ($t_d = 1.5$ years) is likely to require a total manpower of 124 man.years.

Figures 4.1, 4.2, 4.6 and 4.7 adapted from L. H. Putnam, 'A General Empirical Solution to the Macro Software Sizing and Estimating Problem', *IEEE Transactions on Software Engineering*, pp. 345–361, by permission. ©1978 IEEE.

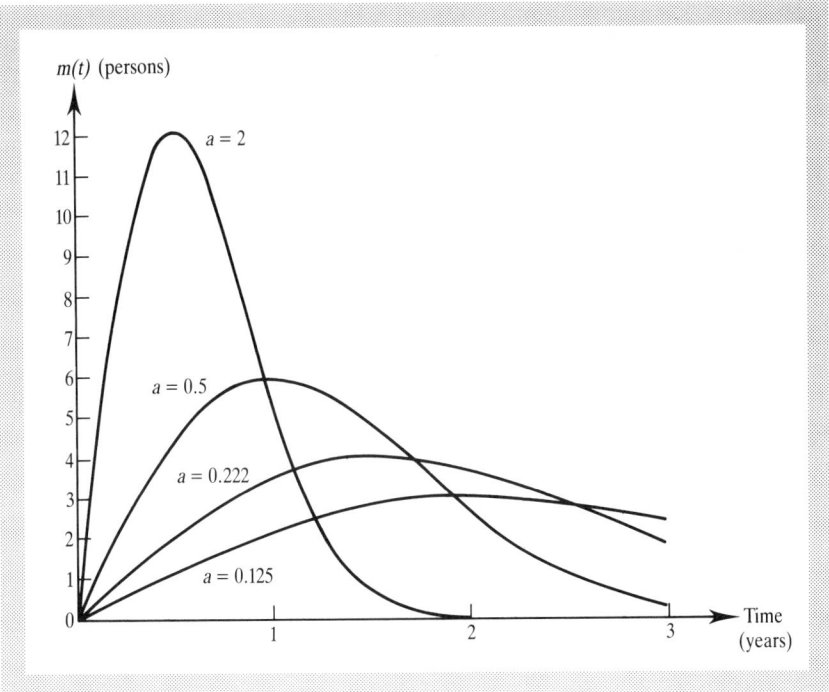

Figure 4.1   Influence of parameter *a* on the manpower distribution.

4.3   The Putnam Model of the Software Life Cycle

The phenomenology of the software development process is not well enough known to develop a complete theory of the Software Life Cycle. However, a number of project managers have noticed that software developments seem to have a life of their own, which can be modelled by a Norden/Rayleigh function. This indicates a purposeful behaviour on the part of the project itself. The practice of project management has also shown that this behaviour is due to imprecise and often changing customer's statements of requirements, and also to the management responding reactively to the project's demands. It can be assumed then, with reasonable approximation, that a software development follows a Norden/Rayleigh manpower distribution, on which is superimposed considerable 'noise', representing the changing requirements and management perturbations. It is from these facts that Putnam has developed an empirical approach to the study of the Software Life Cycle.

In the 1970s, a large quantity of data was collected from more than 200 software developments, mainly from the USA Computer Systems Command. This organization is the US Army Central Design Agency for the Standard Army Management Information Systems that run at each Army installation. It employs about 1700 people in various application areas (data processing and facilities engineering). The size of the projects ranged from 30 man.years to sometimes more than 1000 man.years.

From this vast amount of data, an extensive statistical analysis was carried out to determine the project's functional behaviour. The specific techniques of project description resulting from this analysis are presented in the following subsections.

4.3.1   The manpower distribution revisited

Software developments have two observable parameters: the manpower effort, K, expressed in man.years (or MY for short) and the development time, t_d, expressed in years. For the purposes of this book, K will be referred to as the manpower cost, since it better reflects the reality of the work of the software manager. In his day-to-day work, the software manager has to deal more with numbers of people than with the financial cost. In any case, the manpower cost so defined can be transformed into a financial cost by multiplying it by the appropriate rate for labour.

A.   Properties of the peak manning

In Section 4.2.1, it was found that the project manpower distribution could be modelled by the Norden/Rayleigh function, and it was stated to be:

$$m(t) = 2\,K\,a\,t\,\exp(-a\,t^2) \tag{4.10}$$

Let us now define the parameter a in more detail.

Putnam noticed during his software measurement sessions on large-scale software developments that the manpower distribution curve has its maximum very near the delivery time, t_d. Before this time, effort is spent in specification, design, coding, testing and qualification, while after it the manpower demand corresponds to maintenance, modifications and other on-site work. This observation, made on a large number of projects, constitutes a definition of t_d relative to the peak manning.

As shown in Equation (4.8), the peak manning time is related to a. Therefore, a can be obtained from the peak time as follows:

$$a = \frac{1}{2\,t_d^2} \tag{4.11}$$

The number of people involved in the project at the peak time then becomes easy to determine by replacing a with $1/2\,t_d^2$ in the Norden/Rayleigh Model.

By making this substitution, Equation (4.7) becomes:

$$m(t) = \frac{K}{t_d^2} \, t \, \exp\left(- \frac{t^2}{2 \, t_d^2}\right) \tag{4.12}$$

At time $t = t_d$, the peak manning, $m(t_d)$, is obtained, which is denoted by m_0. Thus, the expression for the peak manning of the project is:

$$m_0 = \frac{K}{t_d \sqrt{e}} \tag{4.13}$$

where K is the total project cost in man.years, t_d is the delivery time in years, e is the base of the natural logarithm ($e = 2.718281828...$) and $\sqrt{e} = 1.648721271...$ and m_0 is the number of persons employed at the peak.

Equation (4.13) can be used to calculate various factors associated with the manning of a project. For example, assuming a software development that is planned to cost $K = 95$ MY and where qualification (see Figure 1.1) will take place in 1 year and 9 months ($t_d = 1.75$ years), this equation can be used to calculate the number of people involved at the peak. In this particular case, the project will require a peak of 33 persons.

The average rate of software team build-up can also be calculated by dividing m_0 by t_d to obtain 18.8 person/year, which leads to a recruitment to the team, on average, of 1.5 person/month, which seems reasonable.

B. Difficulty

The slope of the manpower distribution at start time ($t = 0$) also has some useful properties. By differentiating the Norden/Rayleigh function with respect to time, the following equation is obtained:

$$m'(t) = 2 K a (1 - 2 a t^2) \exp(-a t^2)$$

Then, for $t = 0$:

$$m'(0) = 2 K a = \frac{K}{t_d^2}$$

The ratio K/t_d^2 is called **Difficulty** and is denoted by D, which is measured in person/year:

$$D = \frac{K}{t_d^2} \tag{4.14}$$

This relationship shows that a project is all the more difficult to develop when the manpower demand is high or when the time schedule is short (small t_d).

It is also interesting to observe that difficult projects will tend to have a steeper demand for manpower at the beginning for the same time scale.

Let us now investigate how the quantity D came to be called Difficulty. The first important observation was made by Putnam when comparing some 100 software developments of the US Army Computer Systems Command with their difficulty coefficients. By taking the natural logarithm of the manpower function, as given by Equation (4.12) divided by time, he obtained a linearized manpower curve:

$$\text{Log}\left(\frac{m}{t}\right) = \text{Log}\left(\frac{K}{t_d^2}\right) + \left(-\frac{1}{2\,t_d^2}\right) t^2 \qquad \textbf{(4.15)}$$

When the logarithm of the ratio manpower over elapsed time was plotted against elapsed time squared for all projects under measurement, the plotted projects were located around straight lines modelled by this equation. Since only two quantities are necessary to define a straight line – the intercept and the slope – it follows that $\text{Log}(K/t_d^2)$ is the intercept with the vertical axis and the slope is $-1/2\ t_d^2$ (see Figure 4.2).

Using this representation, Putnam remarked that projects reputed to be easy were grouped around a small value of K/t_d^2 and, inversely, systems that

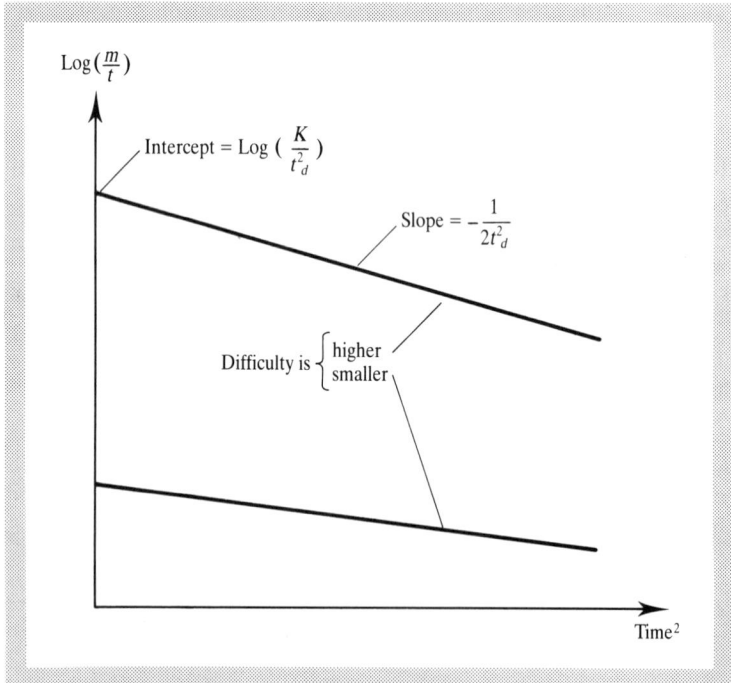

Figure 4.2   Empirical expression of Difficulty.

were reputed to be difficult to develop had a larger value for K/t_d^2. This observation led him to use the ratio $D = K/t_d^2$ as the Difficulty of the project in terms of the programming effort and time to produce it.

If we now consider the peak manning as defined previously by Equation (4.13):

$$m_0 = \frac{K}{t_d \sqrt{e}}$$

we notice that the Difficulty, D, is also related to the peak manning, m_0, and the development time, t_d, by:

$$D = \frac{K}{t_d^2} = m_0 \frac{\sqrt{e}}{t_d} \tag{4.16}$$

Thus, difficult projects tend to have a higher peak manning for a given development time, which is in line with Norden's observations relative to the parameter a (see Figure 4.1).

This argument may be restated as follows:

A project is difficult when one or both of the following conditions apply: the time scale allowed is short and/or the manpower demand is high. If the time scale is short, then firstly Norden's coefficient a is high, and it corresponds to a steep manpower profile; and secondly the peak manning formula, $m_0 = K/t_d \sqrt{e}$, provides a higher value of peak manning, which is consistent with the first point. This also means that the more difficult the project, the higher the number of people to be integrated and the sooner this should be done. This implies a very tight task scheduling with many tasks worked on in parallel, leading to a development plan that is not easily controllable. A difficult project is much more sensitive to perturbations than less difficult ones, and the slightest requirement change out of context or as a result of management reaction will produce a decrease in $a = 1/2 \, t_d^2$; that is, a flattening of the manpower profile with a longer time scale. Naturally, this effect is more accentuated if the manpower demand is higher.

C. Manpower Build-up

The considerations outlined in the previous section regarding the Difficulty led Putnam to examine the behaviour of D more closely. This factor is, in fact, a function of two variables, K and t_d. Let us examine the sensitivity of D relative to each of these variables.

The derivatives of D relative to K and t_d are:

$$D'(t_d) = -\frac{2K}{t_d^3} \quad \text{(person/year}^2\text{)} \tag{4.17}$$

$$D'(K) = \frac{1}{t_d^2} \qquad (\text{year}^{-2}) \tag{4.18}$$

In practice, $D'(K)$ will always be very much smaller than $D'(t_d)$. This difference in sensitivity can be shown by considering two projects:

Project A: cost $=$ 20 MY   and $t_d = 1$ year
Project B: cost $=$ 120 MY   and $t_d = 2.5$ years

The derivative values are:

Project A: $D'(t_d) = -40$ and $D'(K) = 1$
Project B: $D'(t_d) = -15.36$ and $D'(K) = 0.16$

This shows that a given software development is essentially time sensitive.

To demonstrate this finding, let us consider a project expected to involve 250 MY and a development lasting 2.4 years. The Difficulty is $D = 43$ MY/Y^2. If the management now reduces the manpower available by 10%, the new manpower available becomes $K = 225$ MY and the Difficulty $D = 39$ MY/Y^2. Thus, less product is delivered at the planned completion date.

However, as management usually seeks to shorten the development time, in practice, let us consider the effect of a time reduction of five months. In this case, the new development time is $t_d = 2$ years and the Difficulty is $D = 62$ MY/Y^2, which represents an increase in D of 44%. Consequently, problems can be expected during the development, mainly resulting in missed deadlines.

During his study of the US Army Computer Systems Command projects, Putnam observed that the Difficulty derivative relative to time played an important role in explaining the behaviour of software development. He noted that if the project scale is increased the development time also increases to such an extent that the quantity K/t_d^3 remains constant around a value, which could be 8, 15 or 27. This quantity is represented by D_0 and can be expressed as:

$$D_0 = \frac{K}{t_d^3} \qquad (\text{person/year}^2) \tag{4.19}$$

The value of D_0 is related to the nature of the software being developed in the following way:

- $D_0 = 8$ Entirely new software with many interfaces and interactions with other systems.
- $D_0 = 15$ New stand-alone system.
- $D_0 = 27$ The software is rebuilt from existing software.

Putnam also discovered that D_0 can vary slightly from one organization to another depending on the average skill of the analysts, programmers and management involved.

In practice, D_0 has a strong influence on the shape of the manpower distribution. The larger D_0 is, the steeper the manpower distribution is, and the faster the necessary manpower build-up will be. For this reason, the quantity D_0 is called the **Manpower Build-up**. It is also sometimes called the **Manpower Acceleration**, but in this book the former name is preferred.

As D_0 is empirically defined by steps according to the nature of the software under development, it seems reasonable, during the estimating process, to use the maximum possible value of D_0. This maximum value also provides the minimum development time.

For example, if we have to estimate an entirely new software development, the recommended value for D_0 would be 8. Naturally, it would be equally possible to carry out the estimation with any value smaller than 8 (for example, 2, 3, 6.4, 7 or 7.8). The parameter that helps to decide which value to take is the development time. The smaller the value of D_0, the longer the development time. Since we are more interested, in practice, in the shortest development time, this will be obtained with $D_0 = 8$ in our example.

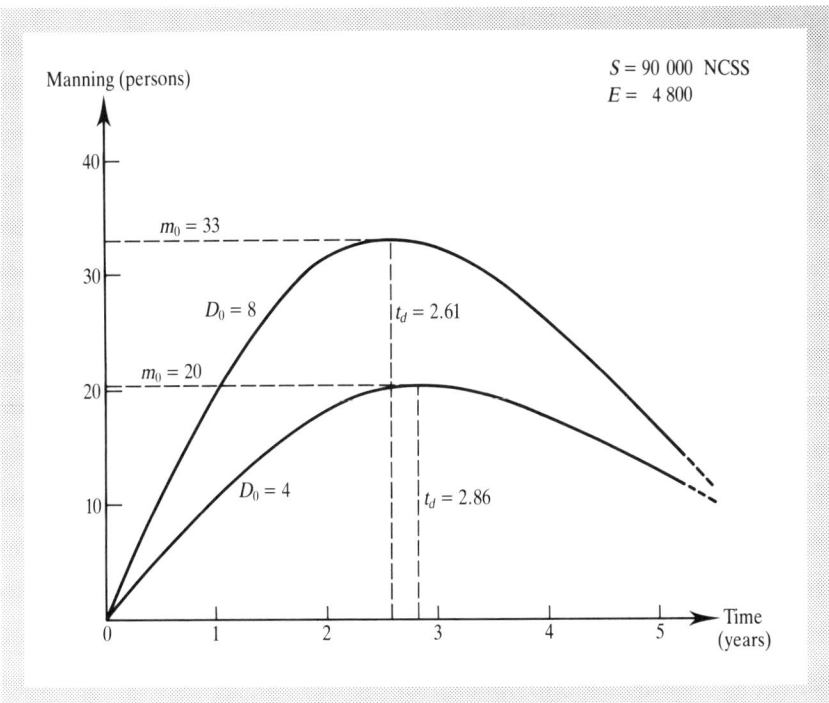

Figure 4.3 Effect of two different Manpower Build-up rates on the manpower profile.

It should be noted here that D_0 demonstrates effects similar to the Difficulty relative to the shape of the manpower profile. The higher the value of D_0 or D, the steeper the profile and the shorter the time scale (see Figure 4.3).

It is also interesting to observe that an easy software development (that is, a stand-alone system) allows the project manager to plan its development with a quick and high build-up of manpower, which means a high D_0 value, in addition to a high D value. This would be regarded as the highest difficulty level a software team can handle with respect to the nature of the software to be produced.

D.   Cumulative manpower cost

We have seen in Section 4.2.1 [see Equation (4.6)] that the cumulative project manpower cost is given, at a given time t, by the expression:

$$C(t) = K \, [1 \, - \, \exp(-a \, t^2)]$$

where C (expressed in MY) gives the manpower cost from the start of the project until time t, K is the total manpower cost (expressed in MY) of the Software Life Cycle, and a is the Norden's coefficient defined by Putnam as being equal to $1/2 \, t_d^2$ [see Equation (4.11)].

During the course of a software project, the cumulative cost increases, from zero, following an S-curve well known in project management (see Figure 4.4). The manpower cost at the delivery time, t_d, can be obtained by substituting $t \, = \, t_d$ in Equation (4.6):

$$C(t_d) = K \left(1 \, - \, \frac{1}{\sqrt{e}}\right) = 0.39 \, K \tag{4.20}$$

Thus, once the developed software system has been delivered to the target processor in an Initial Operational Capability state (see Figure 1.1), only 39% of the total cost K has been expended. The totality of what remains of the manpower is necessary for qualification, maintenance and modifications.

The rate of growth of the cumulative cost is given by its first derivative with respect to time. It can be easily verified that by differentiating the cost function with respect to the time the manpower distribution, $m(t)$, is obtained:

$$m(t) = 2 \, K \, a \, t \exp(-a \, t^2)$$

The cumulative cost increases from zero man.years at the start of the project, as does its growth rate, until time t_d.

At t_d years, the cumulative manpower growth rate is a maximum and equals:

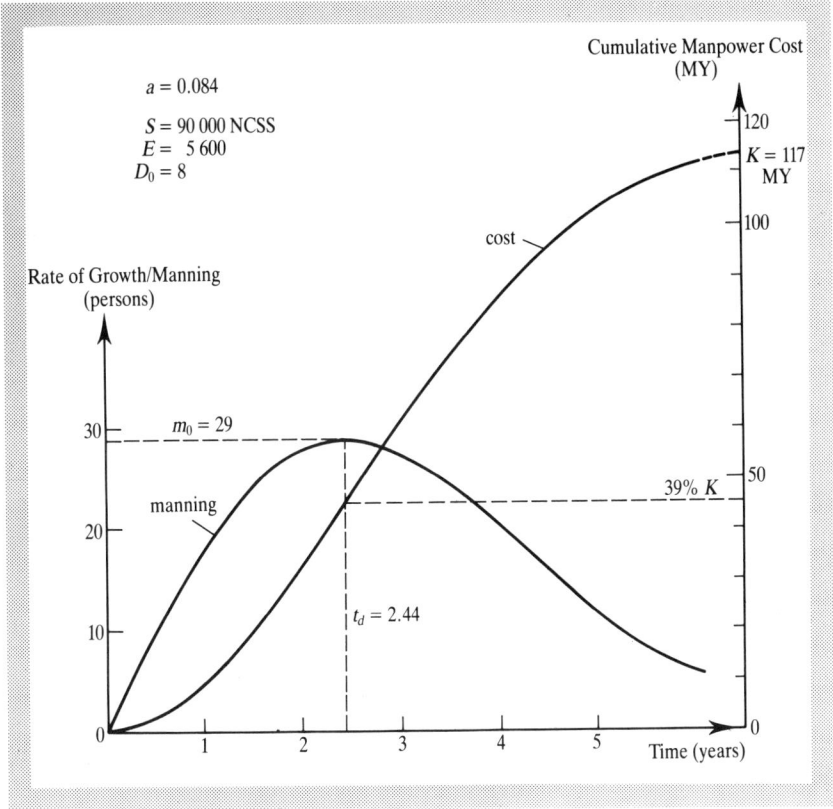

Figure 4.4 Cumulative manpower cost.

$$\frac{K}{t_d \sqrt{e}} \quad \text{(man.year/year)} \tag{4.21}$$

After this time, the growth rate of the cumulative manpower decreases steadily towards zero, which means that the cumulative cost continuously tends towards K (the manpower cost of the Generic Cycle).

A family of normalized curves can be constructed for a set of practical values of the Norden coefficient a (see Figure 4.5) by using the following equation:

$$\frac{C(t)}{K} = [1 - \exp(-a\,t^2)] \tag{4.22}$$

For cost-monitoring purposes, the manpower usage for a fixed cost, K, can be plotted. By comparison with a given curve, this procedure helps to determine potential problems.

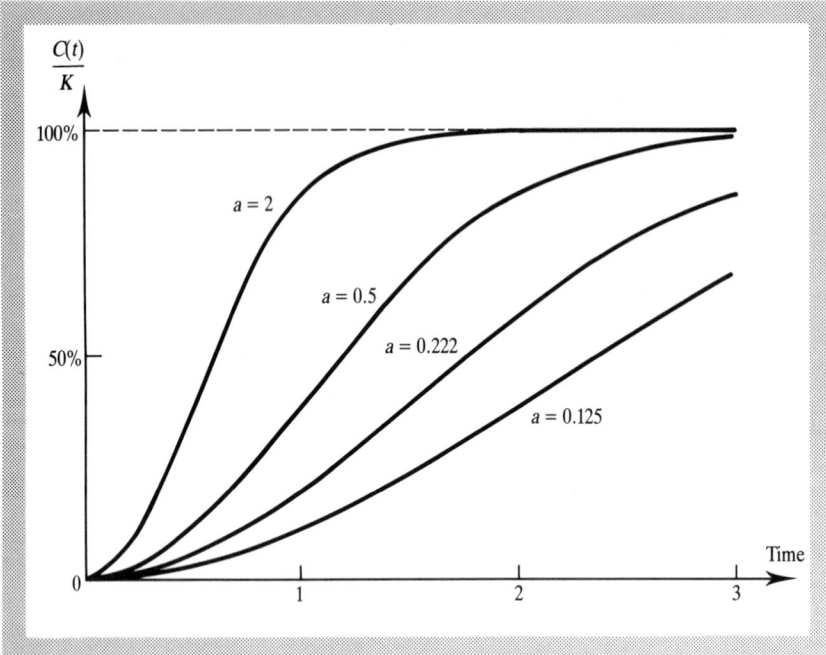

Figure 4.5 Normalized project cumulative cost.

From Equation (4.11) and Equation (4.14), a can be expressed as a function of D, giving:

$$a = \frac{D}{2K} \tag{4.23}$$

This expression clearly shows that the Norden coefficient a is directly proportional to D. This is, in fact, consistent with the view that a project of maximum cost K is regarded as more difficult by a development team when it is developed in a rushed fashion with $a = 2$ than when it is developed in a relaxed fashion with, for example, a equal to 0.222 or 0.125. A high level of managerial and technical skill is required with $a = 2$ to quickly (less than a year) form a development team in an ordered fashion, and to understand the technical problems related to the software to be developed.

4.3.2 The Software Equation

So far, we have looked at the definition of two important parameters of software projects, K and t_d, and how the manning of the project varies with time by means of the Norden/Rayleigh function. The next step is to relate K and t_d to the software product. The best way of doing this is to identify the product as a number of source code statements (see Section 1.7) and to find a relationship between the manpower cost, K, the development time, t_d and the size, S of the delivered software. For reasons of clarity, the method used to produce a reasonable estimate of the software size is delayed to Chapter 5, which is more specifically related to the Putnam-based estimating method.

A. Productivity versus Difficulty

At this stage, it is appropriate to introduce another important finding made by Putnam with respect to the relationship that exists between the overall productivity of the US Army Computer Systems Command projects and their respective difficulty.

By plotting the development productivity (productivity will be defined later in this section) and the Difficulty of each project on log-log paper, Putnam discovered that:

- projects were grouped along three parallel straight lines,
- projects run in the same environment were grouped on the same line.

These three parallel straight lines correspond respectively to the three different locations, called Continental United States, Pacific development environment and European development environment, of the US Army Computer Systems Command, which are shown in Figure 4.6 as lines 1, 2 and 3, respectively. Each of these environments had a consistent and homogeneous set of standards and software practices. When a statistical analysis was carried out on this plot, the slopes of these lines were found to be in the range -0.62 to -0.72. This study was extended to include project data from IBM and General Electric and a family of curves was constructed with similar slopes.

Taken together, these findings were convincing enough to suggest strongly that a fundamental behaviour existed. This was formalized by the equation:

$$Pr = C_n\, D^{-2/3} \tag{4.24}$$

where D is the Difficulty as defined by Equation (4.14), Pr is the productivity defined by the ratio of the delivered source code size, S, (number of statements) to the manpower cost (MY) expended on the project for the production of the software, and C_n is a proportionality constant that depends on the state of technology existing in the environment where the data was captured. In Figure 4.6, the software development environments represented by the lines 1, 2 and 3 are in the order of increasing C_n.

In the Putnam methodology, the productivity factor is not directly usable. Rather, it is either an intermediate working value in the calculation of more useful information or it is an end result which expresses a factor indicating the efficiency of projects. Nevertheless, it is interesting to observe that:

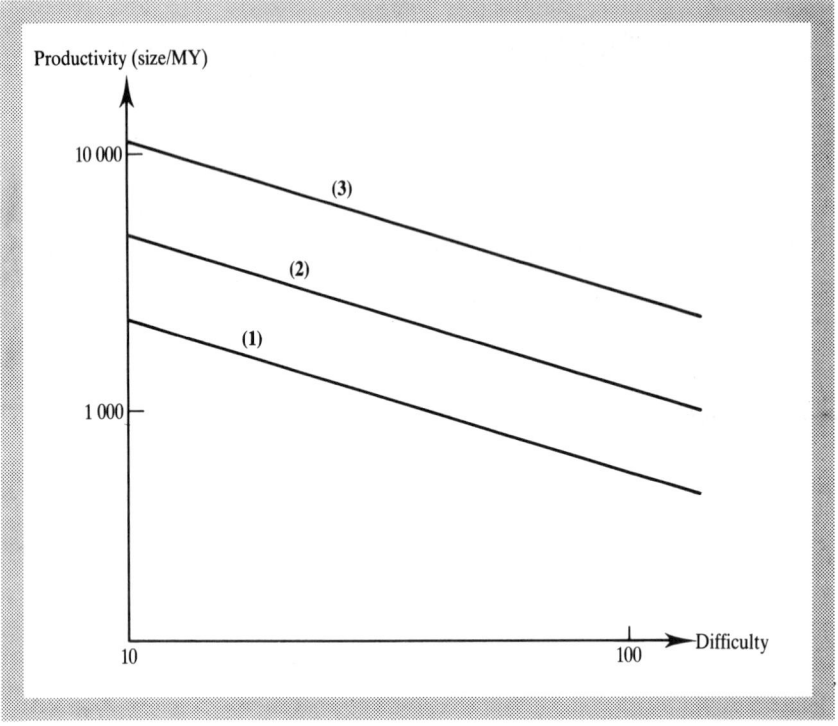

Figure 4.6   Overall setting of the plot productivity versus Difficulty.

- the more difficult a project, the less productive it is;
- the better the quality of the development environment (in terms of tools, methods and management), the more productive the project;

which suggests that premature conclusions on large-scale projects should not be drawn from data collected on small developments. Furthermore, estimates carried out on parts of a project (for example, a subsystem) cannot be added to produce a total project estimate. The Putnam estimating process is not additive: it has to be started at the top level and carried on from there in a top-down fashion. It is based on a macro model.

It is also very important to be aware of the role played by C_n, the state-of-technology factor. If we want to develop a given software product with the least possible manpower, it is very effective to improve the software development environment. This means having adequate support processors, interactive terminals, excellent team capability, good training and management that understands the behaviour of the Software Life Cycle, just to mention a few of the most important items.

B.   Design code subcycle (Development Subcycle)

All that has been described so far is related to the Project Life Cycle, as represented in Figure 4.7 by the project curve. Earlier in this chapter, we saw that the project curve can be modelled by a Rayleigh function, which gives the manning level relative to time and reaches a peak at time t_d. At time t_d, the product is reputed to be operational; hence, the name delivery time when referred to the date and development time when referred to the time duration that has elapsed since the inception of the project. For this reason, we will call this subcycle the Development Subcycle. This name is appropriate as this subcycle is that part of the project cycle that deals directly with the production of the software by such specialists as programmers and analysts, and their direct supervision. Therefore, the Development Subcycle excludes any project-related overheads. Although this definition is sufficient to meet our present objective, we will have to amplify this distinction during the course of Chapter 5.

In practice, the project curve is the addition of two curves called, respectively, the development curve and the test and validation curve. The development curve is a subcycle of the project curve and it has been experimentally verified that it can be modelled by means of a Norden/Rayleigh function. Before developing this subcycle further, it should be mentioned that the test and validation curve is also a subcycle of the project curve and it too can be modelled by a Norden/Rayleigh function.

At the start of a project, the design and coding subcycle matches the project curve. It is also realistic to assume that by the time t_d, what is called coding (testing of the subsystems) is nearly complete. Therefore, the first

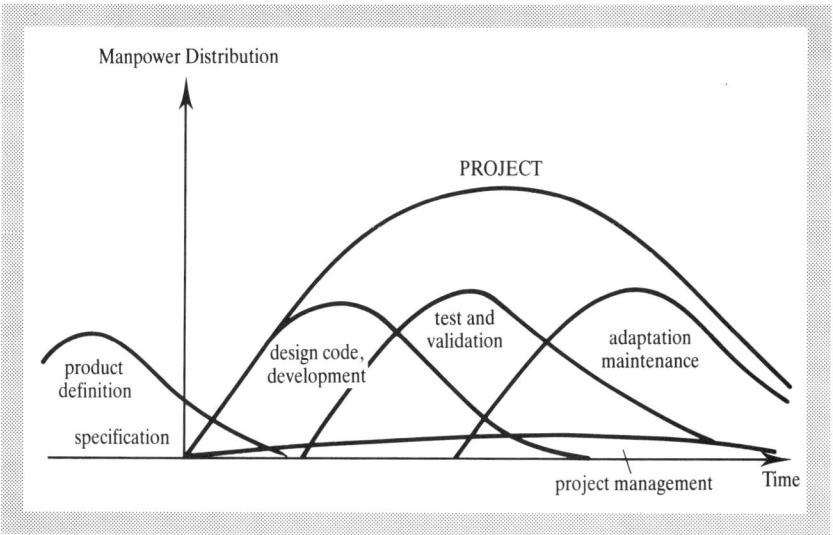

Figure 4.7   Project Life Cycle.

subcycle can be represented by a Norden/Rayleigh function, as for the project curve, but this time some precautions must be taken in determining the peak design manning.

Following these considerations, let $m_d(t)$ and $C_d(t)$ be the design manning and the cumulative design manpower cost. As the manning curve has the same Norden/Rayleigh form as the project curve, these can be represented by:

$$m_d(t) = 2 K_d b t \exp(-b t^2) \tag{4.25}$$

$$C_d(t) = K_d [1 - \exp(-b t^2)] \tag{4.26}$$

An examination of the $m_d(t)$ function shows a non-zero value for m_d at time t_d. This is because the manpower involved in design and coding is still completing this activity after t_d in the form of rework due to the validation of the product. Nevertheless, for the model a level of completion has to be assumed for development.

It is a good practical assumption to assume that the development will be 95% complete by the time t_d. This gives:

$$\frac{C_d(t_d)}{K_d} = 1 - \exp(-b t_d^2) = 0.95 \tag{4.27}$$

It is then legitimate by the set of previous definitions, and by analogy with the Norden coefficient a [see Equation (4.11)], to set:

$$b = \frac{1}{2 t_{0d}^2} \tag{4.28}$$

where t_{0d} is the time at which the development curve exhibits a peak manning. This can then be used to obtain the following relation between the development time, t_d, and the development peak manning, t_{0d}:

$$t_{0d} = \frac{t_d}{\sqrt{6}} \tag{4.29}$$

(all times expressed in years).

To complete the definition of the Development Subcycle, the relationship between K_d (the total manpower cost of the Development Subcycle) and K (the total manpower cost of the Generic Cycle) must be established. This can be obtained by using the observation that at the origin of time both cycles have the same slope. Thus, from Equation (4.14) and by differentiation of Equation (4.25):

$$\left(\frac{dm}{dt}\right)_0 = \frac{K}{t_d^2} = \frac{K_d}{t_{0d}^2} = \left(\frac{dm_d}{dt}\right)_0 \tag{4.30}$$

and considering Equation (4.29):

$$K_d = \frac{K}{6} \tag{4.31}$$

The peak time, t_{0d}, and the total manpower cost of the Development Sub-cycle, K_d, respectively, are therefore proportional to the delivery time, t_d, and the total manpower cost, K, of the Generic Cycle.

The development manpower curve can now be represented by substitution in Equation (4.25) and Equation (4.26) to give:

$$m_d(t) = D\, t\, \exp\left(-\frac{t^2}{2\, t_{0d}^2}\right) \tag{4.32}$$

The development cumulative cost is then represented by:

$$C_d(t) = K_d \left[1 - \exp\left(-\frac{t^2}{2\, t_{0d}^2}\right)\right] \tag{4.33}$$

It should be noted at this stage that the Difficulty, D, is the same whether expressed in terms of K and t_d or K_d and t_{0d}. This is because it is the Difficulty of the total project that is being considered, and it can be applied to the project components and more especially to the development curve. More formally, this can be stated by:

$$D = \frac{K}{t_d^2} = \frac{K_d}{t_{0d}^2} \tag{4.34}$$

This does not apply to the Manpower Build-up, D_0, [see Equation (4.19)] as:

$$D_0 = \frac{K}{t_d^3} = \frac{K_d}{\sqrt{6}\, t_{0d}^3} \tag{4.35}$$

Note here that there is an extra factor, $\sqrt{6}$, when the calculations are made at the subcycle level.

C. Defining the Software Equation

Having determined the Development Subcycle (that is, the subcycle that really produces the source code by involving analysts and programmers) in relation to the Generic Cycle, let us now consider the complementary aspect of the productivity of the development.

As the productivity is defined as a ratio of output over input:

$$Pr = \frac{\text{output}}{\text{input}} \tag{4.36}$$

let the productivity be the ratio, *Pr*, of the total delivered source code constituting the product to the total effort needed to produce this source code:

$$Pr = \frac{\text{size of delivered source code}}{\text{total manpower to produce code}} \tag{4.37}$$

The total effort considered here is the manpower cost expended from the inception of the project to the delivery time, t_d, and, as it happens, this has already been calculated [see Equation (4.20)] to be:

$$C(t_d) = 0.39 \, K \tag{4.38}$$

Therefore, the size, S, of the delivered software at time t_d, expressed in number of source statements, is:

$$S = Pr \times 0.39 \, K \tag{4.39}$$

This equation provides a relationship between the total manpower cost, K, and the quantity of software produced, represented by its size expressed in a number of delivered statements.

All the necessary elements for the determination of the Software Equation are now available. A relationship between productivity and the Difficulty has been previously introduced [see Equation (4.24)], as:

$$Pr = C_n \, D^{-2/3} \tag{4.40}$$

It is now an easy task to link this to the size of the software delivered.

First, from Equation (4.39), by substitution:

$$S = 0.39 \, C_n \, K \, D^{-2/3} \tag{4.41}$$

Then, by substituting for the Difficulty, D, [see Equation (4.14)]:

$$S = 0.39 \, C_n \, K \left(\frac{K}{t_d^2} \right)^{-2/3} \tag{4.42}$$

which leads to:

$$S = 0.39 \, C_n \, K^{1/3} \, t_d^{4/3} \tag{4.43}$$

In the usual form of this expression, the quantity $0.39 \, C_n$ is replaced by a coefficient, E, which is given the name of **Technology Factor**. However, the name **Environment Factor** is also frequently used for E. As was seen at the beginning of this chapter, C_n, and consequently E, is dependent on the state of the technology in the environment where the software is produced. The more efficient the software development methods and tools, and the more skilled the analysts and programmers and their management, the higher the Environment Factor, E.

The **Software Equation** as provided by Putnam can now be written as:

$$S = E \, K^{1/3} \, t_d^{4/3} \tag{4.44}$$

where K is the manpower cost (in man.years) of the Generic cycle, t_d is the development time (in years) and S is the size of the software (in NCSS).

The dimension of the Environment Factor can be expressed in NCSS.person$^{-1/3}$.year$^{-5/3}$, a form that is obviously too complicated to be used each time a result is expressed. Therefore, as the time is always expressed in years when carrying out the calculations, the value of the Environment Factor is assumed to be expressed in the system of units NCSS, person, year. For simplicity, the unit of the Environment Factor will not be shown in the calculations.

Equation (4.44) clearly shows that for a given development time, t_d, and a given amount of manpower involved, K, the quantity of software produced will be higher when the Environment Factor, E, is higher. A high Environment Factor describes a more productive software development capability. In fact, E is the only parameter that is dependent on a given organization. The other coefficients are independent of the organization: they belong to the nature of the Software Life Cycle.

For a specific organization, E can be calculated from past projects. This calculation requires a slight transformation of the Software Equation, as follows:

$$E = \frac{S}{K^{1/3} \, t_d^{4/3}} \tag{4.45}$$

It is easy to use the size, cost and development time of past projects to determine E, and to revise the value of E obtained to model forthcoming projects. This will be presented in detail in Section 6.3.

D. The trade-off of time versus cost

In software projects, time cannot be freely exchanged against cost. Such a trade-off is limited by the nature of software development, as can be shown by the Software Equation.

For a given organization developing a software product of size S, the quantity [from Equation (4.44)]:

$$K^{1/3} \, t_d^{4/3} = \frac{S}{E} \tag{4.46}$$

is constant. Therefore, by raising to the power 3:

$$K\, t_d^4 \tag{4.47}$$

is constant. A compression of the development time, t_d, will produce an increase of manpower cost. This can be shown by calculating the relative differential of Equation (4.47). [*Hint:* The logarithm of Equation (4.47) is constant and its differential is zero, which leads to Equation (4.48).]

$$\frac{\Delta K}{K} = -4\, \frac{\Delta t_d}{t_d} \tag{4.48}$$

Then, if the development time is compressed by 10%, as represented by:

$$\frac{\Delta t_d}{t_d} = -0.1$$

the demand for manpower will increase by four times the time compression – that is, 40% – which could be very considerable. However, not everyone agrees with this particular trade-off behaviour, in practice.

Compression of the development time will also increase the Difficulty, as $D = K/t_d^2$. The same calculation as before shows that:

$$\frac{\Delta D}{D} = \frac{\Delta K}{K} - 2\, \frac{\Delta t_d}{t_d} \tag{4.49}$$

So, the schedule compression just described would give a variation of Difficulty of:

$$\frac{\Delta D}{D} = 0.40 - (-0.20) = 0.60$$

which means an increase in Difficulty of 60%.

Nevertheless, compression of development time is possible. But if compression is excessive, not only would the software development cost much more, but the development would become so difficult that it would run the risk of being unmanageable. This is in line with a remark made by Boehm's that the time scale should never be reduced to less than 75% of its initial calculated value.

4.4 Transportability of the Model

In most of the static models, the values of the parameters of the model are calculated by means of a curve-fitting exercise on a measurement baseline that is either familiar to the model builder (that is, the particular domain of the estimator's software practice) or representative of a wide variety of applications. In both cases, the transportability of the model is most likely to be conditioned by a calibration of the model to the specific organization wanting to use the model, and calibration generally requires curve fitting.

One of the interesting features of the Putnam Model is its transportability. This model has been built to show the relationship between the management parameters (t_d, K, S); it does not pretend to give a direct answer in time and cost, as is done in the static models. The dynamic nature of this model makes it independent of the initial data base. Anyone familiar with elementary mathematics can convince himself of this by examining the equations presented in Section 4.5. Chapter 6 gives the techniques necessary to model any particular project organization.

4.5   Concluding remarks

The Norden problem-solving theory of the development Project Life Cycle describes software development as a series of problem removals. As a consequence, the project expresses a demand for manpower effort which varies during the development. The manpower demand can therefore be represented analytically by means of a Rayleigh function. The resulting Norden/Rayleigh Model shows how the total manpower cost, K, is used in terms of manpower demand during the life of the project for different values of the Norden parameter, a. The general form of Norden's Model, restated here, is:

$$m(t) = 2\,K\,a\,t\,\exp(-a\,t^2)$$

4.5.1   Review of the Putnam Model

The application of the Norden/Rayleigh Model to software developments was made by Putnam, who analyzed a large number of software developments and managed to extract two extremely important parameters. These are the Manpower Build-up, D_0, and the Environment Factor, E. These two parameters constitute a very powerful means of describing any software development by involving the following expressions, which are repeated here for ease of reference.

A.   Manpower distribution

The manpower distribution is expressed by means of a Rayleigh function. Two forms of this function have been introduced. The manpower distribution of the Generic Cycle is:

$$m(t) = D\,t\,\exp\left(-\frac{t^2}{2\,t_d^2}\right) \tag{4.50}$$

and the manpower distribution of the Development Subcycle is:

$$m_d(t) = D\, t\, \exp\!\left(-\frac{t^2}{2\, t_{0d}^2}\right) \tag{4.51}$$

The Putnam Model describes the manpower function as a project's demand for manpower. As the project development proceeds the project manager will try to satisfy this demand by avoiding excessive under- or over-staffing. The manpower demand starts from zero manning, grows steadily, reaches a peak manning and then decreases until project completion (see Figure 4.3).

B.   Software Equation

The Software Equation links the size of the software, determined by the number, S, of NCSS produced within the development time, t_d, and the manpower of the Generic Cycle, K, to the Environment Factor, E.

The Environment Factor, E, sometimes called the Technology Factor, assesses the technical 'goodness' of the programming support environment. E can be measured or derived from past similar projects wherein all variables in the Software Equation are known, thus allowing the estimator to determine E. The determination of E will be explained in Chapter 6.

The Software Equation is:

$$S = E\, K^{1/3}\, t_d^{4/3} \tag{4.52}$$

C.   Manpower Build-up

In the original work [36], this quantity was called the Difficulty gradient; however, the name Manpower Build-up gives this parameter its proper meaning. It expresses the maximum permissible rate of manpower application (or manpower build-up) that a project can sustain and still make forward progress. The names manpower acceleration gradient and/or manpower build-up gradient are also used in the practice of the Putnam Model. It is represented by:

$$D_0 = \frac{K}{t_d^3} \tag{4.53}$$

The statistical analysis performed by Putnam on more than 600 software systems developed for the US Army Computer Systems Command showed that the Manpower Build-up varies by steps as follows:

- $D_0 = 8$ New systems with many interfaces and interactions with other systems.

- $D_0 = 15$ New stand-alone system.
- $D_0 = 27$ Rebuilt or composite system built up from existing systems where large parts are re-used.

These values of D_0 are so central to the Putnam method that they are sometimes indexed 1, 2, 3, ... and called the manpower build-up index (MBI).

D.   Cost

The cumulative manpower cost of the Generic Cycle is expressed by:

$$C(t) = K \left[1 - \exp\left(- \frac{t^2}{2 \, t_d^2} \right) \right] \tag{4.54}$$

and the cumulative manpower cost of the Development Subcycle is expressed by:

$$C_d(t) = K_d \left[1 - \exp\left(- \frac{t^2}{2 \, t_{0d}^2} \right) \right] \tag{4.55}$$

These formulae describe, in a formal fashion, the well-known S-curve of project development cost. An example of this curve is given in Figure 4.5.

E.   Difficulty

The Difficulty, D, is the slope for $t = 0$ of the manpower distribution. It is restated here as:

$$D = \frac{K}{t_d^2} \tag{4.56}$$

This expression shows that a project is all the more difficult when either it requires more manpower, K, or it has to be completed at earlier t_d. The Difficulty gives an idea of how fast a development team can be manned.

4.5.2   Versatility of the Model

A.   The macro model

The Putnam Model of the Software Life Cycle is a macro model in the sense that it addresses directly the large-scale features of a software development (for example, project size, cost and time). The structure of the Software Equation enables the important management variables to be determined without having to manipulate a large quantity of data related to the details of a software development. A single coefficient relates the development process to a particular software organization. This is the Environment Factor, E. It can be easily determined from past projects within a given organization or by an examination of equivalent projects in similar organizations.

B.   Optimum manpower distribution

The use of the Norden/Rayleigh function for manpower distribution guarantees an optimal manning policy. This function represents a demand for manpower in a context represented by a certain management style and development environment. When the manpower available meets this demand the development cost and time become predictable.

C.   Cost/time trade-off

Putnam's Software Equation enables a dynamic behaviour of the management variables; they become interchangeable according to a defined law which provides strategic choices to the project management.

D.   Practicality

The calculations on which the Putnam Model is based can be easily computerized, thus permitting rapid acquisition of important estimating results whatever the project scale.

The following chapters explain how to construct a top-down method of software estimating based on the Putnam Model. They link the model more specifically to the Software Life Cycle and discuss in more detail the significance of the project size. In Chapter 6, the technique is explained and demonstrated by practical cases. This provides the opportunity to show how to estimate the size and the Environment Factor, and to mention some other useful capabilities.

EXERCISES

4.1   In Section 4.2, Norden's Model was constructed from a linear-learning function [see Equation (4.5)]. Consider now a new learning function:

$$p(t) = 2\,a\,t^n$$

where n is a non-nul natural number.

(a)   Express the new functions for both the cumulative manpower cost and the manpower distribution of the Generic Cycle.

(b) Compare these two functions with those resulting from the linear learning function.

4.2 Consider the expression for the cumulative manpower cost of the Generic Cycle as given by Equation (4.6).

(a) By successive differentiation and re-arrangement define the differential equation that generates the Norden/Rayleigh Model; that is:

$$C'' + \frac{t}{t_d^2} C' + \frac{1}{t_d^2} C = D$$

(b) Let $t_d = 2$ years, $D = 30$ person/year and the initial condition zero for $t = 0$. Carry out a numerical integration of this equation using the Runge–Kutta method. (*Note*: Refer to the mathematical package of your computer.) Draw step by step the manpower distribution of the Generic Cycle.

(c) Compare your graph with a graph drawn from Equation (4.50).

(d) Consider a Difficulty increase of 30% at $t = 0.6$ year and by repeating (b) evaluate the delivery time slippage.

4.3 Consider a large-scale project for which the manpower requirement is $K = 600$ MY and the development time is 3 years 6 months.

(a) Calculate the peak manning and peak time of the Generic Cycle.

(b) Calculate the Difficulty and the Manpower Build-up.

(c) What is the manpower cost after 1 year and 2 months?

4.4 A project is being manned at the initial rate of 4 person/month. The delivery is expected in 1 year and 7 months.

(a) Determine the peak manning and the manpower cost of the Generic Cycle.

(b) Determine the Difficulty and the Manpower Build-up.

4.5 A software development requires 90 MY during the total Development Subcycle. The development time is planned for a duration of 3 years 5 months.

(a) Calculate the manpower cost expended until delivery time.

(b) Determine the development peak time.

(c) Calculate the Difficulty.

(d) Calculate the Manpower Build-up.

4.6 A software development for avionics has necessitated 32 MY and produced a size of 48 000 NCSS. The development was started in March 1980 and completed in April 1982.

(a)   Calculate the development time.

(b)   Calculate the total manpower development.

(c)   Calculate the development peak time.

(d)   Calculate the Difficulty.

(e)   Calculate the Manpower Build-up.

(f)   Calculate the Environment Factor.

4.7 What amount of software can be developed in 1 year 10 months in an organization whose Environment Factor is 2400 if a total of 25 MY is permitted for development effort?

4.8 The software development environment of an organization developing real-time software has been assessed at an Environment Factor of 2200. The maximum value of Manpower Build-up for this type of software is $D_0 = 7.5$. The estimated size of the software to be developed is $S = 55\ 000$ NCSS.

(a)   Determine the minimum development time, the total development manpower cost, the Difficulty and the development peak manning.

(b)   The development time determined in (a) is considered too long. It is recommended that it be reduced by two months. What would happen?

Chapter 5
The Putnam Model of Software Development

5.1 Behaviour of the software project

In the previous chapter the background of the model of software development put forward by Putnam was presented. This model was defined by associating:

- a manpower, represented analytically by a Norden/Rayleigh function, with;

- a Software Equation, defined empirically by Putnam while analyzing a large amount of software developments.

Furthermore, we saw that these elements, the manpower cycle and the Software Equation, are linked by two important parameters: the Manpower Build-up, D_0, and the Difficulty, D. The Difficulty coefficient expresses the difficulty as presented by the development to its developers, whereas the Manpower Build-up is a coefficient that has been empirically discovered as determining defined levels of manpower involvement.

In Chapter 4, this model was applied to a basic situation where two manpower cycles were defined; namely, the Generic Cycle and the Development Subcycle. Let us now look at our findings in more detail.

The first manpower cycle was called the Generic Cycle [see Equation (4.50)]. At this stage, we assume that this Generic Cycle has no (not yet) practical and direct use for software estimation. This statement might appear rather harsh, but we will revise it during the course of the chapter, as more elements are introduced. This cycle is called generic because it is an overall and general cycle from which more practical cycles (for example, the Development Subcycle) can be deduced. The total manpower described by the Generic Cycle is K man.years and it is appropriate to note that the same variable K is involved in the Software Equation [see Equation (4.52)], the Difficulty [see Equation (4.56)] and the Manpower Build-up [see Equation (4.53)].

The second manpower cycle considered in Chapter 4 was the Development Subcycle, also called the design code subcycle. This is a subcycle of the Generic Cycle. Let us restate in a summarized fashion why the subcycle concept is used. By means of Equation (4.29), a definition of the subcycle peak time, t_{0d}, was set empirically as a function of the Generic Cycle peak time, t_d. The latter has also been found to be empirically equivalent to the delivery time; that is, the time at which the software is delivered to the destination site – that is, the place where it is going to be qualified, used and maintained. It was then found that, because of the unicity of the Difficulty coefficient [see Equation (4.30)], there was an implied dependency of total manpower under the Development Subcycle, K_d, on the total manpower under the Generic Cycle, K, [see Equation (4.31)]. Furthermore, calculations showed that the factor 6 and its square root, applied respectively to the total generic manpower, K, and the Generic Cycle peak time, enable the Development Subcycle to be deduced from the Generic Cycle.

During the course of this chapter, we will see that this technique can be used in a more general fashion to determine another subcycle, the **Project Subcycle**. But, before adding another subcycle to our collection, we need to introduce some more elements.

A survey of the skills of people involved in a software project leads to a distinction between two groups of tasks necessary for the good achievement of a software project: the development tasks and the support tasks. But note that this distinction is not always clear cut, it depends very much on how the tasks are defined and also on the organizational structure of the project. Nevertheless, the findings of such a practice show that there is good point in attempting this distinction.

Let us first consider the first group of tasks, the development tasks. Note that use of the name 'development' here is consistent with the name used in that part of Section 4.3.2 which introduces the Development Subcycle (or design code subcycle). The manpower in charge of the development tasks is mainly constituted of analysts, programmers and their direct management. This group of people do such work as subsystems and modules specification, design, code and test. These specialists also contribute to various design reviews, code inspection and software benchmarks. At time t_d, the delivery time, they will have produced a software system with a quality level sufficient for the software product to be delivered to the customer for qualification. The distribution of the development manpower with respect to time is modelled by the Development Subcycle (see Figure 5.1). Its analytical expression is given by Equation (4.51).

The second group of tasks is not as clearly defined as the first one; nevertheless, it is important enough to be considered because its role is to support the development process. Manpower involved in these support tasks can belong to various disciplines and the skills might not always be closely related to the development of software. However, it certainly needs a higher level of management whose effort can be solely or partially dedicated to this project. Also in this classification are some clerical staff, engineers who maintain the host processors and provide assistance for specific hardware, planning officers who run the PERT system, and configuration control and change control officers who keep track of the product structure of the software system and its modification, etc. All this manpower is added to the Development Subcycle in Figure 5.1 to form the Project Subcycle. This subcycle can also be modelled by a Norden/Rayleigh function, and will be examined in Section 5.3.2.

5.1.1 Size influence on the project

At this stage, it is presumed obvious that if the product is small enough, say 2000 NCSS, then a single software engineer will be able to do the development work as well as supporting himself; that is, both development and support tasks. If he has enough engineering sense, he will even be able to do

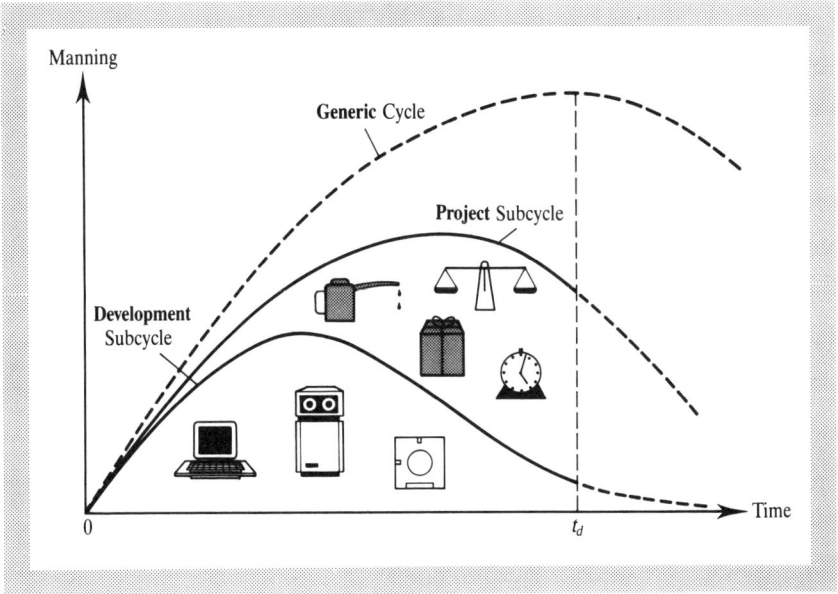

Figure 5.1 Development and support tasks.

the product packaging, the customer's documentation and the qualification on his own. However, by contrast, the development of a large-scale software product of, say, 100 000 NCSS, would be out of reach of a single software engineer. This mammoth task would require a large team of software engineers, supported by a group of support staff and managed by a project manager. Unfortunately, it cannot be assumed that if a single software engineer can develop a 2000 NCSS, then 50 software engineers could develop a 100 000 NCSS product. This would mean that the 100 000 NCSS product could be divided into 50 different and strictly independent modules, which is not generally true, if it is a genuine single product. Even in the rare case where it would be realistic, the management in charge of the 50 small projects would require some planning and co-ordination support work to effectively manage them. Furthermore, on the technical side, to prove that the 50 small modules are independent and different would have previously required adequate specification work from a software system team and also some monitoring and co-ordination with this team to guarantee the conceptual integrity of the product.

In general, a small-scale project is not expected to require any support at all, while a large-scale project will certainly require the development team to be supported by some or all of the specialists previously described. Beyond a certain size, the larger the scale of a project the larger is the amount of required support. Before describing this relation, let us amalgamate another empirical finding made by Putnam relative to project scale [35]:

- a small-scale project is defined by a size less than 18 000 NCSS;
- a medium-scale project is a project whose size is between 18 000 NCSS and 70 000 NCSS;
- a large-scale project is defined by a size greater than about 70 000 NCSS.

Let us now examine each of these three project scales in detail.

5.2   Small-scale projects

5.2.1   Manpower distribution

The manpower distribution for the software development is a subcycle of the Generic Cycle. It is also a Rayleigh function and can be restated from Equation (4.51) (see Figure 5.2) as:

$$m_d(t) = \frac{K_d}{t_{0d}^2} \, t \, \exp\left(-\frac{t^2}{2 \, t_{0d}^2}\right) \tag{5.1}$$

where t_{0d} is the time at which the manning is at a peak (in years) and K_d is the manpower cost (in man.years) corresponding to the product Development

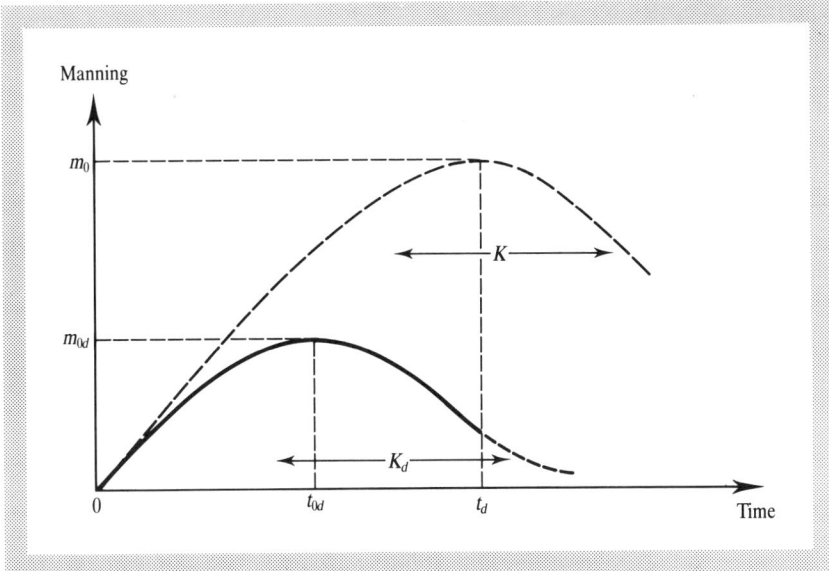

Figure 5.2   Small-scale project.

Subcycle. This manpower is expended on that part of the product development activity starting after the Preliminary Design Review (see Section 1.3.1)
and ends with system test and acceptance. Therefore, it covers subsystems
design, modules specification, design, code, test, subsystems test, and system
test and acceptance. In a small-scale project the overhead efforts (non-
technically orientated efforts) are assumed to be almost negligible. In cases
where they exist they are incorporated into the development effort. Because
of this, the Project Subcycle coincides with the Development Subcycle.

K_d and t_{0d} are related to the Generic Cycle by the following ratios [from
Equation (4.29) and Equation (4.31)]:

$$K_d = \frac{K}{6} \qquad\qquad (5.2)$$

$$t_{0d} = \frac{t_d}{\sqrt{6}} \qquad\qquad (5.3)$$

5.2.2   Peak manning

The expression of the peak manning for small-scale projects, m_{0d}, can be
obtained from Equation (5.1) by simply substituting $t = t_{0d}$:

$$m_{0d} = m_d(t_{0d}) = \frac{K_d}{t_{0d}} \exp\left(-\frac{1}{2}\right)$$

Then:

$$m_{0d} = \frac{K_d}{t_{0d} \sqrt{e}} \tag{5.4}$$

Notice here that the peak manning is expressed in terms of the manpower cost, K_d, and the peak time, t_{0d}, of the Development Subcycle. It can also be expressed as a function of the total manpower cost, K, of the Generic Cycle and its peak time, t_d. This is done by using Equation (5.2) and Equation (5.3) to obtain:

$$m_{0d} = \frac{K}{t_d \sqrt{6e}} \tag{5.5}$$

Thus, the peak manning will go up when either total manpower goes up or the development time scale is reduced. This illustrates the experience that a project time scale reduction should be accompanied by an increased allocation of manpower. A failure to achieve this is likely to entail either a low quality product or a lengthier than planned development time, and this is obviously not what the project manager is looking for.

5.2.3 Cumulative manpower cost

A restatement of Equation (4.55), which expresses analytically the cumulative manpower cost at time t, gives:

$$C_d(t) = K_d \left[1 - \exp\left(- \frac{t^2}{2 \, t_{0d}^2} \right) \right] \tag{5.6}$$

Since the Development Subcycle and Project Subcycle are similar for small-scale projects, this equation also represents the cumulative project cost. (We will come back to this more completely in the next section.)

A quick calculation shows that at peak time, t_{0d}, the project has already expended:

$$\frac{C_d(t_{0d})}{K_d} = 1 - \frac{1}{\sqrt{e}}$$

or:

$$\frac{C_d(t_{0d})}{K_d} \times 100 = 39\% \tag{5.7}$$

In practice, this result may be used as a yardstick to control the progress. If at a certain time the project has already spent 39% of its allocated manpower and if some people are becoming less necessary because planned tasks have been achieved correctly in a timely fashion, then the project manager can genuinely believe to be on the right trajectory (that is, manpower profile). This also means that the total development/project manpower cost is likely to be K_d man.years at the end of the project and also that the delivery deadline is likely to be met.

At this point, it is useful to remark that at delivery time, t_d, the relative manpower cost will be [from Equation (5.6)]:

$$\frac{C_d(t_d)}{K_d} = 1 - \exp\left(-\frac{t_d^2}{2\,t_{0d}^2}\right)$$

Then, with Equation (5.3):

$$\frac{C_d(t_d)}{K_d} = 1 - \exp(-3)$$

Thus:

$$\frac{C_d(t_d)}{K_d} \times 100 = 95\% \qquad (5.8)$$

or, in other words, 95% of the total development/project manpower cost should have been expended at delivery time, t_d. This also means that 5% of K_d remains to be spent in assistance to installation and qualification on site (for example, for defects removal).

5.2.4   The minimum development time example

A software development whose size is estimated at 9000 NCSS is developed in an environment defined by an Environment Factor of 1200. This software is a stand-alone data-processing type program for which a Manpower Build-up of $D_0 = 15$ is selected. Let us determine the Development Subcycle.

From the Software Equation, as presented in Equation (4.52), we get after having divided by E and raised to power 3:

$$\left(\frac{S}{E}\right)^3 = K\,t_d^4$$

Then, dividing by t_d^3 and substituting the Manpower Build-up, K/t_d^3, we obtain:

$$\left(\frac{S}{E}\right)^3 = D_0\,t_d^7$$

Solving for the development time, t_d, we get:

$$t_d = \left[\frac{1}{D_0}\left(\frac{S}{E}\right)^3\right]^{1/7} \tag{5.8a}$$

Referring to Section 4.3.1 on the Manpower Build-up, $D_0 = 15$ is the maximum value for this kind of development (stand-alone program). This value of D_0 corresponds to the minimum development time. Naturally, we could have selected a lower value for D_0, but it is clear that the development time would be longer, which is not the purpose in this example.

From the values given previously, we obtain the minimum development time:

$$t_d \text{ (min)} = 1.6 \text{ years}$$

which is approximately 1 year and 7 months.

We can now calculate the total manpower covered by the Generic Cycle, K. From Equation (4.19) and solving for K, we get:

$$K = D_0\, t_d^3 = 62.7 \text{ man.years}$$

The Difficulty, which is defined by Equation (4.56), can also be calculated:

$$D = \frac{K}{t_d^2} = 24.5 \text{ person/year}$$

This means that the programming team initially grows at the rate of two persons per month, which seems to be feasible with respect to our software team-building experience. We can now determine the total development manpower cost, K_d, from Equation (5.2) to obtain:

$$K_d = 10.5 \text{ man.years}$$

of which 95% [see Equation (5.8)] is expended during the development time, t_d, which is:

$$C_d(t_d) = 9.9 \text{ man.years}$$

and the remaining manpower of 0.6 man.year (or 7.2 man.months) is expended on post-delivery work.

We can now calculate the characteristics of the development peak manning. The peak time is given by Equation (5.3), so we have:

$$t_{0d} = \frac{t_d}{\sqrt{6}} = 0.65 \text{ year}$$

or 7.8 months. Equation (5.4) can provide the number of persons needed at peak manning and we get:

$$m_{0d} = 9.8 \text{ persons}$$

For obvious practical reasons, we will accept to build up the team to 10 persons by the seventh month after the start of the project.

We can verify that the average rate of growth, $m_{0d}/t_{0d} = 15$ person/year (or 1.3 person/month) is lower than the Difficulty ($D = 24.5$ person/year) by drawing a straight line between the peak and the start of the development manpower curve, as shown in Figure 5.2, for example. Note that Equation (5.5) also gives the development peak manning, $m_{0d} = 9.7$ persons, with respect to the rounding used in the calculation.

In the same manner, we can verify Equation (4.34) and we have, when calculating the Difficulty from the Development Subcycle, $D = 24.8$ person/year while still making allowance for the rounding.

Also, according to Equation (5.7) we would have expended 39% of the total development manpower cost; that is:

$$C_d(t_{0d}) = 4.1 \text{ man.years}$$

This provides an extra monitoring element to ascertain the peak time. Naturally, we do not have to confuse progress with motion, this monitoring should be supported by a carefully conducted progress control.

It should now be clear that most of the critical management parameters (for example, cost and time) can be determined by the equations introduced in this section.

5.2.5 The slack time example

Following on from the previous example, let us now assume that, for planning reasons, the customer needs the software product only 2.5 months later. The development time permitted by this new schedule is approximately:

$$t_d' = 1.8 \text{ years}$$

From the Software Equation [Equation (4.52)], we can solve for K' the new total manpower cost of the Generic Cycle:

$$K' = \left(\frac{S}{E}\right)^3 t_d'^{-4} = 40.2 \text{ man.years}$$

which is lower than K, but there is more to come.

The new Manpower Build-up, D_0', is now, from Equation (4.53):

$$D_0' = 6.9 \text{ person/year}^2$$

This lower value of D_0 means that the team would be working at an astonishingly easier pace. The Difficulty can be calculated from Equation (4.56) to give:

$$D' = \frac{K'}{t_d'^2} = 12.4 \text{ person/year}$$

which indeed represents an easier project for the software team than the previous one.

The new total development manpower cost, K_d', would be 6.7 man.years of which 6.4 man.years would be expended before delivery time, t_d'.

The new peak manning can also be calculated. At the peak time, $t_{0d}' = 0.73$ year (or 8.8 months), from Equation (5.4); only six persons would be needed, instead of 10 persons for the previous project.

Finally, let us compare the respective productivities as defined by $Pr = S/K_d$ and $Pr' = S/K_d'$. We obtain:

$$Pr = 857 \text{ NCSS/man.year}$$
$$Pr' = 1343 \text{ NCSS/man.year}$$

This demonstrates that it is very productive to take time in a software development, if this can be allowed by the customer. Naturally, an added condition is to carry out a careful progress control throughout the project in such a way that there is no confusion between slack time and *far niente*.

5.3   Medium-scale projects

In medium-scale projects, the greater the size the greater the proportion of non-direct technical effort (called overheads here) necessary to develop the product. Indeed, more effort in management, configuration control, documentation and quality assurance is added to the development effort. This overhead effort grows with the size and is added to the normal development effort.

The total project manpower distribution is represented by a Rayleigh function (m_p, project curve) inside which can be represented the development manpower distribution (m_d, development curve) (see Figure 5.3). Let us now examine both the Development Subcycle and Project Subcycle.

5.3.1   Development Subcycle

The expressions derived for small-scale projects (see Section 5.2) also describe the Development Subcycle of medium-scale projects. The man-

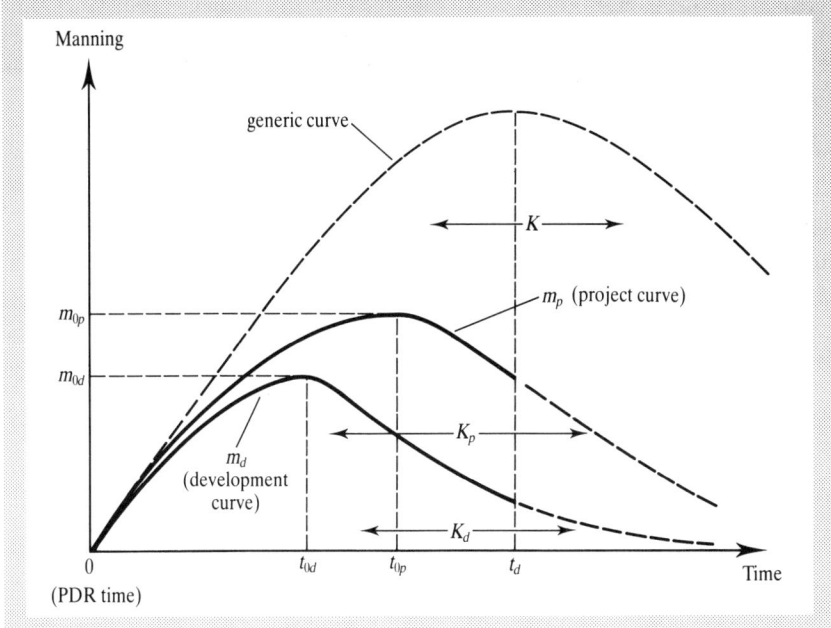

Figure 5.3   Development Subcycle and Project Subcycle.

power distribution is defined by Equation (5.1) where t_{0d}, the development peak manning time, can be calculated from t_d by using Equation (5.3). The same applies to the total development manpower, K_d, which can be calculated from K by using Equation (5.2). The development peak manning can be determined by means of either Equation (5.4) or Equation (5.5).

The cumulative manpower cost is defined by Equation (5.6), hence cumulative development cost at peak manning time, t_{0d}, is still 39% of the total development cost, K_d, [see Equation (5.7)]. And, in the same manner, 95% of this cost has been expended at delivery time, t_d, [see Equation (5.8)].

When the project size passes through the 18 000 NCSS size transition, the Development/Project Subcycle of the small-scale project still exists as a Development Subcycle in the medium-scale project.

5.3.2   Project Subcycle

The Project Subcycle can be defined by means of a Norden/Rayleigh function [see Equation (4.7)]:

$$m_p(t) = 2 \, K_p \, c \, t \, \exp(-c \, t^2) \qquad\qquad (5.9)$$

where $m_p(t)$ is the number of persons employed in the project per time unit (year). The total manpower cost employed by the project from start time $(t = 0)$ to a time infinitely long $(t = $ infinite) is K_p.

The project peak manning will occur at a time t_{0p} such that [see Equation (4.8)]:

$$2\ c\ t_{0p}^2 = 1$$

This expression helps in defining the coefficient c relative to the project peak manning time, t_{0p}, to give:

$$c = \frac{1}{2\ t_{0p}^2}$$

Then, Equation (5.9) becomes:

$$m_p(t) = \frac{K_p}{t_{0p}^2}\ t\ \exp\left(-\frac{t^2}{2\ t_{0p}^2}\right) \tag{5.10}$$

One way of defining this subcycle relative to the Generic Cycle, as expressed by Equation (4.50), is to establish a relation between the manpower, K_d, of the Development Subcycle and the total manpower, K, of the Generic Cycle. Thus:

$$K_p = \frac{K}{\alpha^2} \tag{5.11}$$

where α is a real number whose role is to act as a Form Factor, establishing a dependence of K_p on K. Note that this dependence on K would only affect the amplitude of the project curve; if not, this would entail a lack of consistency with the Generic Cycle and the Development Subcycle. Thus, let us focus our attention on the Difficulty.

Before continuing with this consideration, it is useful to observe that, at any time, the project manpower, K_p, as delineated by the Project Subcycle, consists of the development manpower, as delineated by the Development Subcycle, to which is added the manpower overheads. Consequently, the project curve is always situated between the development curve and the generic curve. This can be expressed as follows:

$$K_d \le K_p, \quad K_p \le K \quad \text{and} \quad \alpha \ge 1$$

Now, returning to the Difficulty, let us recall that the slope of $m(t)$ at time $t = 0$ represents the Difficulty, D. From this, another condition can be imposed on the initial slope; that is, the slope for $t = 0$ of the project curve must equal the same slope for the generic curve. Then, proceeding as was done for Equation (4.30), comparing Equation (4.50) and Equation (5.10):

$$D = \frac{K}{t_d^2} = \frac{K_p}{t_{0p}^2} \tag{5.12}$$

This establishes a relation between t_d, the generic manpower peak time, alias the delivery time, and t_{0p}, the project peak manning time. Using Equation (5.11), this relation can be restated as:

$$t_{0p} = \frac{t_d}{\alpha} \tag{5.13}$$

The expression for the project peak manning, m_{0p}, can be found from Equation (5.10) by replacing t by t_{0p} to give:

$$m_p(t_{0p}) = m_{0p} = \frac{K_p}{t_{0p}} \exp\left(-\frac{1}{2}\right)$$

Thus:

$$m_{0p} = \frac{K_p}{t_{0p}\sqrt{e}} \tag{5.14}$$

This expression enables a calculation of the maximum number of persons employed in a project, m_{0p}, when the total project manpower cost, K_p, and the time, t_{0p}, at which this maximum occurs are known.

At this point, it is a worthwhile exercise to compare Equation (5.14) with Equation (4.13), which defines the peak manning, m_0, of the Generic Cycle. They are similar and also similar to the peak manning, m_{0d}, for a small-scale project, as provided by Equation (5.4). The ratio of Equation (5.14) to Equation (4.13) can be expressed as:

$$\frac{m_{0p}}{m_0} = \frac{1}{\alpha}$$

or:

$$m_{0p} = \frac{m_0}{\alpha} \tag{5.15}$$

Similarly, that for Equation (5.14) and Equation (5.4) is:

$$\frac{m_{0p}}{m_{0d}} = \frac{\sqrt{6}}{\alpha} \tag{5.16}$$

We now have two relations, Equation (5.13) and Equation (5.15), to define the project peak manning relative to the Generic Cycle.

It is noteworthy here that there is a size (for example, 18 000 NCSS) for which the project peak manning, m_{0p}, equals the development peak manning, m_{0d}. Then, Equation (5.16) becomes:

$$\frac{\sqrt{6}}{\alpha} = 1 \quad \text{and} \quad \alpha = \sqrt{6}$$

Transporting this result into Equation (5.13) results in:

$$t_{0p}\,(S = 18\ 000) = \frac{t_d}{\sqrt{6}}$$

which is in fact Equation (5.3), the expression for the development peak manning time. Proceeding similarly with Equation (5.11) implies:

$$K_p\,(S = 18\ 000) = \frac{K}{6}$$

which expresses the total development manpower cost [see Equation (5.2)]. For this size the Project Subcycle coincides with the Development Subcycle.

Proceeding in the same manner with Equation (5.15), accepting for the moment the correspondence with the software size of 70 000 NCSS, would result in a coincidence of the Project Subcycle with the Generic Cycle (see Figure 5.3).

A. Project cumulative cost

Let us now exploit the relation between α and the size to express the project cumulative manpower cost and, with the assistance of some statistical results, model the behaviour of α when the software size varies.

By analogy with Equation (4.54) or by integrating Equation (5.10) gives:

$$C_p(t) = K_p \left[1 - \exp\left(-\frac{t^2}{2\ t_{0p}^2} \right) \right] \tag{5.17}$$

Then, by substituting t_d, delivery time, for t the manpower cost expended in the project until delivery time is obtained:

$$C_p(t_d) = K_p \left[1 - \exp\left(-\frac{t_d^2}{2\ t_{0p}^2} \right) \right] \tag{5.18}$$

Using Equation (5.11) and Equation (5.13) and dividing by K then results in the ratio:

$$Y(\alpha) = \frac{C_p(t_d)}{K} = \frac{1 - \exp\left(-\dfrac{\alpha^2}{2}\right)}{\alpha^2} \tag{5.19}$$

which represents the portion of the total generic manpower expended on the project until delivery time.

Recall here that:

- The Software Equation [see Equation (4.52)] deals directly with the total manpower cost, K, of the Generic Cycle. Thus, by expressing the results relative to K, their introduction into the Software Equation for future estimating use is facilitated.

- The delivery time is a very important time in the life of a project: the work stops in the development organization to be continued at the customer's site - qualification, maintenance, etc. Therefore, this is the time at which expenditure data, such as $C_p(t_d)$, is most likely to be available. This is so even for organizations with a low level of software metrics activity.

It is an interesting exercise, at this point, to make a short study of Equation (5.19) when α is varying along the segment $[1, \sqrt{6}]$. A differentiation of Y provides the first derivative, Y':

$$Y'(\alpha) = \frac{(2 + \alpha^2) \exp\left(-\dfrac{\alpha^2}{2}\right) - 2}{\alpha^3} \tag{5.20}$$

Both functions, Y and Y', are continuously decreasing from 0.39 to 0.16 for Y and increasing from -0.18 to -0.11 for its derivative, Y' (see Table 5.1). The variation of $Y = C_p(t_d)/K$ is represented on the graph $Y(\alpha)$ in Figure 5.4. An increase of the ratio Y is produced in practice by considering larger and larger project scales. This ratio increase is permitted by a decrease of the Form Factor, α.

Table 5.1 Variations of function $Y(\alpha)$.

α	Large-Scale Projects		1	Medium-Scale Projects		$\sqrt{6}$	Small-Scale Projects
Y'	$\dfrac{3}{\sqrt{e}} - 2$		≈ -0.18	$\dfrac{4e^{-3} - 1}{3\sqrt{6}}$		≈ -0.11	
Y	$1 - \dfrac{1}{\sqrt{e}}$		≈ 0.39	$\dfrac{1 - e^{-3}}{6}$		≈ 0.16	

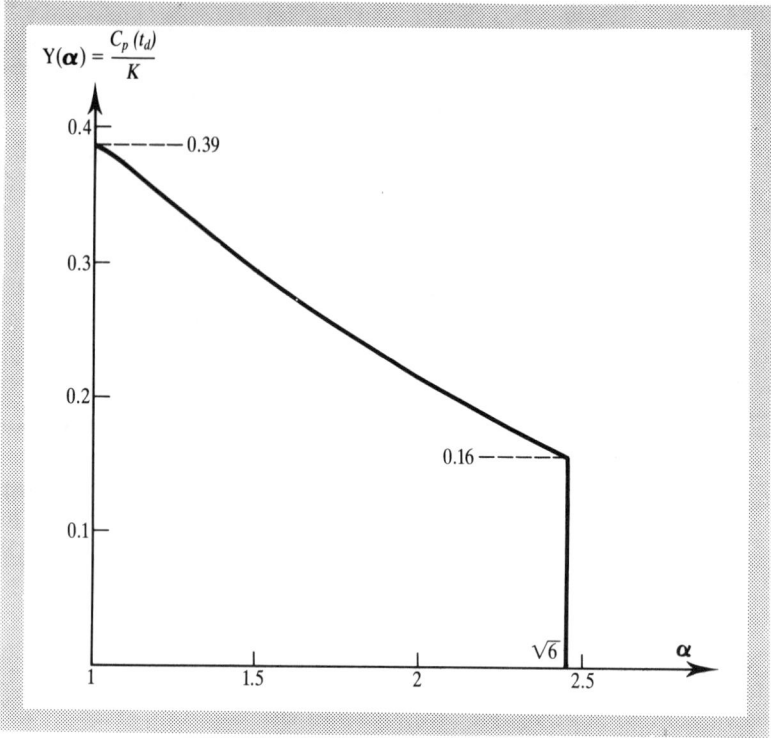

Figure 5.4 $Y(\alpha) = \dfrac{C_p(t_d)}{K}$.

B.   Relation between α and size

Let us now investigate the relation between α and the software size, S. Inevitably, this relation will depend on measurements done on past software projects. However, as the number of software projects under consideration is so large (that is, the Putnam data base), we will assume that it remains stable in future.

Table 5.2 shows results of measurements carried out by Putnam, where F is defined by $t_{0p} = F\,t_d$ [compare with Equation (5.13)]. To facilitate the comparison between Putnam's coefficient F and α, the column $1/F$ has been added, in addition to the column $\alpha(S_k)$. The latter comes from a curve-fitting exercise that is introduced following. Obviously, the variation of $\alpha(S_k)$ is a decreasing function that should pass through $\sqrt{6} \simeq 2.45$ when $S_k = 18$ and tend towards 1 when S_k is approximately 70.

What we are considering here is a simple model, represented by the generic expression:

$$\alpha_a = b\,\exp(m\,S_k)$$

Table 5.2 Empirical relation between α and the software size.

Size (S_k)	$\dfrac{C_p(t_d)}{K}$ (Y)	$\dfrac{t_{op}}{t_d}$ (F)	$\dfrac{1}{F}$	$\alpha(S_k)$
5–15	0.16	0.41	2.44	2.51
20	0.18	–	–	2.29
25	–	0.54	1.85	1.87
30	0.28	0.62	1.61	1.59
40	0.34	0.77	1.30	1.27
50	0.37	0.87	1.15	1.12
70	0.39	0.96	1.04	1.02
100	0.39	1.00	1.00	1.002

Adapted by permission of L. H. Putnam. ©1981 QSM, Inc.

With $m < 0$ and $b > 0$, this function seems likely to represent the variation of $\alpha(S_k)$ provided that the following remark is made: when S_k takes large values (for example, $S_k = 70$), α_a tends towards zero, and the model becomes:

$$\alpha - 1 = \alpha_a$$

The missing term will be re-introduced when all calculations have been done.

By trying several models on a curve-fitting software package, it can be found that the best model is that represented by Equation (5.21), which models $\alpha(S_k)$ with reasonable satisfaction even when considering the following limitations:

Correlation:	$r = -0.998$
Error at 18 000 NCSS:	$< 2.5\%$

$$\text{error} = \frac{1}{7}\sqrt{\sum\left(\alpha - \frac{1}{F}\right)^2} : \quad < 1.2\%$$

Thus:

$$\alpha(S_k) = 1 + 6.23 \exp(-0.079\ S_k) \tag{5.21}$$

This last equation shows that α, the portion of the total generic manpower cost expended on the project until delivery time relative to the generic manpower cost, depends on the size for the value of S_k higher than 18 000 NCSS.

This dependence of α with the size is shown in Figure 5.5. Once the size is known, Equation (5.21) enables the determination of the appropriate value of α, leading to the determination of the project peak manning and project peak time. From this point the Project Subcycle is completely defined.

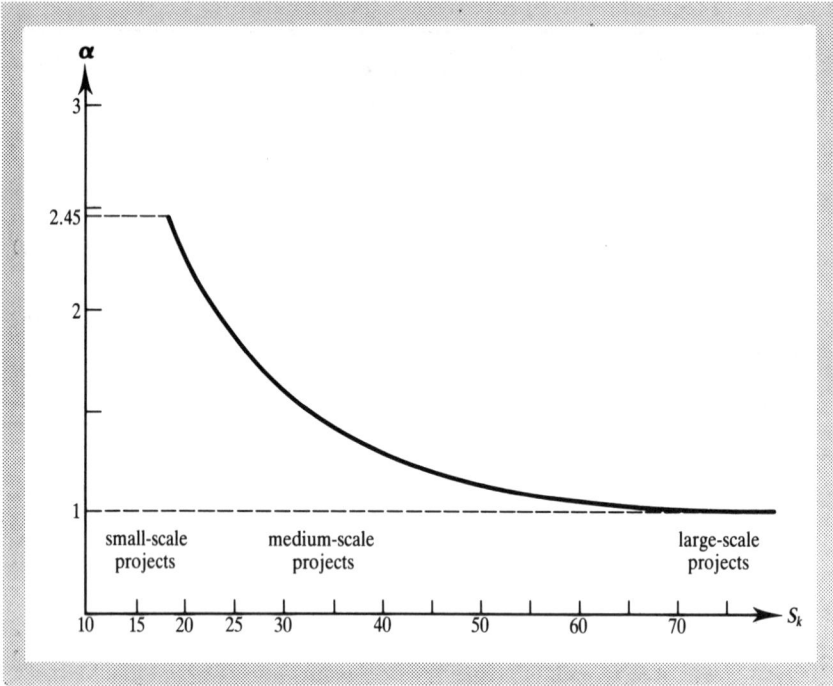

Figure 5.5   Variation of α with the software size.

EXAMPLE

A medium-scale software project consists of developing a program for which the size was estimated at 45 000 NCSS. The 'goodness' of the development environment has been set by an Environment Factor of 2400. It is assumed that we are dealing with real-time software with many interfaces between processes for which the recommended Manpower Build-up is $D_0 = 8$.

As the size is higher than the lower size threshold for medium-scale projects (that is, 18 000 NCSS), we would, therefore, expect that both subcycles exist; namely, the Development Subcycle and the Project Subcycle.

Development Subcycle

Firstly, let us consider the Development Subcycle for the case where we are interested in the minimum development time. If we refer back to Equation (5.8a), derived from the Software Equation, we see that the development time, t_d, is already expressed in terms of the Manpower Build-up, D_0, and the ratio size to the Environment Factor, S/E. Applying this to the present case, with $D_0 = 8$, we find:

t_d (min) $= 2.6$ years

From Equation (4.53), we use the Manpower Build-up to calculate the total manpower cost, K, of the Generic Cycle. Thus:

$$K = D_0 \, t_d^3 = 141 \text{ man.years}$$

This gives the total manpower of the Development Subcycle when substituted in Equation (5.2):

$$K_d = 23.4 \text{ man.years}$$

From Equation (4.56), we obtain the Difficulty:

$$D = \frac{K}{t_d^2} = 21 \text{ person/year}$$

Another interesting quantity to calculate is the peak manning, m_{0d}, and the peak time, t_{0d}, of the Development Subcycle. Using Equation (5.3), it is trivial to find the peak time:

$$t_{0d} = 1.1 \text{ years}$$

and by substituting it into Equation (5.4), we obtain the peak manning:

$$m_{0d} = 12.9 \text{ persons}$$

which could be rounded for practical reasons to 13 persons.

So much for the Development Subcycle. Let us now consider the Project Subcycle.

Project Subcycle

To determine the Project Subcycle we need, in the first instance, to determine the Form Factor, α, of the project manpower curve. Taking advantage of Equation (5.21), after having expressed the size in thousands of NCSS, which gives $S_k = 45$, we then obtain the Form Factor:

$$\alpha(45) = 1.18$$

We verify that this Form Factor value is consistent with the graph provided in Figure 5.5, substitute this figure in Equation (5.11) and solve it for the total Project Subcycle manpower cost. This gives:

$$K_p = 101 \text{ man.years}$$

Note that throughout the project duration, K_p includes the total development manpower cost, K_d.

Another interesting result is the manpower expended in the project from start time until delivery time, t_d. This may be obtained by multiplying the result of Equation (5.19) by K to give first:

$$Y(\alpha) = 0.36$$

Then, using the value of K as previously calculated, we get:

$$C_p(t_d) = 0.36 \, K = 50.8 \text{ man.years}$$

Note that this includes 95% of the development manpower cost, K_d, [see Equation (5.8)]; that is, 22.2 man.years and also nearly 29 man.years for various forms of management, support, qualification, site testing, etc.

Now, regarding the characteristics of the project peak manning, we get from Equation (5.13):

$$t_{0p} = 2.2 \text{ years}$$

which is a little later than one year after the development peak time (we found $t_{0d} = 1.1$ years). At the project peak time, the project manning reaches a peak and this is determined by Equation (5.14):

$$m_{0p} = 28 \text{ persons}$$

Note that the Difficulty as calculated by means of Equation (5.12) on the Project Subcycle is approximately the same as that calculated from the Generic Cycle and is 21 person/year.

5.4 Large-scale projects

We have successively considered the cases of small-scale projects and medium-scale projects when the software size was increasing from a value lower than 18 000 NCSS to a value of 70 000 NCSS. After having observed the coincidence of the Development Subcycle and the Project Subcycle in the case of small-scale projects, we have remarked that the Project Subcycle was detaching itself from the Development Subcycle in the medium-scale projects and this detachment was all the more significant as the scale of the project became larger. When the software size reaches a value of approximately 70 000 NCSS and beyond, the project is said to be large scale. Naturally, large-scale projects, like medium-scale ones, are made up of development effort, represented by a Development Subcycle, to which is superimposed some overhead. Once again, when we consider the addition of the overhead to the development effort we obtain the Project Subcycle, and we will see that for the particular case of large-scale projects the Project Subcycle is quite identical to the Generic Cycle.

Let us now briefly examine the characteristics of both subcycles of large-scale projects.

5.4.1 Development Subcycle

In large-scale projects, the software development work is still modelled by a Development Subcycle, as defined by Equation (5.1) for small-scale projects (see Section 5.2). So, recollecting from Equation (5.2), we observe that the development manpower, K_d, is still linked to the total manpower, K, of the Generic Cycle. Therefore, just as the Generic Cycle grows with the project scale, so does the Development Subcycle while preserving the properties described by Equation (5.2) and Equation (5.3). Moreover, the peak manning is still described by Equation (5.4) and Equation (5.5), the cumulative manpower cost by Equation (5.6), and the useful results provided by Equation (5.7) and Equation (5.8) still hold.

5.4.2 Project Subcycle

The approach here is to focus attention on Equation (5.21), which expresses the Form Factor, α, as a function of the software size, S_k. It shows clearly that when the software size is in the range defined for large-scale projects, then the Form Factor, α, reaches unity. Consequently, Equation (5.11) and Equation (5.13) can be rewritten as follows:

$$K_p \text{ (large-scale)} = K$$
$$t_{0p} \text{ (large-scale)} = t_d$$

Thus, the project peak manning from Equation (5.14) is given by:

$$m_{0p} \text{ (large-scale)} = \frac{K}{t_d \sqrt{e}}$$

Referring back to Equation (4.13), which expresses the peak manning of the Generic Cycle, it can be seen that both peak manning expressions are identical, and so it can be concluded that the Project Subcycle of a large-scale project has reached and remains identical to the Generic Cycle.

Thus, a large-scale project can be modelled as being an association of:

- a Development Subcycle, which is defined exactly as for small-scale projects, and;
- a Project Subcycle, which is in fact the Generic Cycle.

EXAMPLE

As an example of a large-scale software project, let us consider the development of the software of a large local exchange which is used as an international toll centre for a certain European country not disclosed here.

The project started in August 1977 and was completed in April 1981, after having produced 245 000 NCSS of high-level language. This software is certainly real time in nature and would be developed with a low Manpower Build-up (we assume $D_0 = 8$). The manpower expended on the development was 196 man.years. Let us now determine the main characteristics of the software project.

The first element that can be easily determined is the project Form Factor, α. Referring to Equation (5.21), we directly notice that:

$$\alpha(245) = 1$$

Therefore, the Project Subcycle will be exactly positioned on the Generic Cycle. Thus, from Equation (5.11):

$$K_p = K = 6 K_d = 1176 \text{ man.years}$$

Let us bear in mind that this huge amount of manpower is being expended from the start of the project (that is, August 1977, or 77.67) until the end of the Product Life Cycle. But we are more specifically interested in the development period; that is, the period ending in April 1981 (or 81.33) and lasting 3.66 years (t_d). Note that these time units are in decimals of a year; this enables more simple calculations.

From Equation (4.20), we calculate the amount of manpower expended by the project until delivery time, t_d, and obtain:

$$C(t_d) = 0.39 K = 459 \text{ person.years}$$

which represents an average staffing of:

$$\frac{C(t_d)}{t_d} = 125 \text{ persons}$$

In a large-scale project the project peak time, t_{op}, coincides with the delivery time, t_d, so we have:

$$t_{op} = t_d = 3.66 \text{ years}$$

which is nearly 3 years and 8 months.

The previous result given for $C(t_d)$ suggests that some 717 person.years remain to be expended on the project after delivery time. For a project of this scale, it is easy to understand that work will be necessary for some years for maintenance, follow up of the product and various chores not counting the obvious installation work and qualification testing. Let us determine the duration of this Software Life Cycle, assuming that it will end when the last person.year remains to be expended; that is, this person.year will be used to 'bury' the product.

In this case, given t_f the 'funeral' time we would have, using the Generic Cycle since it is similar to the Project Subcycle:

$$C(t_f) = K - 1$$

We write the following equation by using Equation (4.54):

$$C(t_f) = K - 1 = K \left[1 - \exp\left(- \frac{t_f^2}{2\,t_d^2} \right) \right]$$

Thus:

$$K - 1 = K - K \exp\left(- \frac{t_f^2}{2\,t_d^2} \right)$$

or:

$$K = \exp\left(\frac{t_f^2}{2\,t_d^2} \right)$$

and, taking natural logarithms:

$$\text{Log } K = \frac{t_f^2}{2\,t_d^2}$$

$$\text{Log } K^2 = \left(\frac{t_f}{t_d} \right)^2$$

$$t_f = t_d \sqrt{\text{Log } K^2} \tag{5.22}$$

This last expression provides the 'funeral' time of the product as a function only of the development time and the total manpower cost of the Project Subcycle. Substituting appropriate values in this last equation, we get:

$$t_f = 13.8 \text{ years}$$

It is therefore expected that this software product will require some form of maintenance and management, in its current version, until 1992. Naturally, if during this time extra manpower is expended on an enhanced version (that is, K is increased by ΔK), the life of the product would be extended.

Before returning to the Development Subcycle, let us determine the development conditions of this large-scale project; namely, the Manpower Build-up and the Environment Factor.

From Equation (4.53), we obtain the Manpower Build-up, D_0:

$$D_0 = \frac{K}{t_d^3} = 24$$

This figure seems rather high when we compare it with those given for guidance in Section 4.5. However, we have to bear in mind that although this kind of product contains some real-time programming, it also has a great deal of more straightforward programming, which can be speedily developed. Therefore, it was felt by the developers that an energetic approach was possible for this development.

We now proceed to calculate the Environment Factor, E. This requires a transformation of Equation (4.52), as follows:

$$E = \frac{S}{(K \, t_d^4)^{1/3}}$$

After substitution of the values previously calculated or given, we get:

$$E = 4115$$

As shown earlier, in Section 4.5, the Environment Factor assesses the 'goodness' of the programming support environment. If the need for large-scale projects persists, we must build a programming support environment in which the Environment Factor and productivity are high. This is a condition for keeping the development time scale within business reach.

The peak time of the Development Subcycle may be obtained from Equation (5.3); thus:

$t_{0d} = 1.5$ years

from which the peak manning of the Development Subcycle is calculated using Equation (5.4):

$m_{0d} = 79$ persons

It is interesting to compare the peak manning of the Development Subcycle with that of the Project Subcycle, and Equation (5.16) is of great assistance in carrying out this comparison. Since, in our case, $\alpha = 1$, we obtain:

$$\frac{m_{0p}}{m_{0d}} = \sqrt{6}$$

Thus;

$m_{0p} = 193$ persons

and, as previously said, the project peak manning occurs at time t_d in large-scale projects; that is:

$t_{0p} = 3.66$ years

To end this description of a large-scale project let us consider the Difficulty, D. From Equation (4.34) we have:

$$D = \frac{K}{t_d^2} = 88 \text{ person/year}$$

This represents a software team initially building up at a rate of almost four persons per fortnight. This high rate explains the value of the Manpower Build-up previously calculated at 24. Nevertheless, the building of a large team certainly requires this rate, which is acceptable on condition that appropriate management techniques are involved. Here we are thinking about resource control, planning support, task definition, task tracking and progress control, just to mention a few of them.

5.5 Conclusions on project scale

Throughout this chapter we have applied the fundamentals introduced in Chapter 4 to the three scales of software project. Before summarizing our position in terms of project evolution with software size, we need to come back to practical concerns. Indeed, if the concept of a model is to remain useful for software estimation purposes, we need to be quite clear about what part of the software work we are estimating. Thus, let us review what we mean by 'product design'.

The word 'design' is often used with a double meaning. From a product view point, design relates to the activity following the product planning (that is, conceptual planning and product definition, see Section 1.3), which ends with a generic product to be supplied to the software manufacturing facilities. However, the reality is more complex, as it depends on the work organization of each business. As far as software is concerned here, we call this the project phase; its manpower distribution is represented by a project curve and it is modelled by the Project Subcycle. It is that part of the product development activity that starts at the end of the system design phase when the Preliminary Design Review has been accepted by management.

As far as software methodology is concerned, design is also one of several formal activities of software development; it is included in the sequence specification, design, code, test. The design work corresponding to this latter meaning is included within the development curve.

Having satisfied our need to keep in touch with reality, let us see how the model broadly describes a software development from small to large scale. To do this, let us consider a size continuum from small- to large-scale projects and describe how the model represents project evolution as the size changes.

A small-scale project is represented by the curve shown in Figure 5.6(a). It is a subcycle of the Generic Cycle constructed with a total development manpower cost K_d. When the size increases, the development curve and the generic curve get longer, while preserving the manpower to peak time ratio [see Equation (5.2) and Equation (5.3)]; also, development time, t_d, and development manpower cost, C_d, increase.

From a certain size upwards (approximately 18 000 NCSS), the project becomes a medium-scale project and the project curve can be separated from the development curve [see Figure 5.6(b) and (c)]. When the size increases:

- the three curves increase in size (development, project and generic curves);
- the ratio between the generic and development curves remains the same;
- the project curve increases faster at first than the generic curve, but later on it approaches the generic curve [see Figure 5.6(c)].

When the project is large scale (approximately 70 000 NCSS), the project curve meets the generic curve and remains identical to it [see Figure 5.6(d)]. Again, the ratio between the generic and development curves remains independent of size. The development curve accounts for all the technical manpower involved in the project, while the difference between the project curve and development curve is a measure of all the effort of management, configuration management, product certification, marketing, etc.

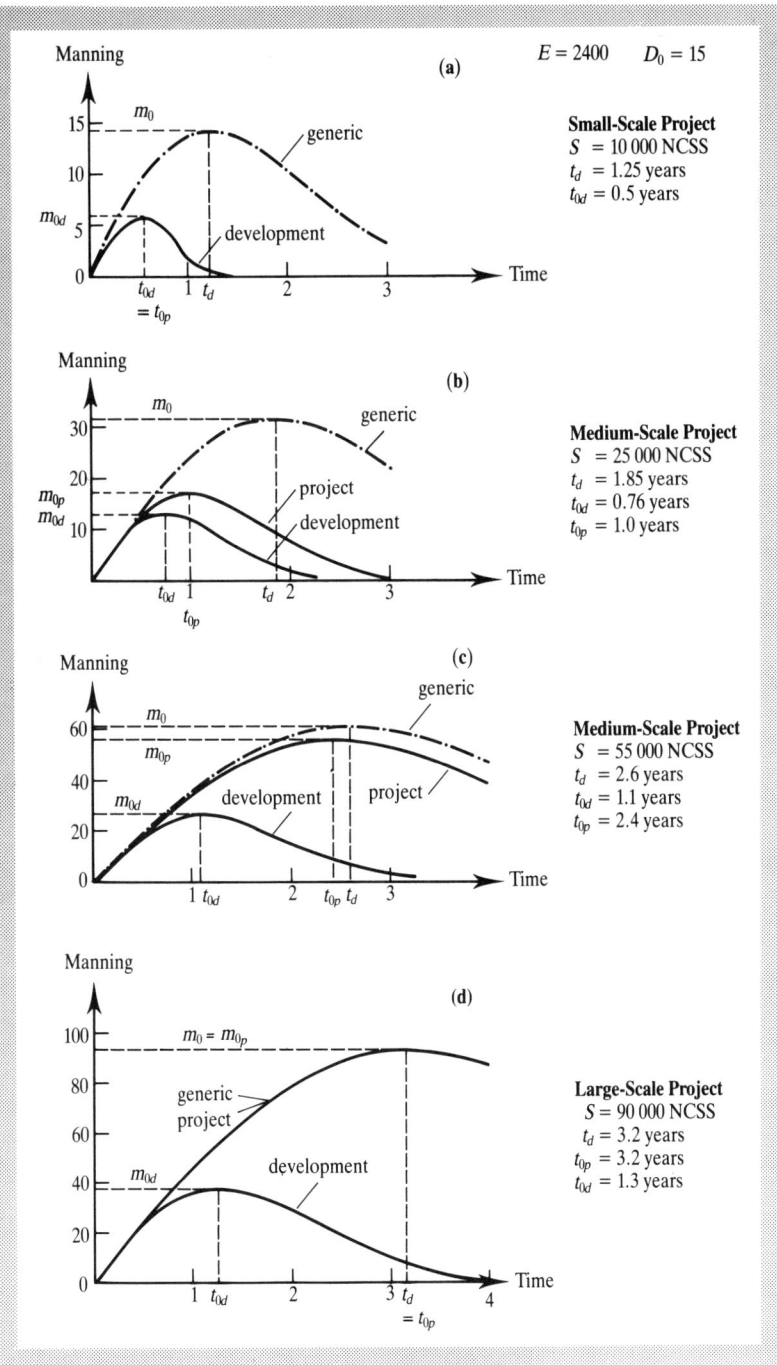

Figure 5.6   Representation of various project scales.

EXERCISES

5.1 A stand-alone project for which the size is estimated at 12 500 NCSS is to be developed in an environment such that the Environment Factor is 1200.

(a) Choosing a Manpower Build-up, $D_0 = 15$, calculate:
- the minimum development time;
- the total development manpower cost;
- the Difficulty;
- the peak manning and the peak time;
- the development productivity.

(b) Consider the case where the development can last two years. Determine the Development Subcycle and compare its development productivity with the productivity of strategy (a).

5.2 A real-time program with an estimated size of 15 000 NCSS has to be developed in one of two companies, A or B. Company A has experienced on similar past projects an Environment Factor of 2400, but because of its current work load could not start for 10 months. Company B, on the other hand, is less experienced, but it is reasonable to assume an Environment Factor of 1400. Moreover, it could start the development immediately. The product delivery is needed in 24 months. By assuming a Manpower Build-up of 8, compare the alternatives and justify your recommendation(s).

5.3 An 18 000 NCSS software project 'A' is being considered by a System House that has experienced an Environment Factor of 1200 on past projects. It is reasonable to carry out the work with a Manpower Build-up, $D_0 = 8$

(a) Calculate:
- the minimum development time;
- the total development cost;
- the peak number of persons to be employed on the project.

(b) Unfortunately, the elapsed time required by the project is found to be too long to be satisfactory for the customer, who requires the product in 1 year and 6 months. Therefore, the management suggested splitting the project into two projects, A_1 and A_2, of 9000 NCSS each, and to run both projects in parallel. For each of these projects calculate the elements as for (a), and compare the results for (a) and (b). Are the management's objectives met, in terms of development time?

(c) Finally, after negotiation, the customer accepts a delivery in 1 year and 10 months. The work starts on both projects and everything progresses well until six months later when the management discovers that the independence assumption made in (b) between A_1 and A_2 was quite wrong. However, the System House is still contracting for a delivery time of 1 year and 10 months. Transform Equation (5.8a) so as to express the new aggregated Manpower Build-up, D_0', and calculate D_0'. Is it realistic?

5.4 A project manager is planning to develop a program estimated at 25 000 NCSS with a delivery deadline in two years. The Environment Factor of his development environment is $E = 1800$. The real-time nature of the software suggests a Manpower Build-up of $D_0 = 8$.

(a) By transforming Equation (5.9), calculate how much of the software product, expressed in size, the project manager can promise for the specified deadline.

(b) Calculate the development time for a second period by re-using the first delivery and assuming that 15% of the first delivery will have to be rewritten. What is the total development time $(t_{d1} + t_{d2})$?

(c) Compare the total development time obtained in (b) with the expected development time, had the development been made in a single run.

5.5 The development of a CHILL compiler started in March 1978 and by September 1981, 47 000 NCSS were developed in a high-level language. The development manpower cost, until September 1981, was 14.8 person.years. This is an example of a medium-scale project with a relatively long development time.

(a) Calculate:
- the Form Factor;
- the total manpower cost of the Generic Cycle and the total manpower cost of the Project Subcycle;
- the development time;
- the Environment Factor;
- the Manpower Build-up;
- the peak development time and manning;
- the peak project time and manning.

(b) Could this compiler be developed on a shorter time scale? Justify your position and produce your estimate.

Chapter 6
A Putnam-Based Estimating Method

6.1 Introduction

The purpose of this chapter is to introduce an estimating method. There are certainly as many methods as there are estimators, ranging from the finger-in-the-air methods to the more sophisticated ones such as that described here. Ideally, the method should consist of a set of defined actions to be carried out in an orderly manner. In that way, any estimator knowledgeable in this method will be able to apply it in the same fashion and be successful even for large-scale projects. Moreover, the results of the estimating process will be observable, assessable and justifiable, and can be criticized; thus, they are amenable to improvements and lead to better understanding.

When this set of defined actions (also called standard practice or method) is subordinated to a group of adequate principles and supported by appropriate tools to make the method more effective, a methodology has been defined. Since from a given set of principles several different valid methodologies can be constructed, this chapter does not pretend to cover the full range of methods. However, the method introduced in this chapter, even if it relies on tools as elementary as paper and pencil, is compatible with the principles developed here and what is more, it gives useful results.

Let us now review the basic principles from which our method has been developed.

(1)   *The method is based on a theory.*

The theory presented in Chapters 4 and 5 aims at constructing a model that behaves like a software project. The establishment of this theory can be summarized as follows. A concept of software development is submitted to experimentation, a measurement baseline is analyzed and the original concept is validated. This provides an understanding of the development process, and this understanding is embodied in a rational model – that is, the Norden/Rayleigh Model as completed by Putnam.

(2)   *The outcome of the method is measurable.*

Some elements are directly measurable – such as the size, development time and manpower cost – while others – such as the Environment Factor – are indirectly measurable. Furthermore, the estimating process is assessable by means of data collected during the development process. The accuracy of the estimate can thus be progressively improved whenever needed.

(3)   *The estimating practice involves the people concerned.*

The size is estimated by the analysts and programmers, and all results can be discussed in an objective fashion. Software development is an activity with a strong human content. It is not wise to ignore it.

(4)   *There is a separation of concerns between estimating and developing.*

The Consulting Estimator is not involved in the project but is responsible for the accuracy of the estimate rather than the result.

Let us preview the successive steps involved in this estimating method (see Figure 6.1). The first thing to do is to estimate the size of the software to be developed. This usually provides a nominal size to which is associated a size range, defined by a standard deviation, inside which the real delivered size is presumed to be. The second thing to do is to determine the Manpower Build-up and the Environment Factor. This is easy to do when statistics results already exist in the organization under consideration. If this is not the case some assumptions have to be made which can be eased by considering statistics of other software organizations. Nevertheless, the results have to be constantly verified during the project duration.

We are now ready, as a third step, to identify the development constraints in terms of manpower cost, development time, peak manning and Difficulty. We might find it advantageous to consider Manpower Build-up as an additional constraint, because it will intervene in the same fashion as other constraints when building the Planning Zone. Naturally, we define these constraints as ranges between maximum and minimum values.

The fourth step consists of constructing the Planning Zone on a rectangular cost–time axis system. The first discovery to be made concerns the existence of the Planning Zone; that is, can we construct a closed area

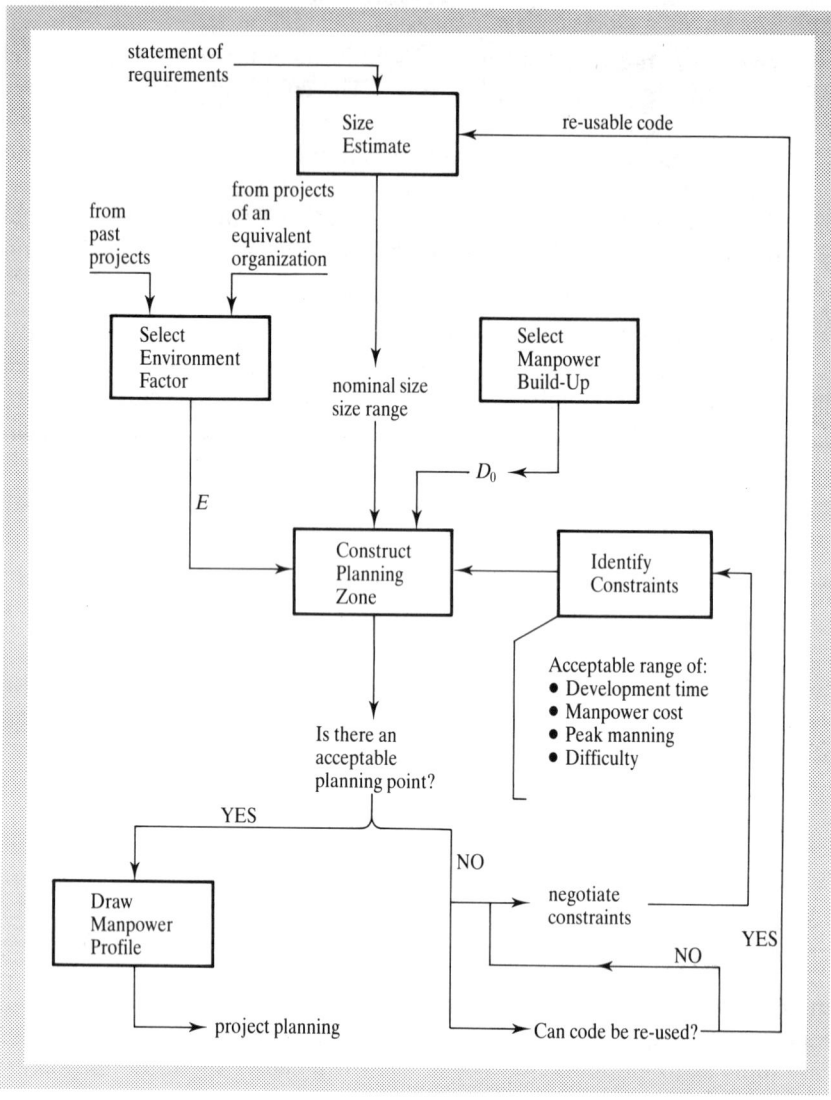

Figure 6.1   Steps of the estimating method.

within which all the constraints are satisfied? The Planning Zone might not exist at first. When this happens we have to start the difficult task of re-negotiating the constraints. We know by experience that this sometimes involves asking the customer to accept a different delivery time – usually a later delivery. An important element of the Planning Zone is the representation of the Software Equation. This poses the hard question: Is there an area within the Planning Zone that permits the software development? A problem often encountered at this point is that the project manager wants to build too much software for the given set of constraints. Thus, we have to put the question: Can we re-use some software instead of developing everything? If this is not possible, then, can we cut out unnecessary modules? In the worst case, we will have to consider seriously postponing some software product functions until an enhanced version is needed by the customer. As we can see, the fourth step is the most dramatic of all and often leads to a tough discussion where the Consulting Estimator needs full mastery of the method.

The final fifth step occurs when an acceptable planning point has been agreed on. We can then draw a manpower profile. This curve gives the distribution of manpower throughout the development time. This is a very useful curve as it enables scheduling of the project's tasks. A realistic manpower profile is a precondition for a correct project plan, irrespective of the project scale.

We presume at this stage that we have a clear global view on the estimating method. It is now time to investigate each of these steps in more detail.

6.2   Size estimate

During the presentation of the size-estimating method, the case of re-used software has been emphasized. Since the beginning of software history a vast quantity of software has been written and made operational at high cost, and this cost is expanding steadily. A possible way of reducing the cost is to re-use as much as possible of existing software. It is contrary to wide-spread opinion to say that re-use of software is expensive. However, it is still cheaper than re-developing everything. It will be even cheaper when a proven method of software re-usability exists. The opportunity is taken here to give the Consulting Estimator a technique for estimating development involving re-used source code. A typical application is software maintenance when part of the software product has to be modified to meet changed requirements.

6.2.1   The full development case

A.   Functional analysis

Sizing up a software project can start as soon as the customer delivers the requirements definition of the product (see Section 1.3.1). A quick functional analysis is carried out by a group of experts in their field. The purpose of this analysis is to break down the product into subsystems, functions and sub-functions, and to arrive at a level of functional entity that can be implemented by one or several small-sized modules (for example, with a size of about 500 NCSS). Naturally, the size estimating can be done with better accuracy during the development phase, and especially for the Preliminary Design Review and the Critical Design Review. At these stages, the design of the product becomes fairly well known, which minimizes sizing errors.

The number of modules per functional entity can vary according to the complexity of the function to be implemented. It is always possible to estimate the number of modules in terms of three figures, called, as in the PERT technique, optimistic, M_o, most likely, M_m, and pessimistic, M_p, where $M_o < M_m < M_p$.

At this point, it is worth mentioning that this analysis is a group activity. Several analysts with knowledge of the requirements pool their resources and try to create possible solutions and allow for difficulties. Further to their knowledge, some might even have specific experience which could be valuable. This practice is very productive when conducted in a brainstorming manner (see Section 1.7.4). The Consulting Estimator adopts the role of chairman and takes careful note of ideas generated by the group.

There is no single technique applicable to size estimating. Any individual approach is acceptable as long as it is incorporated in a consensus-orientated group. When the expert gives his estimate on purely technical grounds, the individual with experience will compare it with different projects, and a realistic participant will be aware of the constraints. All these individual approaches provide different figures for optimistic, pessimistic and most likely quantities; these figures are discussed by the group and adopted when the consensus is established. It is important that all opinions are expressed and taken into account.

In organizations where software metrics exists, tables give the average number of Non-Commentary Source Statements per module and its standard deviation. It is then possible to convert the number of modules per functional entity into a number of NCSS as follows:

Source size = number of modules × number of NCSS per module

Then, to calculate the standard deviation, we can use:

$$S_o = \text{optimistic size} = M_o (N - \sigma_n)$$
$$S_m = \text{most likely size} = M_m N$$
$$S_p = \text{pessimistic size} = M_p (N + \sigma_n)$$

where N is the average module size (in NCSS) and σ_n is the standard deviation of N. In organizations where such a metrics does not exist the estimate can be done directly in terms of S_0, S_m and S_p, which represent the optimistic, most likely and pessimistic module size, respectively.

This practice might appear a bit arbitrary, and with good reason. One reason is that the size of a module is greatly problem oriented. Some algorithms might require many source statements while others need only a few. This tends to produce a large standard deviation value that seems incompatible with the idea of a standard module size. However, the important point to note here is that it is the responsibility of the Consulting Estimator to choose a sizing method and to remain consistent with his choice across projects and throughout the project duration. By acting in this way, the Consulting Estimator gives maximum chance for his size results to be comparable.

Another point worth mentioning at this stage is that some organizations have an existing coding standard. A coding standard is a document that prescribes the rules governing the practice of writing source code for various commonly known algorithms. Wherever this coding standard can be enforced, the structure of modules and their sizes will depend less on the personal style of the programmer (albeit a loose or concise style) and more on the problem at hand. It is therefore to be expected that the size dispersion of modules of the same type would be less and would therefore provide better validation of the sizing in terms of number of modules. Nevertheless, we assume that the ultimate choice is with the Consulting Estimator.

B.   Functional size estimate

Let us assume that a software product can be divided into subsystems, functions and subfunctions, and that each subfunction is divided into modules. This is so because of the functional decomposition as practised during system design.

Module   Let us consider first, the module. For each module, the size is given by a set of three values: S_o, S_m and S_p as previously defined. From these values, the expected module size, S_{md}, can be deduced by the formula:

$$S_{md} = \frac{S_o + 4 S_m + S_p}{6} \tag{6.1}$$

and the standard deviation on the module size is, as usual:

$$\sigma_{md} = \frac{|S_p - S_o|}{6} \tag{6.2}$$

The meaning of the standard deviation is as follows:

Provided that no change occurred in the product requirement definition, the size of the module developed will have a probability of:

99.8% of being between $S_{md} - 3\,\sigma_{md}$ and $S_{md} + 3\,\sigma_{md}$

95% of being between $S_{md} - 2\,\sigma_{md}$ and $S_{md} + 2\,\sigma_{md}$

68% of being between $S_{md} - \sigma_{md}$ and $S_{md} + \sigma_{md}$

Equation (6.1) and Equation (6.2) are the well-known PERT expressions that have been in use for numerous projects since the US Navy created them for the Polaris project in the early 1950s.

Functions   Once the modules are sized up, it is time to take care of the sub-functions. The estimated size of each subfunction is:

$$S_{sf} = \Sigma\, S_{md} \qquad\qquad (6.3)$$

$$\sigma_{sf} = \sqrt{\Sigma\, \sigma_{md}^2} \qquad\qquad (6.4)$$

The expected size of each module of a subfunction is added up to give the size, S_{sf}, of the subfunction. The square of the module standard deviations are added up to give the square of the standard deviation of the subfunctions. These expressions also belong to the PERT sizing technique. Furthermore, they apply when passing from subfunctions to functions and from functions to subsystems.

Overall product   The method just outlined applies to the size estimate of the product. The sizes of the subsystems are added to give the size of the software product. The standard deviation is obtained by taking the square root of the sum of the squares of the standard deviations of the subsystems. It could be fastidious to carry out all these calculations by hand; fortunately, the use of a spreadsheet on a Personal Computer makes this task relatively easy.

EXAMPLE

Let us now see how this method is used in practice on a small example. The Network Signalling Subsystem (NSS for short) is a group of functions aimed at controlling the transfer of information between two stored program control telephone exchanges. NSS runs on four main pieces of hardware connected by means of a multibus. A group of software functions operates on each of these, called CPP (Central Processor Process), SILTEC (Signalling Link Terminal Controller), LOLIC (Local Link Controller) and LOSIP (Local Signalling Process).

A meeting of the analysts involved in the system design and their estimator was arranged, as a result of which a size estimate was produced. The results of the size-estimating session are given in Table 6.1. The expected size was calculated by means of Equation (6.1) applied to the minimum size (optimistic), the maximum size (pessimistic) and the likely size (most likely). In the same way, Equation (6.2) provided the standard deviation of each software part.

Thus, the total size of NSS has a probability of 99.8% of being between 15 324 NCSS and 12 360 NCSS.

6.2.2   The case of re-usable code

The modelling techniques used in software estimating presuppose that all the software whose size is given is obtained by means of a complete development.

Table 6.1   Size estimate for the Network Signalling Subsystem.

Function	Minimum Size	Maximum Size	Likely Size	Expected Size	Standard Deviation
CPP					
Call States Process	2303	4277	3290	3290	329
Maintenance Process	1200	2340	1800	1790	190
Link Device Driver	70	130	100	100	10
Exchange Link Controller	70	130	100	100	10
Background Process	400	800	600	600	67
Linksets Management					
Process	1540	2860	2200	2200	220
CPP Timer	140	260	200	200	20
Total CPP	5723	10797	8290	8280	445
SILTEC	2160	3300	2700	2710	190
LOLIC.Interface	160	250	200	202	15
LOLIC.Driver	140	460	300	300	53
LOLIC.Maintenance	200	300	250	250	17
LOLIC.Executive	320	480	400	400	27
Total SILTEC + LOLIC	2980	4790	3850	3862	200
LOSIP					
LOSIP.P	140	460	300	300	53
LOSIP.C	400	600	500	500	33
LOSIP.Fault Management	400	600	500	500	33
LOSIP.Executive	320	480	400	400	27
Total LOSIP	1260	2140	1700	1700	76
Total NSS	9963	17727	13840	13842	494

This is true when no equivalent software package exists and so it is necessary to specify, design, code and test all processes of a software system. However, this is not always the case. It is becoming more and more common for a desired function to be already implemented in a process compatible with the requirements. This might be so, for example, because the process is available on the market place and it just needs to be adapted to the requirements or, because of a phased-development approach, two functions are almost similar, differing only by a subfunction. In this case, one process is developed completely and the second process is obtained by modification of the first process; that is, the first process source code is re-used.

A re-used process source code of size S_i can have a procedure of size S_p modified by (see Figure 6.2):

- addition of new code of size S_n;
- deleting a size S_d of the initial source code;
- changing a size S_c of the initial source code.

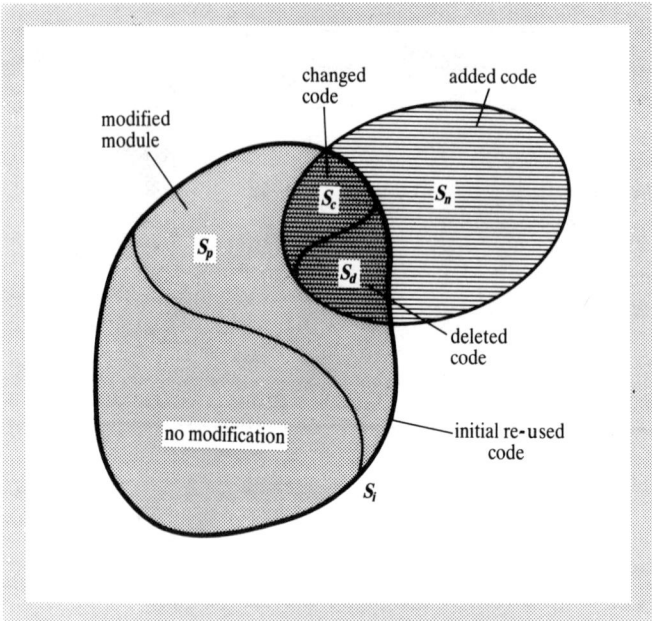

Figure 6.2   The re-used source code case.

The initial re-used code, S_i, is made up of several procedures: one procedure of size S_p has a deleted part, S_d, and a changed part, S_c. What remains unchanged of the S_i code is $S_i - (S_c + S_d)$ (see Figure 6.2).

It is necessary at this stage to give some information about how the source code size is used when determining the manpower allocation. The lowest level of procedure containing the source code creates a need for manpower to specify, design, code and test this procedure, and also to specify, integrate and test higher levels of the structure. Therefore, it has been recognized as good practice to use the following ratios to allocate manpower on each activity. The manpower allocation shown is for the case of a full development (see Table 6.2).

Specification:	9%	
Design:	16%	of manpower generated by the size
Code:	17%	
Unit test:	25%	

$$\overline{\quad 67\% \quad} \tag{6.5}$$

It is assumed here that 67% of the manpower is really used at this level because of the presence of source code at this lowest level. The rest of the manpower (33%) is used at higher levels with the following distribution:

Table 6.2 Comparison between full development and development with re-used code.

Type of Development	Higher Level Specification/ Design	Specification	Design	Code	Unit Test	Higher Level Test	Total
Full development	8	9	16	17	25	25	100%
Re-use – no change	8	2	4	4	6	25	49%
Re-use with change							
Code base, S_i	8	2	4	4	–	25	43%
Procedure modified, S_p	–	–	–	–	6	–	6%
Added code, S_n	8	9	16	17	25	25	100%
Changed code, S_c	–	7	12	13	19	–	51%
Deleted code, S_d	– 8	– 2	– 4	– 4	– 6	– 25	–49%

$$\begin{array}{lr} \text{higher level specification and design:} & 8\% \\ \text{integration and test, total, higher level:} & \underline{25\%} \\ & 33\% \end{array} \qquad \textbf{(6.6)}$$

These figures could be an acceptable starting point in organizations where software metrics does not exist. Since they are independent of the methodology it would be useful for the Consulting Estimator to revise them as soon as he thinks it necessary.

A. Re-use without any change

If the source code of a software part of size S_i was re-used without any change to become part of the new product, then its functions satisfied the specification of the part to be implemented. However, as the re-used part is to become a part of the new product, there is still need for the following:

- rewriting or updating the re-used specification document (2%);
- updating the re-used design document (4%);
- recompiling and checking the compiled source code (4%);
- verifying by a run of the test program that the source code was not contaminated during the transport (6%).

As indicated in Table 6.2, this work represents 16% of the nominal effort. Nevertheless, the re-use of this source code does not avoid higher level specification, design, integration and testing; they are the cause and the consequence of the adoption of this re-used part. Overall, the effort involved is 49% of the effort necessary for a full development. Hence, the equivalent size, S_i (equ), can be taken as:

$$S_i \text{ (equ)} = 49\% \ S_i$$

B. Re-use of a process with change in one procedure

If a process of size S_i is re-used, it is made up of several procedures, one of which of size S_p is modified to meet the specification (see Figure 6.2). This modification consists of:

- adding a size S_n;
- deleting a size S_d;
- changing a size S_c.

Each phase of the Software Life Cycle is affected by the change.

Specification Full specification work will have to be done on changed code, S_c, and added code, S_n, and the specification document will have to be updated for the re-used process less the part involved in the full specification $[S_i - (S_c + S_d)]$. The size of code related to specification effort will be:

$$9 (S_n + S_c) + 2 [S_i - (S_c + S_d)]$$

that is, $2 S_i + 9 S_n + 7 S_c - 2 S_d$.

Design Full design work will have to be done on the changed code, S_c, and added code, S_n, and update of the design document will be done on the re-used process less the part involved in the full design $[S_i - (S_c + S_d)]$. The size of code related to design effort will be:

$$16 (S_c + S_n) + 4 [S_i - (S_c + S_d)]$$

that is, $4 S_i + 16 S_n + 12 S_c - 4 S_d$.

Code Full coding work will be involved on the changed code, S_c, and the added code, S_n, and the rest of the process will need recompilation and various code walk-through effort $[S_i - (S_c + S_d)]$. The size of code related to coding effort will be:

$$17 (S_c + S_n) + 4 [S_i - (S_c + S_d)]$$

that is, $4 S_i + 17 S_n + 13 S_c - 4 S_d$.

Unit test Full testing effort will be required on the new code, S_n, and the changed code, S_c, and the rest of the procedure $[S_p - (S_c + S_d)]$ will need some regression testing and validation work. The size of code related to unit testing effort will be:

$$6 [S_p - (S_c + S_d)] + 25 (S_c + S_n)$$

that is, $6 S_p + 25 S_n + 19 S_c - 6 S_d$.

The effort at higher levels now needs to be identified.

Higher level specification/design The total size remaining after implementation of the change will have to contribute to higher level specification and design $(S_i - S_d + S_n)$. The size of code related to higher level specification/design effort is:

$$8 S_i + 8 S_n - 8 S_d$$

Higher level integration and testing   The total size remaining after unit testing will contribute to higher level integration and testing ($S_i - S_d + S_n$). The contribution to higher level testing is:

$$25 \, S_i + 25 \, S_n - 25 \, S_d$$

C.   Equivalent size of re-used code

Taking the foregoing into account, the size equivalent to a software part built on re-used code can be determined as follows (see Table 6.2):

$$
\begin{aligned}
S \text{ (equ)} = \quad & 43\% \quad S_i \quad \text{(code base)} \\
+ \quad & 6\% \quad S_p \quad \text{(procedure modified)} \\
+ \quad & 100\% \quad S_n \quad \text{(added code)} \\
+ \quad & 51\% \quad S_c \quad \text{(changed code)} \\
- \quad & 49\% \quad S_d \quad \text{(deleted code)} \quad\quad (6.7)
\end{aligned}
$$

Note that this result depends on the rate of manpower allocation, which is different for each organization [see Equation (6.5) and Equation (6.6)]. The calculations have been developed here in such a way that the size equivalent formula can be re-calculated if the organization has a different rate of manpower allocation.

D.   Uncertainty in the size equivalent

As the re-used code base and the procedure to be modified are, in general, known their size can be measured with no uncertainty. However, other sizes S_c, S_d and S_n will be estimated with uncertainty. These are usually deduced as for an entirely new development; thus, Equation (6.1) to Equation (6.4) are used as appropriate.

EXAMPLE

Let us now see how this sizing method is used by constructing an example for the development of a subsystem made up of two processes, CMX and BMX. Each of these processes is constituted of a certain number of procedures – but this number is not relevant here.

The difference between BMX and CMX resides in one procedure (Procedure 6) that needs to be modified to produce CMX by using BMX as a re-used base code. The effort involved is as follows:

Estimated changed code in Proc. 6:   155, 184, 240 NCSS

Estimated deleted code in Proc. 6:   220, 300, 380 NCSS

Estimated added code in Proc. 6:   220, 350, 480 NCSS

Table 6.3 Development of a subsystem consisting of two processes.

Function	Minimum Size	Maximum Size	Likely Size	Expected Size	Standard Deviation
BMX					
Proc. 1	450	620	550	545	28
Proc. 2	220	350	220	242	22
Proc. 3	650	800	700	708	25
Proc. 4	350	550	500	483	33
Proc. 5	680	850	820	802	28
Subtotal	2350	3170	2790	2780	61
Proc. 6	620	830	750	742	35
Total	2970	4000	3540	3522	70
CMX					
43% code base, S_i	1277	1720	1522	1514	74
6% Proc. 6, S_p	37	50	45	44	2
100% added code, S_n	220	480	350	350	43
51% changed code, S_c	79	122	94	96	7
−49% deleted code, S_d	(108)	(186)	(147)	(147)	13
CMX equivalent	1505	2186	1864	1857	99
Total equivalent	4475	6186	5404	5379	121
CMX – real size					
Code base, S_i	2970	4000	3540	3522	70
Added code, S_n	220	480	350	350	43
Deleted code, S_d	220	380	300	300	27
Total CMX – real size	3410	4860	4190	4172	86
Total subsystem – real size	6380	8860	7730	7694	111

Note: Figures in parentheses are negative.

Note here that each set of three figures corresponds to optimistic, likely and pessimistic sizes, respectively (see Table 6.3). As mentioned earlier, the use of a computerized spreadsheet would be very valuable for estimating these figures.

In fact, the real deliverable size will be between 8030 NCSS and 7360 NCSS with a probability of 99.8%, and the size used for estimating the manpower will be between 5750 NCSS and 5000 NCSS with the same probability. Thus, consideration of re-usable code permits a better estimate of the manpower involved.

6.3   Determining predictors

Having determined the size range of the project, we now have to prepare for using the estimating model. Our model makes use of two predictors:

Manpower Build-up, D_0, and Environment Factor, E. Let us consider how to select them.

6.3.1 Manpower Build-up

During the first estimate it is wise to take as a standard a set of values close to those recommended by Putnam, with the following considerations:

- $D_0 = 7.5$ The real-time software has many interfaces with the hardware and other software parts. This software involves many processes in a target environment that has not yet been experienced by the team.

- $D_0 = 15$ The real-time software has some defined interfaces with the environment. The number of processes is significant and there is a relatively high number of interfaces among processes.

- $D_0 = 30$ The software is relatively 'easy' real-time software or conventional sequential software.

- $D_0 = 60$ The conventional sequential software is developed by experienced teams and management.

The justifications for taking this set of values are as follows:

(1)   The variation by steps of D_0 is accepted, as validated by Putnam's statistical work.

(2)   The definition of each step, which is close to the observations made by Putnam, has been found to be both practical and acceptable in developing telecommunications systems.

(3)   The set of values used here are close to those of Putnam. The only difference is that the values used are rounded.

(4)   The accuracy of the figures is not of paramount importance, since the objective of this method is to consistently estimate software development within a given organization, not to compare our performance strictly with those of American software houses. Therefore, the Consulting Estimator will use the figures given here as a standard during the first estimate. When enough data is provided by a measurement campaign the figures can be revised for the organization concerned.

6.3.2 Environment Factor

This can be assessed from past projects by using suitable measurement techniques. In the absence of a historical data base for the organization concerned, similar software developed in a similar environment in other organizations can be taken as a reference for the first estimate. It is then absolutely necessary to implement a measurement scheme for the considered organization (see Section 1.5). It must be remembered that the major role of estimating and re-estimating is to understand, by means of E and D_0, how a large-scale project is behaving before it is too late to take any corrective action.

A.   Determination if one previous development is known

If similar software has been developed with similar methods and equipment in the same or a similar organization, then the following factors will be known:

- the manpower development cost, C_d, in man.years;
- the time elapsed between the start of specification work and the end of integration testing, t_d, in years;
- the size of NCSS.

Therefore, we can deduce K_d from Equation (5.8):

$$K_d = \frac{C_d(t_d)}{0.95}$$

the manpower cost, K, of the Generic Cycle, as in Equation (5.2):

$$K = 6\,K_d$$

and from the Software Equation, Equation (4.52), the Environment Factor is:

$$E = \frac{S}{K^{1/3}\,t_d^{4/3}}$$

which can be easily deduced with the help of a pocket calculator. Let us now try an example to convince ourselves that this works.

EXAMPLE

A project has necessitated 45 MY to produce 35 450 NCSS in 2.5 years. Using the procedure just outlined, we have:

$$K_d = 47.4\,\mathrm{MY} \Rightarrow K = 284\,\mathrm{MY}$$

$$E = \frac{35\ 450}{(284^{1/3}\ 2.5^{4/3})} = 1590$$

For the purpose of a first estimate for a similar project we could take for simplicity $E = 1600$.

B.   Determination if a set of previous projects is known

We can obtain a more accurate value for the Environment Factor if several past projects are known, rather than one, so, for each project, we measure:

- the development manpower cost, $C_d(t_d)$, in man.years;
- the development time, t_d, in years;
- the size of the delivered source code, S, in NCSS.

We invoke once again the Software Equation, as defined by Equation (4.52), and calculate the value:

$$\pi = \frac{S}{C_d} = \frac{E\,K^{1/3}\,t_d^{4/3}}{C_d} \tag{6.8}$$

where:

$$C_d(t_d) = \frac{K\,0.95}{6} = \frac{K}{6.3}$$

which is the combination of Equation (5.2) and Equation (5.8). Then, it follows that:

$$\pi = 6.3\,\frac{E}{D^{2/3}}$$

when we remember that the Difficulty is given by:

$$D = \frac{K}{t_d^2} = 6.3\,\frac{C_d(t_d)}{t_d^2}$$

[see Equation (4.56)]. Taking logarithms of both sides of the expression results in:

$$\text{Log }\pi = \text{Log}(6.3\,E) - \frac{2}{3}\,\text{Log }D \tag{6.9}$$

For each development, we calculate $D = K/t_d^2$ and $\pi = S/C_d$ and plot these values on a log-log scale (see Figure 6.3). We draw a straight line of slope $-2/3$ as close as possible to all the points plotted. Then, taking any practical point along this line, using its co-ordinates π and D, we can calculate the Environment Factor as follows:

$$E = \frac{\pi\,D^{2/3}}{6.3} \tag{6.10}$$

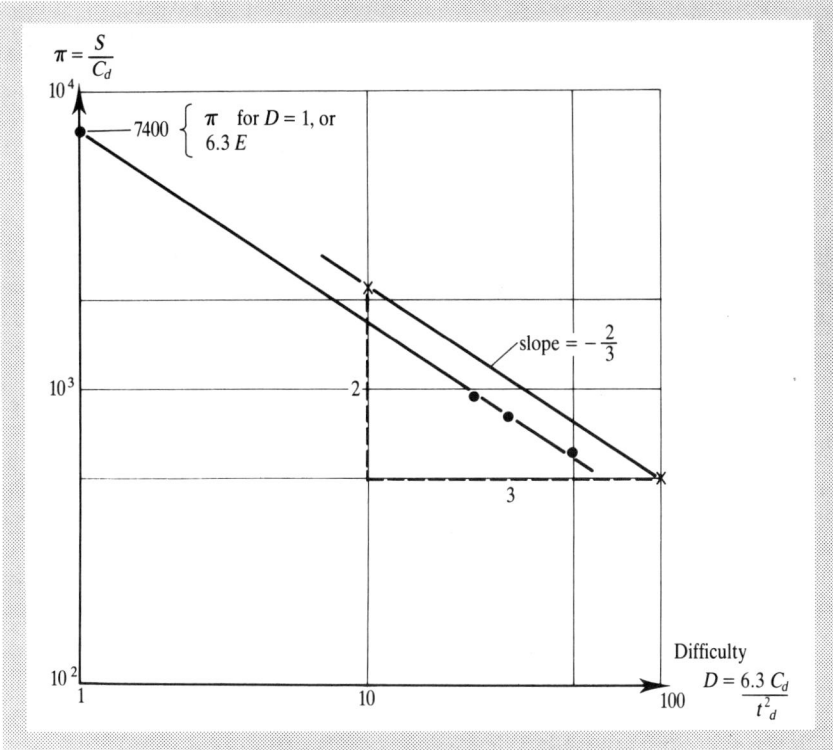

Figure 6.3   Graphical determination of the Technology (or Environment) Factor.

Let us now consider an example to convince ourselves that it is simpler than it seems.

EXAMPLE

Three projects are known to have been achieved in an environment where an estimate has to be carried out. An assessment of the Environment Factor is to be done. These projects are:

P_1: $C_d = 58$ MY, $t_d = 2.7$ years, $S = 35\ 000$ NCSS
P_2: $C_d = 16$ MY, $t_d = 2.1$ years, $S = 15\ 000$ NCSS
P_3: $C_d = 28$ MY, $t_d = 2.4$ years, $S = 23\ 000$ NCSS

The calculation of π and D gives:

P_1: $\pi = 603$ NCSS/MY, $D = 50$ person/year
P_2: $\pi = 938$ NCSS/MY, $D = 23$ person/year
P_3: $\pi = 821$ NCSS/MY, $D = 31$ person/year

A straight line of slope $-2/3$ is drawn as near as possible to the plotted points. Then, taking $D = 1$ we have Log π = Log (6.3 E). The intersect with $D = 1$ gives $\pi = 6.3 E = 7400$ and $E = 1175$ (see Figure 6.3).

6.4   Planning Zone

At this point, it is instructive to consider once again Figure 6.1 to get an idea of the way we have travelled. We know the size and we have determined the Manpower Build-up, D_0, and the Environment Factor, E. We are now ready for the Planning Zone.

6.4.1   Defining the development constraints

For ease of understanding, the mathematical aspect of the construction of the Planning Zone is introduced progressively, and at the same time the Planning Zone technique is illustrated by means of a constructed example.

The primary advantage of the Putnam method is that its equations are related to the most useful management parameters: cost, time, peak manning and the technological characteristics of the software development, as well as the Difficulty and Manpower Build-up. These can easily be thought of in terms of constraints. In this section, we are going to be concerned exclusively with the Development Subcycle (development) of the Software Life Cycle. This can be extended to the project cycle without any problem.

Because of the power law nature of the equations, it is possible to represent all parameters of the software development on a log-log scale. Usually, the manpower cost is represented on the vertical axis and the time on the horizontal axis. On this graph we draw the lines representing the constraints. Some constraints are a maximum not to go beyond; some other constraints are a minimum above which we would like to situate the selected point. The reader might want to glance at Figure 6.4 to verify that the cost time framework is clearly set up. Let us now investigate the meaning of the various straight lines.

A.   The cost and time constraints

Cost and time constraints do not present any difficulty. The maximum and minimum costs require two horizontal straight lines, and the earliest and latest times require two vertical straight lines. These four constraints determine a rectangle. Within this rectangle more refinement is added by considering further constraints.

The maximum cost, cost maxi, is generally established during the conceptual planning phase. An understanding of the market leads to establishing the most reasonable price for the expected product. Consideration of the

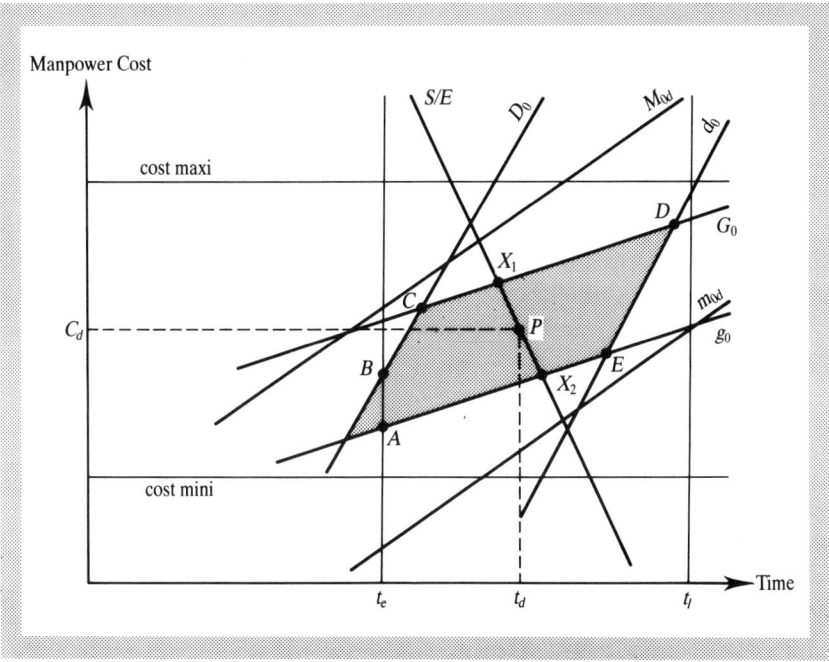

Figure 6.4   Construction of the Planning Zone.

price and expected profit leads to the cost maxi. This can be seen as the cost beyond which the profit is diminished or not possible, or which would lead to losing the contract. (However, consideration of contract costing or pricing is not the purpose here; the reader interested in these matters could read with profit some project management manuals.)

The minimum cost, cost mini, is the cost below which an organization does not wish to be involved in the project development. This could be for various reasons. For example, the small size of the project would not be appropriate for the structure of the organization or its capability: the return on capital employed would not be optimum.

The earliest time, t_e, for delivery is the time before which the customer does not wish to receive the product (it might conflict with some other activities in his organization). The latest time, t_l, is the time at which the customer wants to receive the product for acceptance. It is recommended that the time necessary to ship the product is taken into account here.

B.   The peak manning constraints

Two peak mannings have to be considered: the maximum and minimum. The required peak manning must lie between these two extremes. The peak manning, m_{0d} for the software development is given by Equation (5.5), restated here:

$$m_{0d} = \frac{K}{\sqrt{6e}\, t_d} \tag{6.11}$$

but, as for the manpower cost, what we are interested in is the manpower cost of the Development Subcycle, represented by Equation (5.2). Thus, the expression of the peak manning becomes:

$$m_{0d} = \frac{\sqrt{6}\, K_d}{\sqrt{e}\, t_d} \tag{6.12}$$

Then we have a relation between the development manpower cost, K_d, and the development time, t_d, as follows:

$$K_d = m_{0d} \frac{\sqrt{e}}{\sqrt{6}}\, t_d \tag{6.13}$$

considering that, by taking the logarithm of both sides of the previous equation, we can get:

$$\text{Log } K_d = \text{Log}\left(m_{0d}\, \frac{\sqrt{e}}{\sqrt{6}}\right) + \text{Log } t_d \tag{6.14}$$

This last equation gives a linear representation on a log-log graph and a convenient choice of two points defines the straight line.

The construction of the Planning Zone needs a line for the peak manning maximum and a second line for the peak manning minimum, as shown in Figure 6.4 by the lines M_{0d} and m_{0d}.

The minimum peak manning, m_{0d}, is the manning under which the project manager cannot go. This may be because the resources exist and cannot be re-allocated or, for small projects, it is assumed that a minimum number of persons has to be employed.

The maximum peak manning, M_{0d}, is the manning beyond which the project becomes unmanageable (for example, having more than five subordinates per team leader). Having too many people makes control, co-ordination and planning more difficult, and can put at risk the overall project organization. In many cases, it is not possible to man up to the peak manpower required by the Rayleigh distribution due to shortage of trained personnel.

C. The Manpower Build-up constraints

The Manpower Build-up is given in Section 6.3.1 as a value not to go beyond. It is, nevertheless, practical to choose a value defining a minimum below which we do not wish to work. As well as helping, sometimes, to close the Planning Zone, this can also help to define the longest development time.

The Manpower Build-up is defined by Equation (4.53) and is restated here as:

$$D_0 = \frac{K}{t_d^3} \tag{6.15}$$

The manpower cost we are concerned with, in the Development Subcycle, is:

$$K_d = \frac{K}{6} \tag{6.16}$$

Therefore, by combining Equation (6.15) and Equation (6.16) we have:

$$D_0 = 6\frac{K_d}{t_d^3} \tag{6.17}$$

which expresses the Manpower Build-up as a function of the development manpower cost, not the generic manpower cycle as given in Equation (6.15). We again find an expression of the development manpower cost relative to the development time:

$$K_d = \frac{1}{6} D_0 t_d^3 \tag{6.18}$$

This is easily amenable to a logarithmic expression:

$$\text{Log } K_d = 3 \text{ Log } t_d + \text{Log}\left(\frac{1}{6} D_0\right) \tag{6.19}$$

and can be represented by a straight line on a log-log graph. A first line will be drawn with D_0 (maximum value) as recommended by Section 6.3.1 and a second line will be drawn at a lower level using the value of D_0 selected by the Consulting Estimator. The latter value appears as d_0 in Figure 6.4.

The Manpower Build-up is a parameter that must be found empirically, based on past similar projects. This quantity, d_0 or D_0, has a specific value for different categories of software.

The most critical constraint is D_0, the maximum Manpower Build-up. Where no other measurement baseline includes it, it is recommended to use one of the values given in Section 6.3.1.

The minimum Manpower Build-up, d_0, is not essential. Nevertheless, it may have a role to play in the formation of the Planning Zone.

D.   The Difficulty constraints

The Difficulty gives the Consulting Estimator an idea of how fast a software team can be built up (this is why we also call it team growth; represented as g_0 and G_0 in Figure 6.4). This parameter represents the slope at the origin of the manpower profile. Here, again, two values can be determined by discussion between the Consulting Estimator and the software manager: one maximum value and one minimum value.

The Difficulty is defined by Equation (4.56). Moreover, considerations analogous to those followed with the Manpower Build-up show that the Difficulty is also amenable to a logarithmic expression:

$$\text{Log } K_d = 2 \text{ Log } t_d + \text{Log}\left(\frac{1}{6} D\right) \tag{6.20}$$

Therefore, two straight lines can be drawn for the Difficulty on the log-log graph as G_0 and g_0.

The minimum team growth, g_0, is based on the consideration that as few engineers as possible should be employed in a project. At the beginning, only a few persons whose skill is specialized in the system under development are necessary, while persons having programming skills become increasingly necessary later, during the coding phase. The need for most of these skills becomes less necessary during the testing phase. In other words, it is good practice to start with only a few key engineers and to make the team grow pro-gressively following the natural demand of the project for human resources.

The rate of growth must not be lower than a certain level, g_0, if the team is to attain its peak at the right time. On the other hand, the rate of growth must not be too high, G_0, as each newcomer needs to be correctly integrated in the team organization. The value of G_0 is very dependent on the cohesion of the team organization.

The team growth (g_0, G_0) is expressed as the number of persons per year [see Equation (4.56)].

E.   Constructing the Planning Zone

The foregoing discussion has produced a set of ten straight lines parallel two by two. The considerations of minimum and maximum help in determining an area inside which the ten previous conditions are satisfied. The set of straight lines delimits an area inside which the choice of a set of cost–time values is permitted. This area is the **Planning Zone**. It is represented on Figure 6.4 by the area (A, B, C, D, E). In computerized systems, the Planning Zone is constructed by use of linear programming techniques. Nevertheless, we know at this stage that we can draw it with paper and pencil.

In practice, there are cases where the Planning Zone may not exist. This is a case of early problem detection. The Consulting Estimator has, as a consequence, to reconsider the constraints with the software manager or, in the worst case, with the customer (for example, the constraint being the delivery time).

Everything being considered and correct, a Planning Zone exists and the planning point must be represented by a point situated in the Planning Zone. The final solution must also satisfy the Software Equation.

6.4.2 Defining the software production

A. Representing the Software Equation

The software production can also be represented on a log-log scale by means of a straight line. This is the line that is going to help us determine the amount of software we can produce for a given planning point.

The software production line is defined by the Software Equation, as given by Equation (4.52). By dividing by E and raising to power 3, Equation (4.52) becomes:

$$\left(\frac{S}{E}\right)^3 = K \, t_d^4 \qquad\qquad (6.21)$$

where we can again introduce the development manpower cost by using Equation (5.2). Therefore, we get:

$$K_d = \frac{1}{6} \left(\frac{S}{E}\right)^3 t_d^{-4} \qquad\qquad (6.22)$$

The software production equation can now be represented by means of a straight line by taking the logarithm of both sides:

$$\text{Log } K_d = -4 \text{ Log } t_d + \text{Log}\left[\frac{1}{6}\left(\frac{S}{E}\right)^3\right] \qquad\qquad (6.23)$$

The slope of this line is negative, meaning that, everything else being equal, a lower manpower cost will be achieved by a longer time scale.

Along the line $S/E = $ constant, for a given Environment Factor, the software production is the same (that is, we produce the same amount of source code). When this line is drawn for the software production objective it offers several possible planning points. It then becomes easy to select an acceptable compromise between cost and time.

Another important point here is the role of the ratio S/E. The higher the volume of software to produce, the higher the cost for the same development time, unless the environment is improved. We will return to this point later.

B.   Positioning the planning point

The position of the S/E line depends on the value E, the quality of the environment and the size of the source code to be produced.

The quantity of software produced is related to the 'goodness' of the environment. This factor, E, is at its best when the programming support environment is of good quality which means:

- modern programming practices;
- effective software methodology assimilated by people using it;
- effective procedures;
- effective management methods.

Obviously, this dependence on the environment is difficult to measure; the method was developed in Section 6.3.2. For the same Environment Factor, the larger the source code required the more the line moves to the right. For small projects the software production line will be to the left.

For a given environment there is only one position of the software production line that permits the production of a software product of a given size. At this position, the line intersects the Planning Zone on the segment (X_1, X_2) in Figure 6.4. On this segment, a point P can be selected, called the planning point, which defines a workable relationship between the manpower cost of development, C_d, and the development time, t_d.

For risk avoidance reasons, the planning point cannot be selected too close to X_1 or X_2 since the natural uncertainty regarding the predictors would cause the planning point to move out of the permitted Planning Zone. If minimum risk is expected, then the planning point would be in the middle of the segment (X_1, X_2), and this would correspond to a development manpower cost, C_d, and a development time, t_d, as shown in Figure 6.4.

6.5   Manpower profile

6.5.1   Definitions

The manpower profile is a graphical representation of the variation of the number of persons working on the project during the life cycle of the project.

The manning of the project team is built up once the Preliminary Design Review is agreed on. The most permanent members of the team – for example, analysts, management, etc. – are involved very early in the life cycle and remain so until the end of the development (delivery time).

The manning of the team continues to grow during the design stage when software designers are needed to describe how the product will be implemented. When the design document is agreed on, well before the peak time, t_{0d}, the implementation can start. From this point on, the team is enhanced by the addition of programmers whose objective will be to code the software.

When a module has been tested the programmer is withdrawn and is assigned to another project. As more and more modules are tested so the staffing decreases until only the integration team remains. This team, made up of the most senior engineers, has the task of putting the modules together and testing the product to validate it. When the product is recognized as conforming to its specification, it is then fit for delivery to the customer.

6.5.2   Risk analysis

At this point, it is worth remembering how the model has been computed. A size of source code to be produced has been estimated and a value, S, given. Moreover, as S is an estimate, it is associated with a standard deviation. Assuming a normal distribution, there is a probability of 99.8% for the real size (that is, the size of the software that is effectively delivered) to be between $S - 3\sigma$ and $S + 3\sigma$.

The natural uncertainty in size is already the first source of risk. The other cause of risk arises through the quality of our definitions; that is, the numerical values of the Environment Factor, E, and the Manpower Build-up, D_0. In the absence of any statistical reason to justify the possible uncertainty in E and D_0, it is recommended that a variation of $\pm 15\%$ is assumed for each. Naturally, the Consulting Estimator is quite entitled to increase or decrease this figure according to the confidence he has in his measurement of E and his choice of D_0.

As the equation of the development manpower distribution [see Equation (4.51)] is known, a graph, as shown in Figure 6.5, can be drawn. Two other curves can be drawn describing the pessimistic and optimistic cases. These two curves define the boundaries within which the manning should remain during the development.

6.6   Classification of project environment conditions

To compare development environments or to follow up the evolution of a given development organization, it has been found useful to partition the quality of the environment into environment classes. The lowest class corresponds to a poor environment and can correspond to an Environment Factor $E = 600$. Other classes are determined by multiplying the previous one by 2, thus allowing for five classes of environment from 1 to 5.

The Manpower Build-up is also partitioned into classes, starting with

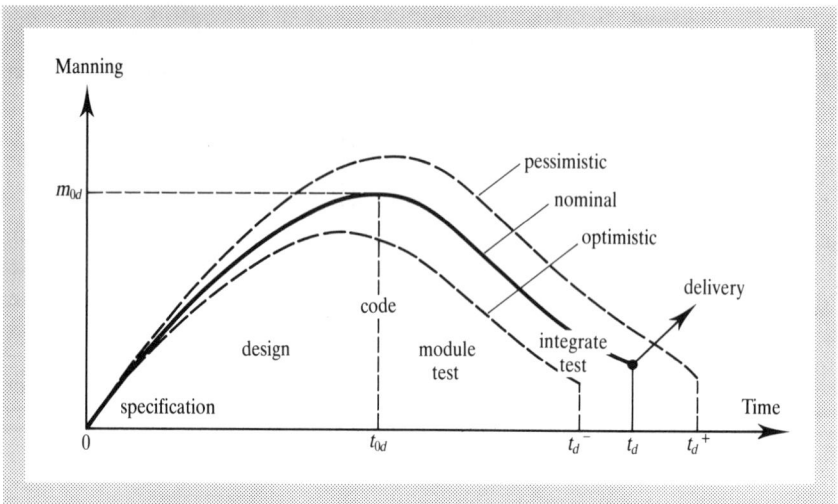

Figure 6.5   Development manpower profile.

the most difficult class ($D_0 = 7.5$) called here class A. As before, multiplying by 2 defines five classes from A to E.

Let us consider the case of a software development of 30 000 NCSS: Figure 6.6 gives the 25 possible developments using the five environment classes and the five classes of permitted Manpower Build-up. Inside each partition, the associated development time, t_d, and development manpower cost, C_d, are given. This can be easily calculated by following the method given in Section 5.2. Remember that the Development Subcycle is calculated the same way whatever the project scale. We have simply considered here the 30 000 NCSS size as it appears to be the run-of-the-mill project size in many organizations. If necessary, the Consulting Estimator can redesign a more convenient classification to satisfy the needs of his own organization.

Let us now examine some features of Figure 6.6. Development time reduction can be done safely only by improving the environment (better equipment and procedures, etc) and this is a strategic decision, which involves procurement time and generally large capital expenditure. Any management decision to shorten the development duration will increase the Manpower Build-up. For this decision to be successful, management must allocate manpower at the right moment, as defined by the new manpower profile. The time scale reduction cannot be as significant as the one obtained by improving the environment. If, further to this, *the time scale shortening is done at constant cost, the slippage is guaranteed.* This is the history of the development of several major software projects.

In a similar fashion, if we consider several software developments of different sizes in the same environment ($E = 1200$) and the same Manpower Build-up ($D_0 = 15$), we can draw the variations of the development man-

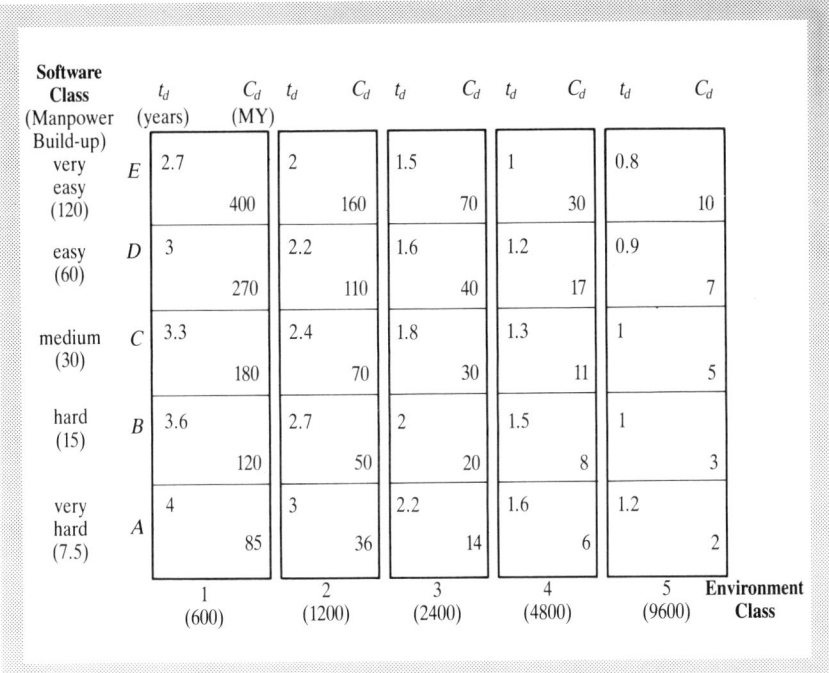

Figure 6.6 Effect of Environment and Manpower Build-up on a development of 30 000 NCSS.

power cost, peak manning and development time on a graph (see Figure 6.7). We find by doing this that there is an exponential growth of development manpower cost with size. This shows how important it is to estimate the size properly from the start.

6.7 The Network Signalling Subsystem case

The project manager responsible for the development of a real-time software subsystem for telecommunications called up his Consulting Estimator to help him prepare a tender for a critical software subsystem. His customer was ready to allow an expenditure of 50 MY for the design (development) of a subsystem that he would commission in 2 years and 4 months. For internal planning reasons, his customer did not want the product delivered before 18 months. This would work out very profitably as the manpower needed to make the development profitable was 5 MY.

The project manager gave all appearances of putting forward a proposal costing 50 MY to the customer and committing himself to providing the product in 2.3 years.

Preliminary discussions were started with the project manager who was

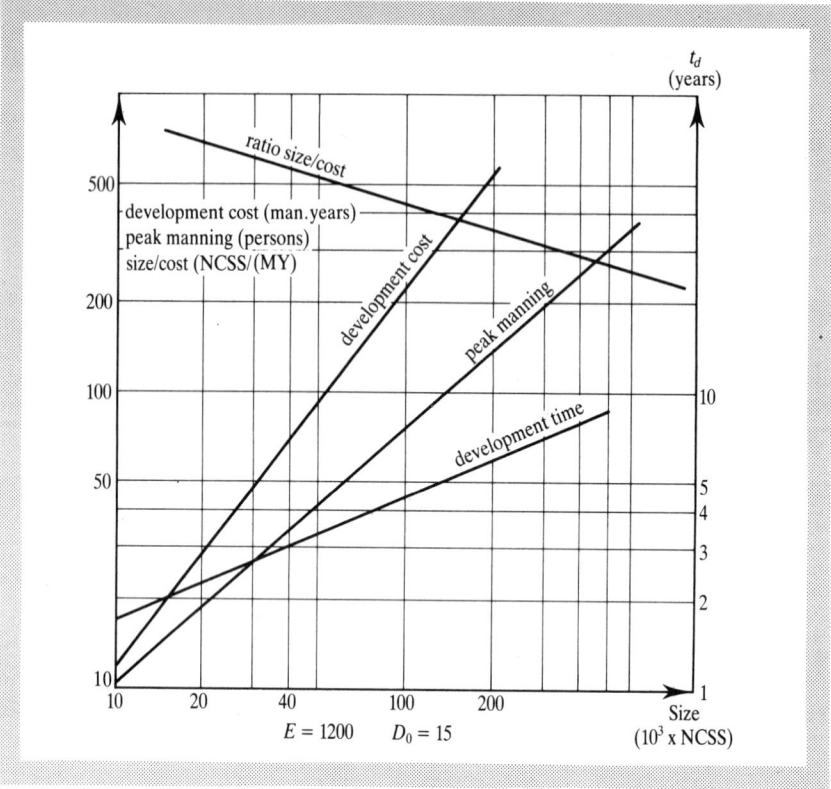

Figure 6.7   Size influence on project characteristics.

very confident, as he was backed up by a good success record in software developments that were similar but with lower manpower requirements. He already had a group of five experienced software specialists whom he had known for a long time and he wanted them to become the backbone of the future team. For some obscure reason he did not want to have more than 22 staff during the project.

As he did not have any measurement baseline the Consulting Estimator investigated some of his past projects and assessed two of his most relevant achievements as follows:

Projects	Size (NCSS)	Cost (MY)	Time (years)
Call processing	5500	9.5	1.5
Call maintenance	9250	12	2.2

His assessment of the Environment Factor resulted in:

Call processing $E = 832$

Call maintenance $E = 777$

As no significant improvement in method, tool, training, standards or procedures occurred, the Consulting Estimator decided that 800 would be a sensible evaluation of the present environment.

Further to this, the main constraints were established and listed as follows:

Constraint	Maximum	Minimum
Development manpower	50 MY	5 MY
Development time	2.3 years	1.5 years
Peak manning	22	4
Manpower Build-up	8	2 (1)
Difficulty	50 (3)	9 (2)

The figures in parentheses here refer to the following notes:

(1) The minimum Manpower Build-up was taken as a quarter of the maximum Manpower Build-up in an almost arbitrary fashion. (This practice is not critical: it just helps to give more consistency to the planning zone.)

(2) The minimum Difficulty was chosen on the basis that in a non-structured team it is difficult to add more than one new engineer every month.

(3) The maximum Difficulty was selected on the assumption that the project manager would rigorously structure the software organization. Then, an average of four new engineers per month would be a maximum.

With the agreement of the project manager, a meeting was organized with the project analysts attending and the Consulting Estimator acting as a facilitator. Obviously, the brainstorming technique was in the estimator's mind; however, it was convenient to let the discussion go on to the objective, which was to estimate the size. Everything went well and after a few hours enough information was generated for the Consulting Estimator to set up a table like that of Table 6.1.

The software consisted of 17 processes grouped in three major processes and the software to be produced in CHILL (as requested by the customer) came to a size of about 13 840 NCSS with a standard deviation of 500 NCSS. This meant that the real deliverable size would be between 12 340 NCSS and 15 340 NCSS with a probability of 99.8%, which is to say that it is practically certain.

Then the Consulting Estimator started the feasibility study. Considering the set of constraints on manpower cost, development time, peak manning, Manpower Build-up and Difficulty, the graphical representation, as shown in Figure 6.8, led to the following calculations.

Two values were obtained for the peak manning, m_{0d}, 25 and 4. Because of Equation (6.13), he knew that the peak manning equation was:

$$\text{Cost} = 0.67 \; m_{0d} \; t_d$$

where 0.67 results from $\sqrt{(e/6)}$ and cost means the total manpower cost of the

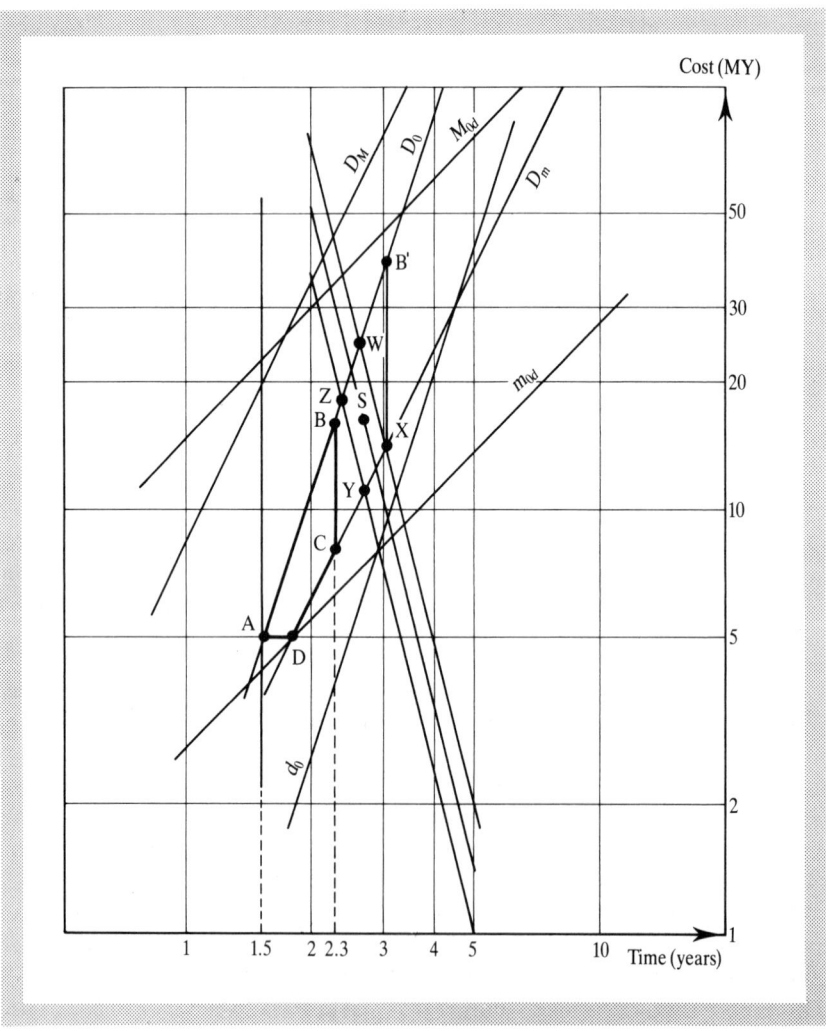

Figure 6.8   Network Signalling Subsystem case.

Development Subcycle, K_d. Then, by replacing the peak manning values, he was able to draw two lines:

Cost maxi $= 14.74 \, t_d$

Cost mini $= 2.68 \, t_d$

It was convenient to take $t_d = 1$ year and $t_d = 5$ years which gave:

t_d (years)	Cost Maxi (MY)	Cost Mini (MY)
1	14.74	2.68
5	73.7	13.4

Then he drew both lines, labelled M_{0d} and m_{0d}, respectively.

The Manpower Build-up was determined in the same way. Using Equation (6.18), restated here as:

$$\text{Cost} = \frac{1}{6} D_0 \, t_d^3$$

with two values of D_0, 8 and 2, he got two equations:

Cost maxi $= 1.3 \;\; t_d^3$

Cost mini $= 0.33 \, t_d^3$

Giving specific values to t_d he could then construct the line, using the following values:

t_d (years)	Cost Maxi (MY)	Cost Mini (MY)
2	10.64	2.64
4	85.12	21.12

Two lines corresponding to the Manpower Build-up were drawn. They are labelled D_0 and d_0, respectively, in Figure 6.8.

Finally, to determine the Difficulty he stated the difficulty equation, as obtained by substituting Equation (5.2) into Equation (4.56):

$$\text{Cost} = \frac{D}{6} \, t_d^2$$

With two values of D, 50 and 9, he obtained two equations:

$$\text{Cost maxi} = 8.3 \, t_d^2$$
$$\text{Cost mini} = 1.5 \, t_d^2$$

These two lines were drawn with the following convenient set of time values:

t_d (years)	Cost Maxi (MY)	Cost Mini (MY)
2	33.2	6.0
3	74.7	13.5

They are labelled D_M and D_m, respectively.

At this stage, a Planning Zone was determined; it is delineated in the figure by A, B, C, D. The practical limits were the time constraints, the Manpower Build-up for a high-cost solution and the Difficulty for a low-cost solution (see Figure 6.8). Two points were of the utmost interest: A and B. Point A represents a low-cost solution:

$$\text{Cost} = 5 \, \text{MY} \qquad t_d = 1.57 \text{ years}$$

Point B represents a maximum cost solution:

$$\text{Cost} = 15.8 \, \text{MY} \qquad t_d = 2.3 \text{ years}$$

It is worth mentioning at this point that the project manager could have developed some software within the previous constraints. Thus, the next stage was to ascertain what could be produced in his technological environment. To determine this, the Consulting Estimator used the Software Equation, as obtained by Equation (6.22):

$$\text{Cost} = \frac{1}{6} \left(\frac{S}{E} \right)^3 t_d^{-4}$$

Before continuing, let us examine the two extreme points, A and B, with respect to what can be produced, knowing that an Environment Factor $E = 800$ must be used. The equation above can be re-arranged to give:

$$\frac{S}{E} = (6 \text{ cost } t_d^4)^{1/3}$$

By substituting appropriate values for cost and t_d for point A (low cost) we obtain:

$$\frac{S}{E} = 5.67 \Rightarrow S = 4536 \text{ NCSS}$$

Similarly, for point B (high cost), we get:

$$\frac{S}{E} = 13.8 \Rightarrow S = 11\ 075 \text{ NCSS}$$

As the objective was to produce a volume of software of between 12 340 NCSS and 15 340 NCSS, in a safe fashion, this is the right moment to announce to the project manager that his development is not possible within the time constraints given.

The next step is to show how the development can be made feasible. It is worth noting at this point that a large number of software developments exist where the project manager did not have any means of having this feasibility study carried out. This resulted in the accepting of contracts including heavy penalties for slippage, and was detrimental for the software industry.

Returning to the Software Equation, three production lines can be drawn on the graph (with $E = 800$) successively for the nominal software production, the high-risk one and finally the low-risk one.

Nominal production: $S = 13\ 840$ NCSS
$$\text{Cost} = 863\ t_d^{-4}$$

High-risk production: $S = 15\ 340$ NCSS
$$\text{Cost} = 1175\ t_d^{-4}$$

Low-risk production: $S = 12\ 340$ NCSS
$$\text{Cost} = 612\ t_d^{-4}$$

These three lines can now be drawn on the graph in the usual way by taking practical values for one variable since they are only downward sloping lines:

t_d (years)	Nominal (MY)	High Risk (MY)	Low Risk (MY)
2	54	73	38
5	1.4	1.9	1
Line passing by	(S)	(W, X)	(Z, Y)

Thus, it becomes clear that the objective can be met by changing the only constraint that can be changed; namely, the latest delivery time. This implies a re-negotiation of the project between the project manager and the customer.

From the view point of the Consulting Estimator, the constraint to be rediscussed is the latest delivery time. If the customer accepts 3.1 years instead of 2 years, the extended Planning Zone would be A, B', X, D and the development would be carried out safely in the area $WXYZ$ (see Figure 6.8).

6.7.1   What can be done?

This is a typical case where the trade-off cost versus time can be made in a controlled fashion. It is not the purpose here to analyze the contracting techniques between project management and customer but to try to describe the main approaches.

A.   The naive approach

The management accepts the contract on the 50 MY and two years basis feeling somewhat anxious about the difficulty, but being mesmerized by the 50 MY budget reward.

A total of 25 engineers will be hired for two years and put to work on a two-year plan. Naturally, the most experienced will not be blind and high turnover will result. The slippage will become more and more clear. When two years have elapsed, if the project manager is still in command, he will have to put forward a three-year time scale development plan to his customer. The product will be achieved at a 75 MY cost, but in three years and with a lot of residual bugs in it. (Yes, this happened!)

B.   The salesman's approach

The management accepts the contract on the 50 MY and two years basis, but plans the work for a 2.5 years development and an effective cost of 20 MY. The cost difference, 30 MY, will be spent in negotiating the penalties between the marketing experts and the customer's counterparts.

The customer will have the right product later than expected. The customer's satisfaction will depend on how clearly the penalties were negotiated.

C.   The diplomatic approach

The management contracts on the two years development time and 20 MY instead of 50 MY. The project team has to convince the customer that he really needs a 7800 NCSS product as Initial Operational Capability. This can be done by suggesting that all unnecessary 'frills' are eliminated from the product. A Full Operational Capability of 13 840 NCSS could be negotiated later.

This approach is interesting if time is of the essence. Customer satisfaction will result from having received on time a product for which the performance was agreed and at a lower price.

D. The technical approach

This approach implies a technical understanding between the customer and the management. The management succeeds in convincing the customer to transform the 50 MY, two years offer into a 30 MY, 2.5 years agreement. If the contract is agreed on, management plans and develops in 2.5 years. This approach minimizes the risk and increases the chance of arriving at mutual satisfaction between customer and developer.

This approach is the easy case where a no-surprise development can be done, as it is possible to exploit the optimum development policy provided by the Rayleigh curve.

6.8 SLIM

The presentation of the Putnam method of software estimating is concluded here by providing a short description of the tool, SLIM. SLIM (Software LIfe Cycle Management) has been designed by Quantitative Software Management, Incorporated, as an automated aid for managers operating in the following areas:

- software budgeting;
- cost, plans and risk assessment of software developments;
- productivity position of their particular software development environment;
- bid evaluation of contractor software development proposals.

SLIM is based on the principles introduced in this book but contains many more features.

6.8.1 Objectives

SLIM aims at providing all levels of managers with information to assist in their software investment decisions by using productivity measures specific to the software development organization. It permits informed decisions to be made on the cost, time and risks of software developments. Productivity measures are possible and help to position organizations with respect to measures for similar developments (business, process control, real time, scientific, command and control systems) in the US, Europe and Japan.

SLIM incorporates, in a practical form, the findings of its originator, L. H. Putnam. Its accuracy has been validated for over 1300 systems. SLIM determines the minimum time to develop a given software system. This time can be used as the starting point for exploiting time/cost trade-off opportunities, permitting the selection of an effective development strategy.

6.8.2 The tool capability

SLIM can be run on IBM-PC compatible equipment. The current version of SLIM provides the following functions:

- Calibration: for productivity measurements;
- Build: to define a new software project;
- Estimate: to identify the minimum development time and corresponding cost for the software project;
- 'What if' functions: for design to cost, design to risk, design to reliability;
- Management constraints: for bid evaluation, parameter changes, trade-off analysis;
- Implementation functions: to define life cycle staffing and cost;
- Development staffing: for risk analysis, definition/specification phase;
- Estimates, cash flow, major milestones, project code production;
- Rates, reliability, staffing categories, Gantt chart;
- Miscellaneous functions: for development/maintenance CPU hours;
- Discounted cashflow; documentation.

A data base of completed projects in SLIM assists the user by checking if the development projections are consistent with similar completed projects.

6.8.3 SLIM deployment

SLIM was first introduced in the US in 1979 and in Europe in 1982. Counting the US and Europe, more than 60 organizations have installed SLIM. Furthermore, it is used by QSM, Incorporated, in its consultancy work in over 1300 software projects. Organizations using SLIM are involved in defence, space, telecommunications, computer manufacturing, process control, business, data processing, etc.

6.8.4 Range of application

SLIM is declared to be suitable for use with software developments that meet two of the following criteria:

- size greater than 5000 executable source statements;
- effort greater than 1.5 man.years;
- over six months' development time.

.   The types of application software supported by SLIM cover most of the known software systems – advanced real time, telecommunications, embedded systems, firmware, scientific, operating systems, office automation, etc.

SLIM, prepared by L. H. Putnam himself, is certainly the most comprehensive tool yet built to support his method.

EXERCISES

6.1 The software for a small digital PABX, SP-1 underwent a size-estimating session which resulted in the following estimates, expressed in NCSS:

Functions	Optimistic Size	Pessimistic Size	Most Likely Size	Expected Size	Standard Deviation
Call control	2800	5450	3650		
Switching control	4700	7200	6400		
Signalling	4100	5400	4200		
Diagnostics	1800	3200	2700		
Maintenance	1100	2500	1800		
Total SP-1					

(a) Calculate the total expected size of the software to be developed for SP-1.

(b) Determine the range of the delivered size with a probability of 99.8%.

6.2 Your client wants to develop SP-2 which is an enhanced version of SP-1. The new product SP-2 will have an additional function, network interface, which permits the connection of the system to a local area network. The estimate for the network interface is: minimum size: 4500; maximum size: 6450; most likely size: 5800 (all values are expressed in NCSS). Further to this addition, signalling will have a most likely addition of 2000 NCSS, but it could be between 890 NCSS and 2500 NCSS. Diagnostics is likely to be increased by 800 NCSS at least with a maximum of 1200 NCSS and the maintenance function will be increased by a likely 950 NCSS, which is also considered as a maximum, the minimum being estimated at 560 NCSS.

(a) Calculate the probable delivered size range of SP-2 with a probability of 99.8%.

(b)   Calculate the equivalent size range and the equivalent expected size, in view of estimating the development.

6.3   Consider the case where the size-estimating group is not sufficiently aware of the product design; thus, they provide a most likely value, S_m, which reflects the overall volume of the software product. On the other hand, optimistic and pessimistic values are given by a $\pm \Delta s$ operation made on the likely size. This leads to:

$$S_o = S_m - \Delta s$$
$$S_p = S_m + \Delta s$$

What are the consequences on the expected size and the standard deviation?

6.4   Consider another way of biasing estimates where the pessimistic size, S_p, and the optimistic size, S_o, are derived from the most likely sizes by multiplying and dividing, respectively, by the same number, n, greater than 1. This would lead to:

$$S_o = \frac{S_m}{n}$$
$$S_p = n\, S_m$$

What are the consequences on the expected size and the standard deviation?

6.5   Consider the case of the project manager who sets a rigorous time constraint, t_d, for the development of a software product of size, S. From this, the allowed time scale, t_d, and the volume of software to be developed, S, is known. (Numerical application: $S = 45\ 000$ NCSS; $t_d = 2$ years.)

(a)   From the expressions of the Software Equation and the Manpower Build-up, find a relation between the Environment Factor, the Manpower Build-up, the size and the development time.

(b)   Assume that the environment can be improved to help meet the deadline. Derive from the previous relation the expression for the Environment Factor. Taking $D_0 = 7.5$, calculate E.

(c)   Assume that the Manpower Build-up can be set up freely. Find the expression giving D_0 as a function of the other variable. Taking $E = 1200$, calculate D_0.

(d)   Knowing that $E = 1200$ and the software project is such that a Manpower Build-up of 15 must be considered as a maximum, prepare your recommendations to the project manager.

(e)   Verify your answers using SM10.

6.6 Consider the Software Equation, Equation (4.44), and the peak manning expression, Equation (5.5).

(a) Find the expression giving the peak manning, m_{0d}, as a function of the size, S, the Environment Factor, E, and the development time, t_d. What can you say about the influence of a development time contraction on the peak manning, m_{0d}?

(b) A software development of 24 000 NCSS has to be developed in 2 years and 3 months in an environment such that $E = 1200$. What development peak manning can you predict? Calculate the Manpower Build-up.

(c) Despite some discussion, the customer insists on a development time reduction of three months. Calculate the new development peak manning and Manpower Build-up.

(d) Compare the development productivity for both cases.

6.7 Consider the following situations A, B, C and D which are to be operated in an environment for which $E = 1200$:

Situation	Manpower Cost (MY)		Development Time (years)	Peak Manning (persons)	Manpower Build-up	Difficulty (person/year)
A	Max:	40	3	40	15	48
	Min:	12	2.5	10	4	18
B	Max:	20	1.5	18	15	50
	Min:	10	0.8	5	4	20
C	Max:	20	1.5	15	15	40
	Min:	5	0.8	5	8	15
D	Max:	70	3.5	50	7.5	60
	Min:	20	3	15	2	40

(a) Draw the Planning Zone on log-log graph paper. Does the Planning Zone exist?

(b) For each situation, position a planning point approximately at the centre of the Planning Zone. Draw the Software Equation line and give in each case the size of the software that can be developed with the development manpower cost and time.

6.8 Consider again situation A of Exercise 6.7. It is necessary to develop some software for which the size is 35 000 NCSS with a standard deviation $\sigma = 2200$ NCSS.

(a) The Environment Factor for the organization considered here is
$E = 1800$. Draw on the Planning Zone for A the three Software
Equation lines corresponding to the nominal, pessimistic and
optimistic cases. Choose a maximum security planning point and
give its co-ordinate, cost and time. Determine the segment centred
on the planning point, which links the pessimistic point to the
optimistic point, and give the co-ordinates, cost and time for both
points.

(b) Draw the three manpower profiles corresponding to the
pessimistic, nominal and optimistic cases.

Chapter 7
A Look Ahead

Most software developments are estimated by a practice of intuitive consensus, encompassing various practices such as rule of thumb, bottom-up analysis, past projects comparison, etc., often carried out by a group of experts. This generally leads to a first optimistic estimate followed by a series of replanning exercises, which result in a heavy cost overrun.

This book has presented a global method based on a macro model that aims at giving a once-and-for-all valid estimate. But, like most estimating methods, it is based on a preliminary size estimate. The natural uncertainty about a size prediction and its late measurement necessitates carrying out some re-estimates during the development of the software. This is a weak point. However, the method presented here, as it is based on a macro model, tends to minimize most of the uncertainty about the results of the estimate. In this sense, it is believed that it represents real progress in the technique of estimating.

Naturally, the goal of the practising estimator is to improve his method. This will certainly tend towards the replacement of size as an estimating tool by parameters that can be assessed early in the Software Life Cycle, preferably during the specification phase.

The role of the specification phase is to describe in an unambiguous way what is going to be developed. This 'what' aims to technically represent the customer's informal requirements. Unfortunately, the specification process makes great use of natural language (for example, English). However good it

163

is for everyday use, a natural language does not help in describing a customer's problem. This language is not only inadequate but it can also add confusion, and does not permit checking for consistency and completeness. Furthermore, it does not allow a rigorous definition of the customer's requirements so that a check can be made to ascertain that what is going to be developed is really what the customer wants.

Fortunately, some progress is being made in software engineering that may offer a formal and rigorous method of specifying problems. Of course, these methods are mathematically founded and their adoption will go hand in hand with a change in the culture of the software practitioners. It is possible to mention such methods as VDM [20], CCS [25], etc., which are at the moment at various levels of development.

Formal and rigorous methods might provide new descriptors for software products on which to base an estimating method, such as that built around the macro model described. The role of a measurement baseline will be to create metrics that link these formal descriptors to the management parameters (for example, size, cost, elapsed time). Then, the full advantage of a macro model will be realized and higher software productivity will be possible.

Appendix 1
Software Project Modelling – SM10

A small-scale estimating tool is easy to implement on a small Personal Computer. The program described here, called SM10, was developed by the author for use with the model described in Chapter 6. Although simple, it has been used to size up several large-scale, real-time software developments.

A small program tool running on a pocket-size Personal Computer presents some valuable advantages, such as:

- The program is stored either on the computer's permanent memory or on a small cassette; thus, the tool set can be easily transported (to the office, the home, meetings, etc.).

- The speed of the calculation is reasonable.

- It is sufficiently user friendly for the Consulting Estimator who is used to running it.

Nevertheless, there are some disadvantages when compared with more powerful tools:

- Project modelling on pocket computers does not take full advantage of the graphic facilities offered by the method described in Chapter 6 (for example, linear programming, graph drawing, etc.); thus, the reliance is on a single figure displayed on a small screen.

165

- SM10 is an individual tool; it does not encourage communication between two persons.
- It is not very practical for calibrating the Manpower Build-up and the Environment Factor automatically to historical data. A manual method has to be used.

Software Modelling 10 (SM10)

The program can be easily keyed in and stored for repeated use (see Figure A1.1 and Table A1.1). Although this program is written in Basica for the IBM-PC it can be easily adapted to the portable Personal Computer accepting the language BASIC.

The program can perform the following functions:

(1) **Input and verify:** Size, Environment Factor and Manpower Build-up.

(2) **Direct run:** All results are calculated. This contains a slack time option of 0.2 years.

(3) **Display results:** Results concerning the Development Subcycle and the Generic Cycle can be displayed. For the Development Subcycle, the following can be determined:

- development time, t_d, in years;
- peak time, t_{0d}, in years;
- development manpower cost, K_d, in man.years;
- development peak manning, m_{0d}, in number of persons;
- productivity in NCSS/MY.

Table A1.1 User guide for SM10.

Step	Prompt	Answer	Result
1	SM10		
	Enter project data (E) direct run (R)	E	to step 2
	Run with constraint (C)		
	Display: Development (D) Generic (G)		
	(– E: permit to update S, E and D_0;	R	to step 3
	– R: calculate the results;	C	to step 4
	– C: enter some target results and do		
	preliminary calculations;	D	to step 5
	– D & G: display results).	G	to step 6
		other	to step 1
2	**Update: Size (S)**		
	Environment (E) Do (D)	S	to step 2.1

Table A1.1   (cont.)

Step	Prompt		Answer	Result
	(Update the size, the Environment Factor and Manpower Build-up; exit this step by **X**).		E D X other	to step 2.2 to step 2.3 to step 1 to step 2
2.1	**Size = ###### New size=**	(1)	**New size**	to step 2
2.2	**E = ##### New E=**	(1)	**New E**	to step 2
2.3	**Do = ###.# New Do=**	(1)	**New Do**	to step 2
3	**Run with Slack time (S)?:** (Calculate the manpower profile with slack time of 0.2 year (**S**) or without (any other key))		S other	to step 1 to step 1
4	**Enter Constraint** **Productivity (P) Time (T)** **Peak Manning (M)** (If a target of Productivity (**P**), development time (**T**) or peak manning (**M**) is needed, step 4 carries out the preliminary calculations before starting step 3, by key **X**)		P T M X any	to step 4.1 to step 4.1 to step 4.1 to step 3 to step 4
4.1	**Adapt (E, Do):** (**E** or **Do** is adapted to meet the constraint)	(2)	E D other	to step 4.2, 4.3 or 4.4. to step 4.1
4.2	**Productivity (Ncss/m.y), P=**	(3)	Productivity target	to step 4
4.3	**Development time (y), Td=**	(4)	Time target	to step 4
4.4	**Peak manning (Persons), Mod=**	(5)	M_{0d} target	to step 4
5	(Display the values of the Development Subcycle calculated during step 3)			Display t_d, t_{0d}, M_{0d}, D, K_d and P to step 1
6	(Display the values of the Generic Cycle calculated during step 3)			Display t_d, m_0 and K to step 1

(1) If no change is required just press **Enter**.

(2) When E or D_0 is adapted to meet the constraint the adapted value can be read by a step 2.

(3) The minimum productivity constraint is initialized at 100 NCSS/MY. Also, productivity = $S/C_d(t_d)$.

(4) The minimum development time constraint is initialized at 0.5 year (6 months).

(5) The minimum peak manning target is initialized at 1 person.

```
 10 REM    ••••••••••••••••••••••••••••••••••••••••••••
 20 REM    •••                                     •••
 30 REM    •••            SM10                      •••
 40 REM    ••••••••••••••••••••••••••••••••••••••••••••
 50 REM basica-ibm-pc SM10    (B:SMI.BAS)
 60 DIM A$(3),B$(4),C$(3)
 70 READ S,E,D,Z
 80 FOR I=0 TO 4:READ B$(I):NEXT I
 90 FOR I=0 TO 3:READ C$(I):NEXT I
100 FOR I=0 TO 3:READ A$(I):NEXT I
110 GOSUB 1070
120 PRINT "Enter project data      (E)     Direct run   (R)"
130 PRINT "Run with constraint     (C)   "
140 PRINT "Display: Development  (D)      Generic      (G)" :PRINT
150 INPUT "Enter your Choice : ",Y$
160 FOR I=0 TO 4 :IF Y$=B$(I) THEN 180
170 NEXT
180 ON I+1 GOSUB 210,520,440,620,720
190 GOTO 110
200 REM
210 GOSUB 1070
220 PRINT "Update:" :PRINT
230 PRINT "Size (S) Environment (E) Do (D) : "
240 PRINT
250 INPUT "Enter your Choice [Exit (X)] :",Y$
260 FOR I=0 TO 3 :IF C$(I)=Y$ THEN 280
270 NEXT
280 ON I+1 GOSUB 320,360,400
290 IF Y$="X" THEN 300 ELSE 210
300 RETURN
310 REM                 Change size
320 PRINT USING "Size= #####";S;
330 INPUT " New size=",W
340 IF W<=0 THEN 210 ELSE S=W:RETURN
350 REM                 Change Environment Factor
360 PRINT USING "E= ####";E;
370 INPUT " New E=",W
380 IF W<=0 THEN 210 ELSE E=W:RETURN
390 REN                 Change Manpower Build-up
400 PRINT USING "DO= ###.#";D;
410 INPUT " New Do=",W
420 IF W<=0 THEN 210 ELSE D=W:RETURN
430 REM
440 PRINT :PRINT "Enter Constraint"
```

Figure A1.1   SM10 program.

```
450  PRINT "Productivity (P) Time (T)    Peak Manning (M)"
460  PRINT : INPUT "Enter your Choice [Exit (X)] : ", Y$
470  FOR I=0 TO 3:IF A$(I)=Y$ THEN 490
480  NEXT
490  ON I+1 GOSUB 800,880,950
500  IF Y$="X" THEN 520 ELSE 440
510  REM
520  PRINT : INPUT "Run with Slack time (S)? : ",Y$
530  T=((S/E)^3/D)^(1/7) :K=D*T^3
540  IF Y$="S" THEN GOSUB 600
550  M=K/(SQR(EXP(1))*T)
560  L=K/6       :N=T/SQR(6)
570  R=.95*L     :P=S/R
580  Q=L/(N*SQR(EXP(1)))
590  F=K/T^2     :RETURN
600  T=T+Z :K=(S/E)^3/T^4:D=K/T^3 :RETURN
610  REM
620  PRINT
630  PRINT USING " Td (y)          =      ##.##";T
640  PRINT USING " Tod (y)         =      ##.##";N
650  PRINT USING " Mod (persons) =      ##";Q
660  PRINT USING " Difficulty      =      ###";F
670  PRINT USING " Kd (m.y)        =      ###.#";L
680  PRINT USING " P (Ncss/m.y)  = #####";P
690  PRINT : INPUT "Enter any key:",Y$
700  RETURN
710  REM
720  PRINT
730  PRINT USING " Td (y)          =      ##.##";T
740  PRINT USING " Mo (persons)  =      ###";M
750  PRINT USING " K (m.y)         =      ###";K
760  PRINT : INPUT "Enter any key:",Y$
770  RETURN
780  REM
790  REM              Productivity constraint
800  GOSUB 1030
810  INPUT "Productivity (Ncss/m.y),P= ",P
820  IF P< =100 THEN 810
830  L=S/(.95*P)
840  ON X GOSUB 850,860
850  E=(D^4/(6*L)^7)^(1/9)*S :RETURN
860  D=(E/S)^(9/4)*(6*L)^(7/4) :RETURN
870  REM
880  GOSUB 1030              :REM Delivery time constraint
```

Figure A1.1   (cont.)

```
890  INPUT "Development time (y), Td= ",T
900  IF T< =.5 THEN 890
910  ON X GOSUB 920,930
920  E=S/(D•T^7)^(1/3)     :RETURN  :REM Adapt Environment
930  D=(S/E)^3/T^7          :RETURN  :REM Adapt Manpower Build-up
940  REM                    Peak manning constraint
950  GOSUB 1030
960  INPUT "Peak manning (Persons),Mod= ",Q
970  IF Q< =1 THEN 960
980  H=(Q•SQR(6•EXP(1)))^(7/6)/S
990  ON X GOSUB 1000,1010
1000 E=D^(5/6)/H            :RETURN  :REM Adapt Environment
1010 D=(H•E)^(6/5)          :RETURN  :REM Adapt Manpower Build-up
1020 REM
1030 INPUT "Adapt (E,Do): ",Y$
1040 IF Y$="E" THEN X=1  :RETURN  :REM Adapt environment, keep Do
1050 IF Y$="D" THEN X=2  :RETURN  :REM Adapt Do, keep Environment
1060 GOTO 1030
1070 CLS :PRINT :PRINT :PRINT "SM10" :PRINT :RETURN
1080 REM
1090 DATA 25000,2400,15,.2       :REM Initialise Size, Environment
1100 DATA E,R,C,D,G              :REM factor, Do (Manpower Build-up)
1110 DATA S,E,D,X                :REM and slack time.
1120 DATA P,T,M,X
1130 END
```

Figure A1.1   (cont.)

(4)   **Running SM10 with constraints**:   SM10 can be run with constraints on development time, t_{0d}, peak manning, m_{0d}, or productivity, P. The constraint is arrived at by either keeping Manpower Build-up constant whereupon the program adapts the Environment Factor value, or by keeping the Environment Factor value constant and adapting the Manpower Build-up.

By choosing **Adapt E**, the Manpower Build-up will remain at the input value and the program will adapt the Environment Factor value to meet the constraint.

By selecting **Adapt D**, the Environment Factor value will remain at the current value and the program will adapt the Manpower Build-up to satisfy the constraint.

Productivity constraint: SM10 asks for the productivity constraint to be entered, calculates the necessary adaptation, then calculates the results.

Development time constraint: SM10 asks for the target development time and calculates the results, after having carried out necessary adaptations.

Peak manning constraint: SM10 operates as before once the peak manning constraint has been input.

Appendix 2
Modelling on a Personal Computer – PA2

General

The successful use of SM10 created the need for a more elaborate tool. The facilities offered by the IBM-PC prompted the author to write PA2, making it possible to take advantage of the graphics capability offered by the video monitor.

In comparison with SM10, PA2 has the following additional capabilities:

- Planning Zone and manpower profiles can be represented on the video screen and printed out;
- useful results can be obtained within a short time;
- the Consulting Estimator and his client can discuss and select an appropriate strategy together in front of the screen.

The IBM-PC estimating station

The hardware used is an ordinary IBM-PC with the following configuration:

- IBM monitor 24 × 80 display;
- keyboard;

- dual 5″ floppy disk unit;
- video monitor for the representation of graphs;
- dot-matrix printer.

The program, PA2, standing for Planning Aid Number 2, resides on a 5″ floppy disk. It can be loaded in the usual way for the IBM-PC (or similar machines) **(Ctrl, Alt, del)**. A menu then appears on the display monitor offering a choice between the Planning Zone Function (PLZ) and the Manpower Profile Function (MPR). Once selected, the function provides a special menu on the video monitor. From that moment, the user is guided by a self-explanatory menu using the function keys of the keyboard. Figures A2.1 and A2.2 show an example of the use of PA2.

Curve -type	Based	Time	Cost	Source Code	Env.	S/E	Manpwr Build-up	Man Peak	Time	Difficulty	Prod
1 SEMI-QUICK	0	1.94	18.2	13842	1200	11.5	15.0	14	0.8	29.1	762
2 MARGIN +	1	2.02	20.7	15342	1200	12.8	15.0	15	0.8	30.4	740
3 MARGIN -	1	1.84	15.7	12342	1200	10.3	15.0	13	0.8	27.7	787

Profile No.	Time (Year)	Cost (MY)	Date (YYWW)
1	0.47	3.10	8625
1	0.69	6.00	8637
1	0.90	9.10	8648
1	1.26	13.70	8714

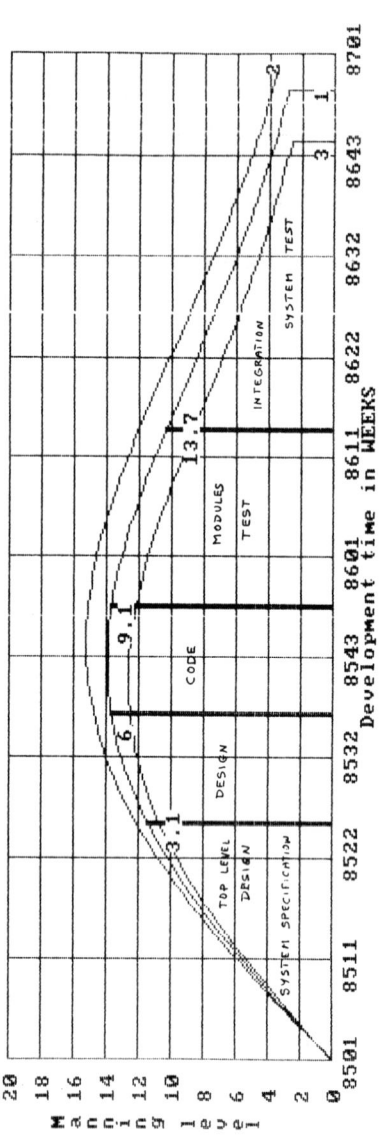

Figure A2.1 Manpower profile for project NSS.

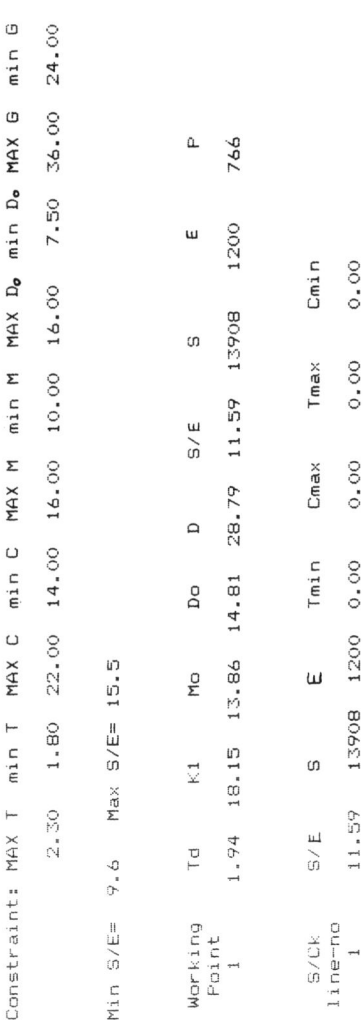
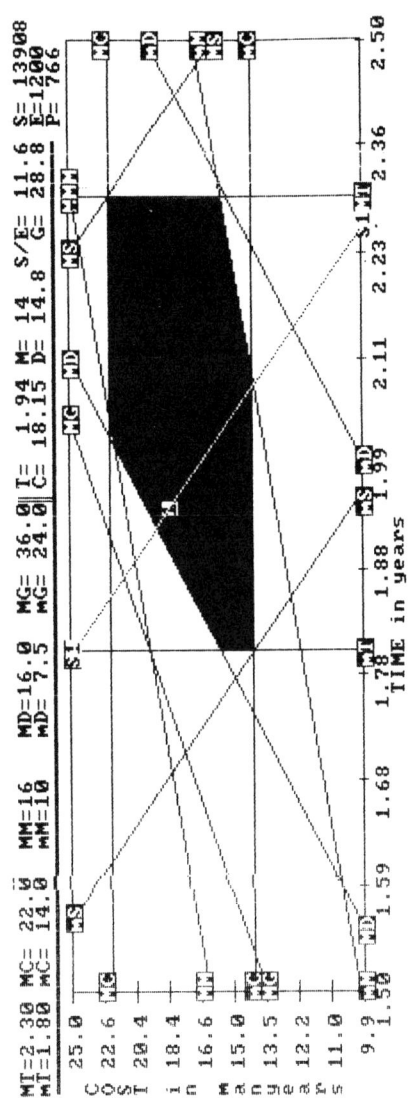

Figure A2.2 Planning Zone for NSS.

Appendix 3
Modelling with a Spreadsheet

The spreadsheet has become very popular since the advent of the Personal Computer, from which it takes the name of Electronic Spreadsheet. A spreadsheet is a matrix made up, typically, of 63 columns and 255 rows, as is the case for Multiplan developed by Microsoft, Incorporated. Each cell can contain literal or numerical data on which can be performed logical and arithmetic operations, and also complex functions. The spreadsheet can be a very effective supporting tool for the Consulting Estimator interested in practising the method described in Chapter 6 in an elementary fashion.

Minimum development time

To see how a spreadsheet is used, let us consider the case of the minimum development time, as outlined in the example in Section 5.2, and solve the problem by means of a Multiplan spreadsheet.

We start with the assumptions that the size, S, has been evaluated, and that the Environment Factor, E, and the Manpower Build-up, D_0, have been selected. From the Software Equation, as expressed by Equation (4.52), and the expression of the Manpower Build-up [see Equation (4.53)], we can deduce the development time, t_d, and arrive at Equation (5.8a), which is restated here as:

176

$$t_d = \left[\frac{1}{D_0} \left(\frac{S}{E}\right)^3\right]^{1/7}$$

The minimum development time, t_d (min), is obtained from this equation by using the maximum Manpower Build-up permitted, D_0 (max). Thus:

$$t_d \text{ (min)} = \left[\frac{1}{D_0 \text{ (max)}} \left(\frac{S}{E}\right)^3\right]^{1/7} \tag{A3.1}$$

and the development manpower cost, K_d, is obtained by:

$$K_d = \frac{1}{6} D_0 \text{ (max)} \, t_d^3 \text{ (min)} \tag{A3.2}$$

The time, t_{0d}, at which the peak manning occurs is [see Equation (5.3)]:

$$t_{0d} = \frac{t_d}{\sqrt{6}} \tag{A3.3}$$

and the peak manning, m_{0d}, is then [from Equation (5.5) and Equation (4.53)]:

$$m_{0d} = \frac{D_0 \text{ (max)} \, t_d^2 \text{ (min)}}{\sqrt{6e}} \tag{A3.4}$$

and the Difficulty, D, is:

$$D = D_0 \text{ (max)} \, t_d \text{ (min)} \tag{A3.5}$$

Installing the spreadsheet

We now have all the necessary equations to construct the example on the spreadsheet; hence, Size, S, (row 6), Environment, E, (row 7) and Manpower Acceleration, D_0, (row 8) can be positioned easily (see Figure A3.1). (The reader is assumed to be familiar with the documentation *Multiplan Electronic Worksheet* by Microsoft.)

As Multiplan offers a large variety of mathematical functions, we can use them in order to define the following:

(1) *Development Time (row 12)*: We enter here Equation (A3.1):

ROUND ((((R[−6]C/R[−5]C)ˆ3)/R[−4]C)ˆ(1/7),1)

#1	1	2	3	4	5	6
1	COST/TIME ESTIMATE					
2						
3						
4	INPUTS \ OPTIONS	A	B	C	D	E
5						
6	Size (ncss) S:	27000	30000	33000	30000	30000
7	Environment E:	1200	1200	1200	2400	1200
8	Manpwr. Accel. Do:	15	15	15	15	30
9						
10	RESULTS	A	B	C	D	E
11						
12	Develp. Time(y) Td:	2.6	2.7	2.8	2	2.4
13	Cost (m.y) K1:	43.9	49.2	54.9	20	69.1
14	Pk-Man.Time (y) To:	1.1	1.1	1.1	0.8	1
15	Peak-Manning(p) mo:	25	27	29	15	43
16	Difficulty D:	39	40.5	42	30	72
17						
18						
19						
20						

Figure A3.1   Example of how to use a spreadsheet.

(2) *Manpower cost (row 13)*: We enter here Equation (A3.2):

ROUND ((R[−5]C*R[−1]C^3)/6,1)

(3) *Peak time (row 14)*: From Equation (A3.3), we enter:

ROUND(R[−2]C/6^(1/2),1)

(4) *Peak manning (row 15)*: We describe Equation (A3.4) as follows:

ROUND((R[−7]C*R[−3]C^2)/((EXP(1)*6)^(1/2)),0)

(5) *Difficulty (row 16)*: In the same manner, we input Equation (A3.5):

ROUND(R[−8]C*R[−4]C,0)

These functions are the Multiplan representations of the equations given for the minimum time software development. Once installed, the spreadsheet can be saved on a floppy disk and re-used when necessary.

EXAMPLE

The example shown in Figure A3.1 is only intended to give an outline description of the possibilities of a spreadsheet. The reader may extend the scope of this example to any other cases (for example, medium-scale and large-scale projects).

Note that five options or 'whatif' situations are labelled from A to E on row 4 of the spreadsheet. Naturally, Multiplan allows the user to replace these letters by more explicit titles.

Option B represents a project whose size is evaluated to be 30 000 NCSS. This project is intended to be developed in an environment assessed to be $E = 1200$ with a Manpower Build-up $D_0 = 15$. The main results are calculated by the spreadsheet on rows 12 to 16; namely:

- development time;
- manpower cost;
- peak time;
- peak manning;
- Difficulty.

A standard deviation, σ, on the size is assumed to be 1000 NCSS. Option A represents the optimistic case where the size is the nominal size minus 3σ; that is, a size of 27 000 NCSS. Multiplan automatically computes all the results in column 2. The same calculations are done in column 4 for the pessimistic case (size = 33 000 NCSS).

The comparison between the three cases becomes easy. For example, the development would take between 2.6 years and 2.8 years according to the conditions shown in rows 6, 7 and 8, and especially, the natural uncertainty on the size.

If the environment was improved to, say, $E = 2400$, then option D immediately gives the new development time, two years. By contrast, if the Manpower Build-up is increased to $D_0 = 30$, instead of improving the environment, option E shows that the development would be 2.4 years at a significantly increased cost of 69 MY. The development would be completed only 3.6 months earlier.

As option D shows, there is undoubtedly great advantage in improving methods, tools, standards, training and general conditions of working if a low development cost is to be obtained.

Appendix 4
A Putnam-Based
Representation of COCOMO

We have seen in Chapter 3 that the COCOMO method can be used for estimating the project cost (K_n, in man.months) and the development time (t_d, in months). Naturally, as a preliminary to this, some evaluations are needed regarding the size of the software to be developed and the 15 cost drivers used by the COCOMO intermediate model.

The Putnam method also aims at estimating the project cost (C_p, in man.years) and the development time (t_d, in years). Moreover, to arrive at this, the evaluation of the size of the software development (in number of NCSS) is necessary. This later model makes use of two parameters: the Environment Factor, E, and the Manpower Build-up, D_0. In contrast to the 15 COCOMO cost drivers, which describe the software environment from the 'bottom end', these two parameters of Putnam describe the software environment from the 'top end', in a macroscopic fashion.

In this section, we will consider how a COCOMO estimate would be represented in Putnam's terms. Put in a different way, a software project has been estimated by means of COCOMO's 15 cost drivers and we want to know what values for the Environment Factor and the Manpower Build-up would give the same manpower cost and manpower time estimates for any given software project.

Assumptions

A set of assumptions has to be made if the comparison is to be meaningful. These assumptions will have a bearing on what is compared and the means of describing what is compared.

(1) *The project*   The same software project is assumed to be examined by both Boehm's and Putnam's methods.

(2) *The size*   The size, S, of the software product is expressed in number of NCSS. This expression is assumed to be acceptable by both methods.

(3) *The manpower cost*   The COCOMO manpower cost expressed in man.months can be easily converted to man.years. The nature and effectiveness of the work done by the project team is such that it is acceptable by both methods, and it is assumed that the COCOMO cost is the project manpower cost expended from $t = 0$ (start of development) until $t = t_d$ (delivery time). The manpower cost considered in both methods is that expended from the Preliminary Design Review (PDR) stage to the Full Operational Capability (FOC) stage (see Section 1.3).

(4) *The development time*   The development time, t_d, has the same meaning for both methods: it is the time that has elapsed between the PDR and the FOC stages.

Analytical background

We saw in Section 5.3 that the project manpower cost expended from PDR time until time t is given by Equation (5.17), which can be restated as:

$$C_p(t) = K_p \left[1 - \exp\left(-\frac{t^2}{2\, t_{0p}^2} \right) \right]$$

(A4.1)

The COCOMO project manpower cost is the cost that has been expended at time t_d (delivery time). It can be expressed by:

$$C_p(t_d) = K_p \left[1 - \exp\left(-\frac{t_d^2}{2\, t_{0p}^2} \right) \right]$$

(A4.2)

The project peak manning time, t_{0p}, is related to the delivery time, t_d, by α in such a way that, restating Equation (5.13):

$$t_{0p} = \frac{t_d}{\alpha}$$

(A4.3)

Therefore, the exponential quantity in Equation (A4.2) can be expressed by:

$$\frac{t_d^2}{2\,t_{0p}^2} = \frac{\alpha^2}{2} \tag{A4.4}$$

Then, the COCOMO cost can be re-expressed by substituting the result of Equation (A4.4) into Norden's expression of cumulative manpower cost, Equation (A4.2). Thus, we get:

$$C_p(t_d) = K_p \left[1 - \exp\left(-\frac{\alpha^2}{2} \right) \right] \tag{A4.5}$$

The full manpower cost, K_p, of the Project Subcycle can now be expressed directly relative to the cost, K, of the Generic Cycle. Taking advantage of Equation (5.11) we obtain:

$$K_p = \frac{K}{\alpha^2} = \frac{C_p(t_d)}{1 - \exp\left(-\dfrac{\alpha^2}{2} \right)} \tag{A4.6}$$

Then, solving for K:

$$K = \frac{\alpha^2\, C_p(t_d)}{1 - \exp\left(-\dfrac{\alpha^2}{2} \right)} \tag{A4.7}$$

This equation links the project manpower cost from COCOMO, $C_p(t_d)$, to the total manpower cost of the Generic Cycle, K, and thus to the Software Equation.

Once the size, S, of the software to be developed is known, the project Form Factor can be determined, since the α curve, as shown in Section 5.3, is known. From the project manpower cost and the development time given by COCOMO, it is then possible to determine a generic Norden manpower distribution starting from zero at initial time. Although the zero starting manpower has been criticized by Boehm and Parr, we should bear in mind here that we are omitting the product definition cycle, which is ending at this time.

From the expression of the Software Equation, as given in Section 4.5 [see Equation (4.52)], we can calculate the Environment Factor by:

$$E = \frac{S}{K^{1/3}\, t_d^{4/3}} \tag{A4.8}$$

Since the three variables S, K and t_d are known, it is possible to calculate the Environment Factor. As we intend to solve this problem by numerical methods, we do not need to develop the full formula for E.

Some other results can also be obtained, such as:

- the Difficulty, $D = K/t_d^2$;
- the Manpower Build-up, $D_0 = K/t_d^3$;
- the peak manning time of the Project Subcycle, $t_{0p} = t_d/\alpha$;
- the total manpower cost of the Development Subcycle, $K_d = K/6$;
- the peak manning time of the Development Subcycle, $t_{0d} = t_d/\sqrt{6}$.

We can conclude then that it is possible to define a Norden/Rayleigh manpower distribution curve and both the Putnam parameters, E and D_0, from a COCOMO cost/time estimate. To carry out this exploration we use the program tool called CCMO. The IBM-PC Basic version (Basica) of CCMO is given in Figure A4.1 and the CCMO user guide is shown in Table A4.1.

The CCMO tool

CCMO can be easily keyed in on an IBM-PC or other compatible machines or, after a slight adaptation, on any Personal Computer accepting Basic. For repeated use, CCMO can be stored on a cassette or a diskette.

The size of the software to be estimated and the COCOMO cost drivers are input, then CCMO calculates and displays the Putnam description of the software development.

Exploring the COCOMO cost drivers

This section aims to find out what values of the Environment Factor and the Manpower Build-up satisfy the COCOMO estimates for a given software developed in various environments. Thus, let us consider how a software development of an estimated size of 30 000 NCSS is seen by a Putnam model for several different steps of difficulty.

We will consider six different software development conditions, A to F (see Table A4.2). The combination of very low, low, nominal, high, very high and extra high have been chosen in such a way as to cover the range of the cost drivers as defined in Table 3.1.

In environment A, we are describing the best possible conditions for software development. The personnel is very experienced and knowledgeable. Tools and methods are excellent. The computing capability is at its best. Therefore, to express this level of 'goodness' some cost drivers have been chosen low (VIRT, TURN) and some very high (ACAP, AEXP).

Environment B is an intermediate software capability between environment A and the nominal environment C where all cost drivers are nominal. Thus, environment C is supposed to be the mid-range of COCOMO.

From environment D to environment F, the software development

Table A4.1   CCMO user guide.

Step	Prompt		Answer	Result
1	CCMO			
	Cost-drivers update (C), Size update (S)		C	step 2
	Cocomo run (K) Slack time run (L)		S	step 3
	Display: Development (D) Project (P)		K	step 4
			L	step 5
			D	step 6
			P	step 7
			other	step 1
2	Cost Driver Name:		CD [1]	step 2.1
			X	step 1
			other	step 2
2.1	CD = ###.# New Value=	[2]	New value	step 2
3	Size = ###### New size=	[3]	New size	step 1
4	Mode (O, S, E):		O	step 4.1
	(O: organic mode		S	step 4.1
	S: Semi-detached mode		E	step 4.1
	E: Embeded mode)		X	step 1
			other	step 4
4.1	Cp (Td) (m.y) = ###.#	[4]		
	Td (y) = ##.##			
	Enter any key:		X	step 1
5	Cp (Td) (m.y) = ###.#			
	Td (y) = ##.##			
	New Td (y) =		New Td	
	Enter any key:		X	step 1
6	Td (y) =			
	Tod (y) =			
	Mod (persons) =			
	Difficulty =			
	Kd (m.y) =			
	P (NCSS/m.y) =			
	Do =			
	E =			
	Cost Drivers =			
	Enter any key: =		X	step 1
7	Top (y) = ##.##			
	Mop (persons) = ###			
	Kp (m.y) = ###.#			
	Cp (Td) (m.y) = ###.#			
	Form factor = #.##			
	Overhead (m.y) = ###.#			
	Enter any key:		X	step 1

[1]   Input the two first characters of the cost driver's names as defined in Table 3.1.

[2]   The new value must be >0.7 and <1.66. **Enter** or the value 0 does not change the previous value.

[3]   If no change is required just press **Enter**.

[4]   This displays the manpower in man.years and the time in years.

```
10  REM    ••••••••••••••••••••••••••••••••••••••••••••
20  REM    •••                                      •••
30  REM    •••             CCMO                     •••
40  REM    ••••••••••••••••••••••••••••••••••••••••••••
50  REM
60  REM CCMO – Basica – ibm-pc      (B:CCMOI.BAS)
70  DIM A(14),B$(14),C$(6)
80  GOSUB 1040
90  PRINT :PRINT :PRINT "CCMO":PRINT
100  GOSUB 1090                      :REM Initialisation A,B$,C$
110  PRINT "Cost-drivers update   (C)      Size update    (S) "
120  PRINT "Cocomo run            (K)      Slack time run (L) "
130  PRINT "Display: Development (D)      Project        (P) "
140  PRINT :INPUT "Your Choice is: ",Y$
150  FOR I=0 TO 5
160  IF C$(I)=Y$ THEN 180   :REM Verify, index input character
170  NEXT
180  ON I+1 GOSUB 210,360,740,420,810,940
190  GOTO 90                     :REM Unknown character
200  REM
210  INPUT "Cost Driver Name: ",Y$
220  FOR I=0 TO 14
230  IF B$(I)=Y$ THEN 290         :REM Verify, index the name
240  NEXT
250  IF Y$ > < "X" THEN 210.      :REM Unknown name. Redo
260  Z=1 :FOR I=0 TO 14
270  Z=Z*A(I)    :NEXT            :REM Calculate cost multiplier
280  RETURN
290  PRINT Y$;"=";A(I);           :REM Display actual CD
300  INPUT "New Value=",N
310  IF N=0 THEN 340              :REM No new value detection
320  IF (N<.7) OR(N>1.66) THEN 300      :REM Limit the value
330  A(I)=N                       :REM The value is accepted
340  GOTO 210                     :REM Next cost driver
350  REM
360  PRINT USING "Size= #####";S;  :REM actual size
370  INPUT " New size= ",W
380  IF W<=0 THEN 390 ELSE S=W :REM No change range
390  GOSUB 1090                   :REM Size accepted
400  RETURN
410  REM
420  PRINT :INPUT "Mode (O,S,E): ",Y$
430  IF Y$="O" THEN 490           :REM Organic mode
440  IF Y$="S" THEN 510           :REM Semidetached mode
```

Figure A4.1   CCMO program.

```
450  IF Y$="E" THEN 530          :REM Embedded mode
460  IF Y$ < > "X" THEN 420       :REM Unknown mode or exit
470  RETURN
480  REM
490  U=3.2  :V=1.05  :W=.38       :REM Parameters for organic
500  GOSUB 560          :RETURN
510  U=3    :V=1.12  :W=.35        :REM Param. for semidetached
520  GOSUB 560          :RETURN
530  U=2.8  :V=1.2   :W=.32        :REM Param. for embedded
540  GOSUB 560          :RETURN
550  REM
560  X=Z•U•(S/1000)^V   :T=2.5•X^W  :REM Cocomo results
570  X=X/12   :T=T/12             :REM Transformation in years
580  PRINT
590  PRINT USING "Cp(Td) (m.y)= ###.#";X
600  PRINT USING "Td     (y)  =  ##.##";T
610  REM
620  R=1+6.23•EXP(-.079•S/1000)  :REM Form factor
630  Q=X/(1-EXP(-.5•R^2))          :REM Project manpower-Kp
640  K=Q•R^2   :F=K/6   :REM Generic & Development mnpwr
650  E=S/((K•T^4)^(1/3))           :REM Environment Factor
660  G=T/SQR(6) :H=T/R    :REM Peak time (develop. & project)
670  L=K/((SQR(6•EXP(1)))•T)       :REM Development peak manning
680  J=K/(R•SQR(EXP(1))•T)         :REM Project peak manning
690  M=K/T^2    :D=K/T^3 :REM Difficulty & Manpower Build-up
700  P=S/(F•.95)                   :REM Productivity
710  PRINT :INPUT "Enter any key: ",Y$
720  RETURN
730  REM
740  PRINT :PRINT
750  PRINT USING "Cp(Td) (m.y)   = ###.#";X
760  PRINT USING "Td     (y)     =  ##.##";T  :REM Slacked time
770  PRINT :INPUT "New Td (y)     =  ",W
780  IF W< =.5 THEN 790 ELSE T=W :REM Time limit 6 months
790  GOSUB 620  :RETURN           :REM Time accepted
800  REM
810  GOSUB 1090                    :REM Display results
820  PRINT USING "Td (y)       =   ##.##";T
830  PRINT USING "Tod (y)      =   ##.##";G
840  PRINT USING "Mod (persons) =  ##";L
850  PRINT USING "Difficulty    =  ##";M
860  PRINT USING "Kd (m.y)      =  ###.#";F
870  PRINT USING "P (Ncss/m.y)  = #####";P
880  PRINT USING "Do           =   ###.#";D
```

Figure A4.1   (cont.)

```
890   PRINT USING "E            = #####";E
900   PRINT USING "Cost Drivers =   ###.##";Z
910   PRINT :INPUT "Enter any key: ",Y$
920   RETURN
930   REM
940   GOSUB 1090
950   PRINT USING "Top (y)         =    ##.##";H
960   PRINT USING "Mop (persons) =    ###";J
970   PRINT USING "Kp (m.y)        =    ###.#";Q
980   PRINT USING "Cp (Td) (m.y)   =    ###.#";X
990   PRINT USING "Form factor    =     #.##";R
1000  PRINT USING "Overhead (m.y) = ###.#";X-.95*F
1010  PRINT :INPUT "Enter any key: ",Y$
1020  RETURN
1030  REM
1040  FOR N=0 TO 5  :READ C$(N) :NEXT
1050  FOR N=0 TO 14 :READ B$(N) :NEXT :READ S
1060  FOR N=0 TO 14 :A(N)=1      :NEXT
1070  Z=1               REM Initialise cost multiplier
1080  RETURN
1090  CLS :PRINT :PRINT :PRINT "CCMO": PRINT :RETURN
1100  REM
1110  DATA C,S,L,K,D,P           :REM Commands
1120  DATA RE,DA,CP,TI,ST,VI,TU,AC,AE,PC,VE,LE,MO,TO,SC
1130  DATA 25000                 :REM Initial size
1140  END
```

Figure A4.1 (cont.)

capability becomes worse: the computer turnaround is getting lengthier, the personnel is constituted of more junior programmers new to the profession, tools and methods are very simple. Environment F represents the worst case by COCOMO standards. We must recognize that it is difficult to establish a metric on the cost drivers as expressed in COCOMO. The idea used here is to cover the full COCOMO range by progressing the rating by steps around the nominal environment labelled C.

Note that the last line of Table A4.2 provides the values of the product of all cost drivers. From the best conditions of software development (A) to the worst conditions (F), the cost drivers range from 0.1 to 72 (rounded values). As this value has a multiplier effect on the nominal manpower cost, it is clear that the manpower demand for a given project can vary from 10% of the nominal manpower (A) up to 72 times this nominal manpower (F). It is current practice to define the productivity of software development by means of the ratio of size to development manpower employed. The best feature of COCOMO is to capture, by means of the 15 cost drivers, those elements governing the productivity of a given organization.

Table A4.2 Definition of software environments A to F.

COCOMO Attributes	Software Environments					
	A	B	C	D	E	F
Product						
RELY	VL	L	N	H	VH	VH
DATA	L	L	N	H	VH	VH
CPLX	VL	L	N	H	VH	EH
Computer						
TIME	N	N	N	H	VH	EH
STOR	N	N	N	H	VH	EH
VIRT	L	L	N	H	VH	VH
TURN	L	L	N	H	VH	VH
Personnel						
ACAP	VH	H	N	L	VL	VL
AEXP	VH	H	N	L	VL	VL
PCAP	VH	H	N	L	VL	VL
VEXP	H	H	N	L	VL	VL
LEXP	H	H	N	L	VL	VL
Project						
MODP	VH	H	N	L	VL	VL
TOOL	VH	H	N	L	VL	VL
SCED	VH	H	N	L	VL	VL
All CD	0.098	0.26	1.0	5.02	34.58	72.33

Note: The symbols used in this table represent the COCOMO ratings (see Table 3.1): VL: very low; L: low; N: nominal; H: high; VH: very high; EH: extra high.

Conclusions

This appendix has attempted to find a link between two completely different models: Boehm's and Putnam's model. Naturally, this is a very difficult or almost impossible task, because one model is a micro model and the other is a macro model – these offer two opposite views of the same problem. The best we can do is to verify that there is no contradiction between them.

The approach we have taken here is to use the cost driver ratings to define six software development environments (A to F) representing various conditions of software development from the best (A) to the worst (F) and to find how they are represented by the macro model. The results are shown in Table A4.3.

Four groups of cost drivers (CD) (that is, product, computer, personnel and project, as referred to in Table 3.1) are assessed using the Table A4.2. The products of all cost drivers are given for each environment condition

Table A4.3   Environment Factor and Manpower Build-up equivalence (S = 30 000 NCSS, embedded mode).

COCOMO	Software Environments					
	A	B	C	D	E	F
Product CD	0.49	0.70	1.0	1.43	2.11	2.68
Computer CD	0.76	0.76	1.0	1.45	2.35	3.87
Personnel CD	0.35	0.57	1.0	1.85	3.69	3.69
Project CD	0.75	0.86	1.0	1.31	1.89	1.89
All CD	0.098	0.26	1.0	5.02	34.58	72.33
Manpower cost (m.m)	16.09	43.78	165.84	829.23	5738	12 002
Development time (m)	6.08	8.38	12.83	21.47	39.88	50.50
Putnam equivalent						
Environment Factor	44 170	20 720	7526	2213	509	291
Manpower Build-up	36	38	40	42	46	47

under the label 'All CD'. Then, using the intermediate mode formula, the COCOMO manpower and development time are given – they are expressed, respectively, in man.months (m.m) and months (m), in Table A4.3.

At this stage, the use of CCMO (see Table A4.1) enables the calculation both of the Putnam parameters; namely, the Environment Factor, E, and the Manpower Build-up, D_0. The results are given in Table A4.3.

From Table A4.3, it can be seen that when the development conditions get worse, from environment A to environment F (this is expressed in COCOMO by the cost driver multiplier increasing from 0.1 to 72), the Environment Factor decreases from 44 170 to 291. This is in line with the idea that the Environment Factor evaluates the 'goodness' of the software development environment. The more effective the environment, the easier it is to develop the software, so the manpower cost is smaller and the development time is shorter. This trend can be observed by comparing the values of the Environment Factor, the manpower cost and the development time.

It is also possible to observe the variation of the Manpower Build-up, D_0. This increases when the development conditions become worse. A basic Putnam model would have shown a nearly constant Manpower Build-up; but with the COCOMO model, a variation of 13% around the median value of 41.5 is obtained.

Solutions to Selected Exercises

Chapter 1

1.4 FOUR56 is made up of five modules of 960 NCSS each.

(b) The manpower necessary for the development of FOUR56 is $52 \times 4800/1200 = 208$ mw.

(c) The manpower demand (in mw) generated by the module size of 960 NCSS is $52 \times 960/1200 = 41.6$ mw.

At module level and for each module:

Specification:	$41.6 \times 9\% =$	3.7 mw
Design:	$41.6 \times 16\% =$	6.6 mw
Code:	$41.6 \times 17\% =$	7.1 mw
Module test:	$41.6 \times 25\% =$	10.4 mw
Total:	$=$	27.8 mw

At FOUR56 level and for the full package the remaining manpower is $5 \times 41.6 \times 33\% \simeq 68.6$ mw, which is shared between:

Specification and design:	$208 \times 8\% =$	16.6 mw
Integration and test:	$208 \times 25\% =$	52.0 mw
Total:		68.6 mw

This makes a total for FOUR56 of 207.6 mw (value not rounded).

Chapter 2

2.1 (a) If $Y = \text{Log } y$, $A = \text{Log } a$ and $X = \text{Log } x$, then $Y = A + b X$.

(b) $Z = \Sigma(Y_i - A - b X_i)^2$.

(c) If $\partial Z/\partial A = 0$, then $\Sigma(Y_i - A - b X_i) = 0$.
Therefore, $\Sigma Y_i = NA + b \Sigma X_i$.

If $\partial Z/\partial b = 0$, then $\Sigma(X_i Y_i - A X_i - b X_i^2) = 0$.
Therefore, $\Sigma X_i Y_i = A \Sigma X_i + b \Sigma X_i^2$.

(d) $A = \dfrac{\Sigma Y_i - b \Sigma X_i}{N}$; $b = \dfrac{\Sigma X_i Y_i - \dfrac{\Sigma X_i \Sigma Y_i}{N}}{\Sigma X_i^2 - \dfrac{(\Sigma X_i)^2}{N}}$.

2.2 (a) The coefficients are $a \simeq 3$ and $b \simeq 1.2$. The regression model is then $E = 3 L^{1.2}$.

(b) The predicted manpower cost is $E = 122.5$ man.months.

2.3 The amount of manpower involved is 96 man.months.

(a) Number of lines of source code can be obtained by reversing Equation (2.2) and Equation (2.5) to give:

$$L = \left(\frac{E}{a}\right)^{1/b}$$

Then:

$$L \text{ (SEL)} = 94\ 264 \text{ LOC}$$
$$L \text{ (W–F)} = 24\ 632 \text{ LOC}$$

(b) Duration in months can be calculated by means of Equation (2.4) and Equation (2.6):

$$D \text{ (SEL)} = 15 \text{ months}$$
$$D \text{ (W–F)} = 13 \text{ months}$$

(c) Average manning is:

$$M \text{ (SEL)} = 6.4 \text{ person/month}$$
$$M \text{ (W–F)} = 7.4 \text{ person/month}$$

(d) Productivity is:

$$P \text{ (SEL)} = 11\ 783 \text{ LOC/MY}$$
$$P \text{ (W–F)} = 3\ 079 \text{ LOC/MY}$$

Thus, it seems that SEL can produce four times as much software as IBM for the same manpower and time scale.

Chapter 3

3.1 (a) Manpower cost, K_m = 192 man.months [from Equation (3.3)];
development time, t_d = 13.4 months [from Equation (3.4)].

(b) For a probability of 99.8%, 3σ = 4650 NCSS. Thus for the
pessimistic case:

$$S_p = 32\ 150 \text{ NCSS}$$
$$K_{mp} = 232 \text{ man.months}$$
$$t_{dp} = 14.3 \text{ months}$$

and for the optimistic case:

$$S_o = 22\ 850 \text{ NCSS}$$
$$K_{mo} = 154 \text{ man.months}$$
$$t_{do} = 12.5 \text{ months}$$

Thus, the manpower ranges from 154 man.months to 232
man.months, while the development time ranges from 12.5
months to 14.3 months.

3.2 For the three modes, we have $K = a\ S_k^b$, and with $Pr = S/K$, we get:

$$Pr = \frac{(1000)^b}{a\ S^{b-1}}$$

then:

(a) *Organic mode*:

$$Pr_o = \frac{588.6}{S^{0.05}} \text{ NCSS/man.month}$$

Semi-detached mode:

$$Pr_s = \frac{764}{S^{0.12}} \text{ NCSS/man.month}$$

Embedded mode:

$$Pr_e = \frac{1106}{S^{0.2}} \text{ NCSS/man.month}$$

(b)

S_k	Pr_o	Pr_s	Pr_e
10	371	253	175
20	359	233	153
30	351	222	141
40	346	214	133
50	343	209	127
60	340	204	122
70	337	200	119
80	335	197	116
90	333	194	113

3.3 **(a)** From the surface of the trapezoid and the time relation we obtain:

$$K_m = m_0 (t_r + t_s)$$
$$t_d = 2 t_r + t_s$$

Remembering that the slope, r, is given by:

$$r = \frac{m_0}{t_r}$$

and eliminating t_r and t_s, the expression is:

$$m_0^2 - r t_d m_0 + r K_m = 0 \tag{3.3.1}$$

In a similar fashion, we get:

$$r t_r^2 - r t_d t_r + K_m = 0 \tag{3.3.2}$$
$$r t_s^2 - r t_d^2 + 4 K_m = 0 \tag{3.3.3}$$

(b) Solving Equation (3.3.3) for t_s, we get the condition for which t_s exists (that is, this represents the triangular limit):

$$t_d^2 - 4 \frac{K_m}{r} \geq 0$$

Or:

$$r \geq \frac{K_m}{\left(\frac{t_d}{2}\right)^2}$$

That is, with $B = K_m / (t_d/2)^2$:

$$r \geq B \tag{3.3.4}$$

(c) The same kind of calculation as for (b) gives:

$$m_0 = r \frac{t_d}{2} \left[1 \pm \text{sqrt}\left(1 - \frac{B}{r}\right)\right]$$

$$t_r = \frac{t_d}{2} \left[1 \pm \text{sqrt}\left(1 - \frac{B}{r}\right)\right]$$

Note that the condition (3.3.4) still holds.

(d) From Equation (3.3) and Equation (3.4), substituting t_d and K_m, we obtain:

$$B \simeq S_k^{0.43} \text{ (person/month)}$$

(e)

S_k	K_m (m.m)	t_d (m)	B (p/m)	M_0 (max) (p)	m_0 (p)
30	213	13.9	4.4	31	18
50	394	16.9	5.5	46	30
90	797	21.2	7.1	75	56

3.4

Attributes	Range		Ratio
Product	0.49	2.68	5.5
Computer	0.76	3.87	5.1
Personnel	0.35	3.69	10.5
Project	0.68	1.89	2.8

Chapter 4

4.1 (a) From Equation (4.4), by substituting $p(t) = 2\,a\,t^n$, we obtain:

$$C(t) = K \left[1 - \exp\left(- \frac{2\,a}{n+1}\, t^{n+1} \right) \right]$$

Then, by differentiating, the manpower expression would be:

$$m(t) = 2\,K\,a\,t^n \exp\left(- \frac{2\,a}{n+1}\, t^{n+1} \right)$$

and:

$$m'(t) = 2\,K\,a\,t^{n-1}\,(n - 2\,a\,t^{n+1}) \exp\left(- \frac{2\,a}{n+1}\, t^{n+1} \right)$$

If $n = 1$, we obtain the equations of Chapter 4. The peak manning for $t_p = (n/2\,a)^{1/n+1}$ is:

$$m\ (\text{peak}) = 2\,K\,a \left(\frac{n}{2\,a} \right)^{\frac{n}{n+1}} \exp\left(- \frac{n}{n+1} \right)$$

(b) The slope at the start time is zero (or, $D = 0$) and the peak time is:

$$t_d' = \left(\frac{n}{2\,a} \right)^{\frac{1}{n+1}}$$

instead of:

$$t_d = \frac{1}{\sqrt{2\,a}}$$

For the same value of a, substituting t_d for t_d', gives:

$$t_d' = (n\,t_d^2)^{\frac{1}{n+1}}$$

We can verify here that when n increases the time scale is reduced. An increase of n gives a sharp rise of the peak manning relative to its value for $n = 1$. Therefore, a non-linear learning curve would give an early more peaky model which would not be helpful to represent the reality of software development [28].

4.2 (a) From Equation (4.6), we have:

$$C(t) = K \, [1 - \exp(-a \, t^2)]$$

with $a = 1/2 \, t_d^2$. By differentiation, we obtain:

$$C'(t) = 2 \, K \, a \, t \, \exp(-a \, t^2)$$

$$C''(t) = 2 \, K \, a \, (1 - 2 \, a \, t^2) \, \exp(-a \, t^2)$$

Thus:

$$C''(t) - 2 \, K \, a \, \exp(-a \, t^2) + 4 \, K \, a^2 \, t^2 \, \exp(-a \, t^2) = 0$$

$$C'' + 2 \, K \, a - 2 \, K \, a \exp(-a \, t^2) + 4 \, K \, a^2 \, t^2 \exp(-a \, t^2) = 2 \, K \, a$$

$$C'' + 2 \, a \, C + 2 \, a \, t \, C' = 2 \, K \, a$$

resulting in:

$$C'' + \frac{t}{t_d^2} \, C' + \frac{1}{t_d^2} \, C = D$$

(b) Any Runge–Kutta package will do.

4.3 (a) From Equation (4.13), we have:

$$m_0 = 104 \text{ persons}$$

The peak time is 3.5 years.

(b) Equation (4.14) gives the Difficulty:

$$D = 49 \text{ person/year}$$

Then, from Equation (4.19), we get the Manpower Build-up:

$$D_0 = 14 \text{ person/year}^2$$

(c) From Equation (4.6) and Equation (4.8), we have:

$$C \, (1.17) = 32.6 \text{ MY}$$

4.4 (a) $m_0 = 46$ persons; $K = 120$ MY.

(b) $D = 48$ person/year; $D_0 = 30$ person/year^2.

4.5 (a) From Equation (4.27), $C_d(t_d) = 85.5$ MY.

(b) From Equation (4.29), $t_{0d} = 17$ months.

(c) From Equation (4.14), $D = 46$ person/year.

(d) From Equation (4.19), $D_0 = 13.5$ person/year^2.

4.6 (a) Start date $= 80.25$; delivery date $= 82.33$; development time $= t_d = 2.08$ years.

(b) $K_d = 32/0.95 = 33.7$ MY.

(c) $t_{0d} = t_d/\sqrt{6} = 0.85$ year (or 10 months).

(d) $K = 6 K_d = 202$ MY; $D = K/t_d^2 = 46.7$ person/year.

(e) $D_0 = 22.5$ person/year^2.

(f) $S/E = 15.6$; then $E = 3077$.

4.7 This is an almost straightforward application of the Software Equation with $t_d = 1.8$ years and $K = 150$ MY; then, $S = 27\ 920$ NCSS.

4.8 (a) By transforming Equation (4.44), we have:

$$\left(\frac{S}{E}\right)^3 = K\, t_d^4$$

which is also equivalent to:

$$\left(\frac{S}{E}\right)^3 = D_0\, t_d^7$$

Then:

$$t_d = \left[\frac{1}{D_0}\left(\frac{S}{E}\right)^3\right]^{1/7}$$

Since $S/E = 25$, t_d (min) $= 3$ years. As $K = D_0\, t_d^3 = 202$ MY, the total development manpower cost is therefore 33.75 MY. The Difficulty is $D = D_0\, t_d = 22.5$ person/year and the peak time is $t_{0d} = 1.2$ years. Substituting in Equation (4.32), we get the peak manning:

$$m_{0d} = D\, t_{0d}\, \exp\left(-\frac{1}{2}\right) = 16 \text{ persons}$$

(b) Development time reduction means either developing the software at a higher Manpower Build-up or producing less software.

(i) Increase Manpower Build-up: The Software Equation can be re-arranged as follows:

$$D_0 = \frac{1}{t_d^7}\left(\frac{S}{E}\right)^3$$

The new development time would be 2.8 years and the new Manpower Build-up is:

$$D_0' = 11.6 \text{ person/year}^2$$

Then, $K = D_0\, t_d^3 = 254$ MY and the total development manpower cost $= 42.4$ MY. The new Difficulty is $D' = D_0'\, t_d = 32.5$ person/year. The peak time is $t_{0d} = 1.14$ years and, as previously done, the new peak manning is $m'_{0d} = 22$ persons. Note the huge increase in peak manning and manpower cost.

(ii) Produce less software: The Software Equation can be re-written as follows:

$$\left(\frac{S}{E}\right)^3 = D_0\, t_d^7 = 7.5 \times 2.8^7 = 10\ 120$$

Thus, $S/E = 21.6$. Then for $E = 2200$, the size of software delivered is $S = 47\ 586$ NCSS. The problem is now to decide which software functions can be cut down.

Chapter 5

5.1 (a) From Equation (5.8a), t_d (min) $= 1.85$ years (1 year 10 months). As the peak time $= 0.75$ year (9 months), the generic manpower cost is, from Equation (4.53):

$$K = D_0\, t_d^3 = 95\ \text{MY}$$

Then, the total manpower development is:

$$K_d = 15.8\ \text{MY}$$

From Equation (4.56) and Equation (4.53), the Difficulty is:

$$D = D_0\, t_d = 27.75\ \text{person/year}$$

From Equation (5.4), the peak manning is:

$$m_{0d} = 13\ \text{persons}$$

The development productivity is the ratio of the size produced divided by the development manpower used to develop this size; thus:

$$Pr = 791\ \text{NCSS/MY}$$

(b) The development can last two years. By re-arranging Equation (5.8a), we obtain the effective Manpower Build-up:

$$D'_0 = \frac{1}{t_d^7}\left(\frac{S}{E}\right)^3$$

Then, $D'_0 = 8.8$ person/year^2 and the peak time is 0.8 year. From Equation (4.53), the generic manpower cost is:

$$K = D'_0\, t_d^3 = 70.4\ \text{MY}$$

and the total manpower development cost is:

$$K'_d = 11.7\ \text{MY}$$

and, from Equation (4.56) and Equation (4.53), the Difficulty is:

$$D' = D_0\, t_d = 17.6 \text{ person/year}$$

Equation (5.4) gives the peak manning:

$$m'_{0d} = 9 \text{ persons}$$

The development productivity is:

$$Pr' = 1068 \text{ NCSS/MY}$$

It is to be noted that a longer development time scale provides better development conditions.

5.2   All the calculations are summarized as follows. (Note that these calculations can be carried out either by using the formulae introduced in this chapter or by means of SM10 presented in Appendix 1.)

Factor	Company	
	A	*B*
Environment Factor	2400	1400
Manpower Build-up	8	8
Development time	1.63 years	2.05 years
Peak time	0.67 year	0.84 year
Generic manpower cost	34.65 MY	68.92 years
Development cost	5.77 MY	11.5 MY
Peak manning	5 persons	8 persons

The most important point, in the present case, is the delivery time. Company *A* cannot deliver before 1.63 years for development time plus 10 months (0.83 year) for delay, which makes a delivery date of 2.46 years (2 years and 5.5 months). Therefore, Company *B* seems to be the best choice as it can guarantee 24 months.

5.3   (a)   and (b) can be calculated by means of SM10 (see Appendix 1):

Factor	Case	
	a	*b*
Size	18 000 NCSS	9000 NCSS
Development time	2.37 years	1.76 years
Development cost	17.8 MY	7.3 MY
Peak manning	11 persons	6 persons

Even by having two developments of 9000 NCSS carried out in parallel, we do not meet the goal of 1.5 years.

(c)   The equivalent Manpower Build-up is D_0' such that:

$$D_0' = \frac{1}{t_d^7} \left(\frac{S}{E}\right)^3 = 48.5$$

Compared with values recommended in Section 4.5.1, the value found for D_0' is very high, which is a sign of project slippage.

5.4 (a)   From Equation (5.8a), we solve for the size:

$$S = E (D_0 t_d^7)^{1/3} = 18 \ 143 \ \text{NCSS}$$

(b)   During the second period, a size of 25 000 − 18 143 = 6857 NCSS will remain to be developed. Since this extra part will have to work with the part developed during the first period, we will have to take into account the manpower demand created by the existence of this first period software. This is equivalent to 15% of 18 143 NCSS. Therefore, the size equivalent for the second period will be 9578 NCSS. Using SM10, we calculate the development time for the second period, t_{d2}:

$$t_{d2} = 1.5 \text{ years (1 year and 6 months)}$$

The total development time is:

$$t_d \text{ (tot)} = t_{d1} + t_{d2} = 3.5 \text{ years}$$

(c)   SM10 allows us to calculate the one-go development time, to obtain:

$$t_d = 2.3 \text{ years (2 years and 3.5 months)}$$

which is obviously shorter than t_d (tot). However, in the practice of (b) we would take advantage of the manning decreasing in the first period to build up the second period project earlier. This would provide a shorter overall development time.

5.5 (a)   From Equation (5.21), we obtain the Form Factor:

$$\alpha = 1.15$$

The generic manpower cost is obtained from Equation (5.2), so $K = 93.5$ MY. The total Project Subcycle manpower cost is obtained from Equation (5.11):

$$K_p = \frac{K}{\alpha^2} = 70.7 \text{ MY}$$

The development time is 81.75 − 78.25 = 3.5 years. The Environment Factor can be obtained from Equation (4.52) to give:

$$E = \frac{S}{(K\,t_d^4)^{1/3}} = 1950$$

The Manpower Build-up, from Equation (4.53), is:

$$D_0 = \frac{K}{t_d^3} = 2.2 \text{ person/year}^2$$

The development peak time, t_{0d}, from Equation (5.3), is:

$$t_{0d} = 1.4 \text{ years (1 year and 5 months)}$$

The development peak manning, m_{0d}, from Equation (5.4), is:

$$m_{0d} = 7 \text{ persons}$$

The project peak time, t_{0p}, from Equation (5.13), is:

$$t_{0p} = \frac{t_d}{\alpha} = 3 \text{ years}$$

The project peak manning, m_{0p}, from Equation (5.14), is:

$$m_{0p} = 14 \text{ persons}$$

(b) The value of the Manpower Build-up calculated in (a) is not the maximum value that could be recommended. We could have planned this development with $D_0 = 7.5$. Thus, the minimum development time can be derived from Equation (5.8a) to give (with $E = 1950$ previously calculated):

$$t_d \text{ (min)} = 2.9 \text{ years (2 years and 11 months)}$$

Then, we can determine all the other parameters: total generic manpower cost, $K = 183$ MY; total development manpower cost, $K_d = 30.5$ MY; total project manpower cost, $K_p = 138.4$ MY; development peak time, $t_{0d} = 1.18$ years; project peak time, $t_{0p} = 2.5$ years; development peak manning, $m_{0d} = 16$ persons; and project peak manning, $m_{0p} = 34$ persons. Note the increase of peak manning and manpower due to the time scale contraction.

Chapter 6

6.1 (a) The total expected size of SP-1 is $S = 18\,875$ NCSS with a standard deviation of $\sigma_s = 725$ NCSS.

(b) The range of the delivered size for SP-1 is defined by $S_r = S \pm 3\,\sigma_s$; that is, size (max) = 21 050 NCSS and size (min) = 16 700 NCSS.

6.2 (a) The added software size is:

Addition	Size	σ
Nl	5692	325
Signalling	1883	283
Diagnostics	867	67
Maintenance	885	65
Total	9327	441

and the expected delivered size of SP-2 would be S (del) = 28 202 NCSS with σ (del) = 849 NCSS. Therefore, the expected addition is S_n = 9327 NCSS and σ_n = 441 NCSS.

(b)   Using Equation (6.7), the equivalent size for the estimation of SP-2 is:

$$S \text{ (equ)} = 43\% \, S + S_n$$
$$= 17\ 443 \text{ NCSS}$$

and σ (equ) = 540 NCSS.

6.3   From Equation (6.1), we have:

$$S_{md} = \frac{S_m - \Delta s + 4 S_m + S_m + \Delta s}{6}$$

Then, $S_{md} = S_m$ and:

$$\sigma_{md} = \frac{S_m + \Delta s - S_m + \Delta s}{6}$$
$$= \frac{\Delta s}{3}$$

The expected size will be the most likely size, which is a sign that the uncertainty in the size is not captured.

6.4   From Equation (6.1), we have:

$$S \text{ (exp)} = \frac{n^2 + 4 n + 1}{6 n} S_m$$

As the expected size will always be higher than the most likely size:

$$\sigma_s = \frac{n^2 - 1}{6 n} S_m$$

The range of the standard deviation would be between 0 and $S_m/6$.

6.5 (a)   From Equation (4.44) and Equation (4.53), we obtain
$S = E (D_0 \, t_d^7)^{1/3}$.

(b) $E = \dfrac{S}{(D_0\, t_d^7)^{1/3}} = 4562.$

(c) $D_0 = \left(\dfrac{S}{E}\right)^3 t_d^{-7} = 412$ person/year^2.

6.6 (a) $m_{od} = \left(\dfrac{S}{E}\right)^3 \dfrac{1}{\sqrt{6e}\ t_d^5}$: A development time contraction creates a demand for a higher development peak manning. Note the power 5 on the development time.

(b) $m_{od} = \dfrac{1981}{t_d^5} = 34$ persons; $D_0 = 27.4$ person/year^2.

(c) $m_{od} = 62$ persons; $D_0 = 62.5$ person/year^2.

(d) $C_{d1}(t_d) = 49.42$ person.years; $C_{d2}(t_d) = 79.17$ person.years; $Pr_1 = 486$ NCSS/MY; $Pr_2 = 303$ NCSS/MY.

6.7 The following table gives the approximative values for the planning points selected:

Situation	S (NCSS)	K_d (MY)	t_d (years)	m_{od} (persons)	D_0 (person/year^2)	D (person/year)
A	26 100	30	2.75	16	8.6	23.8
B	No Planning Zone (reason: D_0 (max) too small)					
C	6 200	5.2	1.45	5	10.2	15
D	35 445	38.5	3.25	18	6.7	21.9

6.8 Because of the higher Environment Factor, $E = 1800$, we have to expect to produce more software for the same planning point ($K_d = 30$ MY, $t_d = 2.75$ years). We would have:

$$S \ \ = 39\ 157\ \text{NCSS}$$
$$D_0 = 8.6\ \text{person/year}^2$$
$$m_{od} = 16\ \text{persons}$$
$$D \ \ = 23.8\ \text{person/year}$$

The quantity of software produced does not match the requirements of $S = 35\ 000$ NCSS. Hence, we have to move the planning point to an earlier time defined by:

$$t_d = \left[\dfrac{1}{6\,K_d}\left(\dfrac{S}{E}\right)^3\right]^{1/4}$$

obtained by re-arranging the Software Equation. Then, with $K_d = 30$

MY we get $t_d = 2.53$ years. For this new planning point, we have approximately, for $S = 35\ 000$ NCSS:

$m_{0d} = 18$ persons
$D_0 = 11$ person/year^2
$D = 28$ person/year

Three Software Equation lines can be drawn, represented by $(K_d = 1/6\ (S/E)^3\ t_d^{-4})$:

Optimistic: $K_d = 655\ t_d^{-4}$
Nominal: $K_d = 1225\ t_d^{-4}$
Pessimistic: $K_d = 2057\ t_d^{-4}$

It is worth noting that any point along a given Software Equation line gives the same amount of software. This is so for different costs and times, and more especially for a different Manpower Build-up, D_0. We can choose the three points in such a way that the Manpower Build-up remains the same, $D_0 = 11$. We get the approximate following results:

Case	S (NCSS)	t_d (years)	K_d (MY)	m_{0d} (persons)	D
Optimistic	28 400	2.31	22.6	15	25
Nominal	35 000	2.53	29.6	17	28
Pessimistic	41 600	2.73	37.3	20	30

The only risk is to have produced the software too early ($t_d = 2.3$ years).

Glossary

Notation	Definition	Reference
a	Norden's coefficient $(= 1/t_d^2)$	68
α	Form Factor: it defines the Project Subcycle relative to the Generic Cycle	104
$C(t)$	Cumulative manpower cost used in the Generic Cycle until time t	67
$C_d(t)$	Cumulative manpower cost used in the Development Subcycle until time t	82
C_n	Proportionality coefficient used in Putnam's productivity study	79
$C_p(t)$	Cumulative manpower cost used in the Project Subcycle until time t	106
D	Difficulty (person/year)	71
D_0	Manpower Build-up (person/year^2)	74
ϵ	Assessment of the estimating process	12
E	Environment Factor, also called Technology Factor	84
K	Total manpower cost of the Generic Cycle from $t = 0$ to infinity	66

Notation	Definition	Reference
K_d	Total development manpower cost of the Development Subcycle from $t = 0$ to infinity	82
KLOC	Unit of size of a piece of software expressed in a number of thousands of lines of source code	22
K_m	Manpower cost for COCOMO, basic model	48
K_n	Manpower cost for COCOMO, intermediate model	50
K_p	Total project manpower cost of the Project Subcycle from $t = 0$ to infinity	103
LOC	Unit of size of a piece of software expressed in a number of lines of source code	22
$m(t)$	Manning of the Generic Cycle at time t	68
m_0	Peak manning of the Generic Cycle	68
m_{0d}	Peak manning of the Development Subcycle	97
m_{0p}	Peak manning of the Project Subcycle	105
$m_d(t)$	Manning involved in the Development Subcycle at time t	82
$m_p(t)$	Manning involved in the Project Subcycle at time t	102
MY	Unit of manpower, man.year (or person.year)	3
M_0	Optimistic number of modules	126
M_m	Most likely number of modules	126
M_p	Pessimistic number of modules	126
N	Size of a standard module expressed in NCSS	126
NCSS	Unit of software size: it stands for Non-Commentary Source Statements	23
$p(t)$	Learning function used in Norden's model	67
Pr	Productivity	83
S_0	Optimistic size	126
S_m	Most likely size	126
S_p	Pessimistic size	126
S_{md}	Expected module size	127
σ_{md}	Standard deviation of the expected module size	127
σ_n	Standard deviation on the size of a standard module	126
S	Size of a piece of software expressed in NCSS	84
S_k	Size of a piece of software expressed in kilo.NCSS	48

Notation	Definition	Reference
t	Time variable	67
t_{0d}	Peak time of the Development Subcycle	82
t_{0p}	Peak time of the Project Subcycle	105
t_d	Development time, when referred to the duration	70
	Delivery time when referred to the end of development	70
	This assumes that the development/project starts at time zero	
	Peak time of the Generic Cycle	68
t_f	Final time of the Project Subcycle	115
$Y(\alpha)$	Ratio of the cumulative manpower cost of the Project Subcycle until time t_d on the total generic manpower cost	107

References

[1] Albrecht, A. J. and Gaffney, J. E., Jr. 'Software Function, Source Lines of Code, and Development Effort Prediction: A Software Science Validation', *IEEE Transactions on Software Engineering*, **SE-9**, **6**, pp. 639–647, 1983.

[2] Aron, J. D. 'Estimating Resources for Large Programming Systems', in *Software Engineering Techniques*, NATO Science Committee, J. N. Buxton and B. Randell (eds.), 1970.

[3] Basili, V. R. 'Resource Models', in *Models and Metrics for Software Managements and Engineering*, IEEE, pp. 4–9, 1980.

[4] Boehm, B. W. *Software Engineering Economics*, Prentice-Hall, 1981.

[5] Boehm, B. W. 'Software Engineering Economics', *IEEE Transactions on Software Engineering*, **SE-10**, January 1984.

[6] Booch, G. *Software Engineering with Ada*, Benjamin/Cummings, 1983.

[7] Brooks, F. P. *The Mythical Man-Month*, Addison–Wesley, 1982.

[8] Buck, F., *et al. A Cost-by-Function Model for Avionics Computer System*, Vol. 1, Naval Air Development Center, NADC-SD-7088, 1971.

[9] Conte, S. D., Dunsmore, H. E. and Shen, V. Y. *Software Engineering Metrics and Models*, Benjamin/Cummings, 1986.

[10] Daly, E. B. 'Management of Software Development', *IEEE Transactions on Software Engineering*, pp. 229–242, May 1977.

[11] Farr, L. and Zagorski, H. J. 'Quantitative Analysis of Programming Cost Factors: A Progress Report', in *Economics of Automatic Data Processing*, ICC Symposium Proceedings, Rome, Frielink, A. B. (ed.), North-Holland, 1965.

[12] Frederic, B. C. *A Provisional Model for Estimating Computer Program Development Costs*, Tecolote Research Inc., 1974.

[13] Freiman, F. R. and Park, R. E. 'PRICE Software Model – Version 3: An Overview', in *Proceedings IEEE–PINY*, Workshop on Quantitative Software Models, IEEE Catalog No. TH0067-9, pp. 32–41, October 1979.

[14] Gilb, T. *Software Metrics*, Chartwell-Bratt Ltd (England) and Student Litteratur (Sweden), 1976.

[15] Halstead, M. H. *Elements of Software Science*, Elsevier, North-Holland, Inc., 1977.

[16] Heldman, R. K. 'Top Down Planning: Part 1 – Conceptual Planning, Part 2 – Requirements Definition, Part 3 – Product Definition', in *Telephone Engineer & Management*, pp. 79–80 and 84, June 1982, pp. 100, 105–107, July 1982, pp. 87–90, September 1982.

[17] Herd, J. R., *et al.* 'Software Cost Estimation Study – Study Results', Final Technical Report, RADC-TR-77-220, Vol. I (of two), Doty Associates Inc., Rockville, MD, 1977.

[18] James, T. G. 'Software Cost Estimating Methodology', in *IEEE Proceedings of National Aerospace Electronic Conference*, 1977.

[19] Jensen, R. W. and Tonies, C. C. *Software Engineering*, Prentice-Hall, 1979.

[20] Jones, C. B. *Software Development: A Rigorous Approach*, Prentice-Hall, 1980.

[21] Kustanowitz, A. L. 'System Life Cycle Estimation (SLICE): A New Approach to Estimating Resources for Application Program Development', in *Proceedings IEEE*, COMSAC, 1977.

[22] McCabe, T. J. 'A Complexity Measure', *IEEE Transactions on Software Engineering*, **SE-2**, 4, pp. 308–320, December 1976.

[23] Tom de Marco *Structured Analysis and System Specification*, Yourdon Press, April 1981.

[24] Tom de Marco *Controlling Software Projects*, Yourdon Press, 1982.

[25] Milner, R. *A Calculus of Communication Systems*, Springer-Verlag, Lecture Notes in Computer Science, **92**, 1980.

[26] Mohanty, S. N. 'Software Cost Estimation: Present and Future', *Software-Practice and Experience*, **11**, pp. 103–121, 1981.

[27] Nelson, E. A. *Management Handbook for the Estimation of Computer Programming Costs*, AD-648-750, Systems Development Corporation, 1966.

[28] Norden, P. V. 'Useful Tools for Project Management', in *Management of Production*, M. K. Starr (ed.), Penguin, 1970.

[29] Norden, P. V. 'On the Anatomy of Development Projects', *IRE Transactions on Engineering Management*, PGEM, **EM-7**, **1**, pp. 34–42, March 1960.

[30] Osborn, A. F. *Applied Imagination*, Charles Scribner's Sons, 1963.

[31] Parr, F. N. 'An Alternative to the Rayleigh Curve Model for Software Development Effort', *IEEE Transactions on Software Engineering*, **SE-6**, **3**, May 1980.

[32] Putnam, L. H. 'Progress in Modelling the Software Life Cycle in a Phenomenological Way to Obtain Engineering Quality Estimates and Dynamic Control of the Process', *IEEE Computer Society Publication*, No. 78CH1390-4C, August 1978.

[33] Putnam, L. H. and Fitzsimmons, A. 'Estimating Software Costs', *Datamation*, pp. 189–198, September 1979, *Datamation*, pp. 171–178, October 1979 and *Datamation*, pp. 137–140, November 1979.

[34] Putnam, L. H. 'A General Empirical Solution to the Macro Software Sizing and Estimating Problem', *IEEE Transactions on Software Engineering*, pp. 345–361, July 1978.

[35] Putnam, L. H. 'The Real Economics of Software Development', in *The Economics of Information Processing*, Vol. 2, Operations, Programming and Software Models, John Wiley & Sons, pp. 167–176, 1982.

[36] Putnam, L. H. *The Influence of the Time–Difficulty Factor in Large Scale Software Development*, Digest of Papers, IEEE Fall COMPCON 77, Fifteen IEEE Computer Society International Conference, Washington DC, pp. 348–353, September 1977.

[37] Thibodeau, R. 'An Evaluation of Software Cost Estimating Models', Rome Air Development Center, Air Force Systems Command, Griffiss Air Force Base, New York 13441, *Final Technical Report*, RADC-TR-81-144, 1981.

[38] Walston, C. E. and Felix, C. P. 'A Method of Programming Measurement and Estimation', *IBM Systems Journal*, **16**(1), pp. 54–73, 1977.

[39] Warburton, R. D. H. 'Managing and Predicting the Costs of Real-Time Software', *IEEE Transactions on Software Engineering*, **SE-9**, **5**, September 1983.

[40] Wolverton, R. W. 'The Cost of Developing Large-Scale Software', *IEEE Transactions on Computers*, **C-23**, **6**, pp. 615–636, June 1974.

[41] Zelkowitz, M. V. 'Advances in Software Engineering: Resource Estimation', in *Advances in Computer Programming Management*, T. A. Rullo (ed.), Vol. 1, Heyden & Son Inc., 1980.

Index